D1431654

Advance praise for *The Constitution of Knowledge*

"Long one of the country's wisest and most honest voices, Jonathan Rauch has written a hugely valuable and necessary book, an illuminating exploration of the flight from fact. If, as the Gospel of John put it, the truth shall set us free, then count Rauch among the liberators."

—JON MEACHAM,
historian; author of *His Truth Is Marching On: John Lewis and the Power of Hope*

"Liberty, of course, requires constant vigilance, but who would have thought until recently that the idea of truth needed defending? Sadly, we now see that it does, but happily, Jonathan Rauch has come to the rescue of both truth and liberty in this thought-provoking, essential work."

—MITCHELL E. DANIELS, JR.,
president, Purdue University;
former governor of Indiana

"Once waged primarily on the turf of government censorship, the battle for free speech and an open society has shifted toward the new terrains of social media, cancel culture, and rampant disinformation. Starting from first principles and applying them to headlines as recent as the storming of the U.S. Capitol in 2021, *The Constitution of Knowledge* provides the map we've been waiting for. In my forty years of work on behalf of the values our democracy depends on, I've seen a handful of landmark books come along. This is one of them."

—NADINE STROSSEN,
John Marshall Harlan II Professor of Law, Emerita,
New York Law School; former president,
American Civil Liberties Union, 1991–2008

"Why can't we have shared facts anymore? The most profound and useful answer is contained in this book. Jonathan Rauch shows us how it is that societies ever come to know things. It is only after we appreciate the miracle of knowledge production (the "constitution" of knowledge) that we can understand the tragedy befalling us now, as key institutions and practices decay. This book is a magnificent integration of psychology, epistemology, and history. It is a joy to read—deep insight after deep insight, embedded in playful writing, about one of the most important problems of the 2020s."

—JONATHAN HAIDT,
Thomas Cooley Professor of Ethical Leadership,
NYU-Stern School of Business;
author of *The Righteous Mind*; co-author of
The Coddling of the American Mind

"The digital age was supposed to bring about the blessings of unlimited knowledge fueled by radically egalitarian free speech allowing everyone to access, share, and learn from freely available information to the benefit and progress of all. Instead, an epistemic crisis supercharged by viral disinformation and indifference to truth has bred deep cynicism about the benefits of free speech and the liberal ideals that underpin this increasingly unpopular idea. In his unputdownable new book, Jonathan Rauch provides both a surgically precise diagnosis and a promising cure for the ailments that torment the twenty-first century with its crisis of authority, distrust, and rampant tribalism. We ignore Rauch's warning and prescription at our own peril."

—JACOB MCHANGAMA,
founder and CEO, Justitia

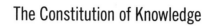
The Constitution of Knowledge

The Constitution
of Knowledge

A Defense of Truth

JONATHAN RAUCH

BROOKINGS INSTITUTION PRESS
Washington, D.C.

The Brookings Institution is a private nonprofit organization devoted to research, education, and publication on important issues of domestic and foreign policy. Its principal purpose is to bring the highest quality independent
research and analysis to bear on current and emerging policy problems. Interpretations or conclusions in Brookings publications should be understood to be
solely those of the authors.

Library of Congress Control Number: 2021936756

ISBN 9780815738862 (hc)
ISBN 9780815738879 (ebook)

9 8 7 6 5 4 3 2

Typeset in Sabon Pro

Composition by Elliott Beard

For my father
Oscar C. Rauch
In loving memory

Write if you get work.

Contents

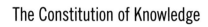

The Constitution of Knowledge

1

"A Terrible Statement Unless He Gets Away with It"

Chaos and conformity have caused an epistemic crisis

In the public square of Athens, a homely, snub-nosed, bulgy-eyed old man encounters a homely, snub-nosed, bulgy-eyed young man. Hailing the young man and remarking on their resemblance, Socrates begins a conversation with Theaetetus and sets out to determine whether they also resemble each other in their love of philosophy. Theaetetus protests that he is no great intellect; philosophical puzzles make him quite dizzy, "wondering whatever they can mean." Ah! Then you *are* a philosopher: "This sense of wonder is the mark of the philosopher," insists Socrates. "Philosophy indeed has no other origin."

With that, in a conversation imagined by Plato 2,400 or so years ago, the old man commences to lead his new friend on an expedition into the densest thickets of epistemology. What is knowledge? What is error? How does error arise? Why is error even possible? Each question would seem to have an obvious answer, yet each obvious answer collapses upon examination.

Perhaps knowledge is correct perception of the world? But perception varies between individuals; it varies, too, *within* individuals. A wine which tastes sweet when I am well may taste bitter the next day, when I am ill. There are dreams and hallucinations, all imaginary yet seeming real. Each of us is a parade of changing perceptions, but our shifting personal palimpsest can never be the same as knowledge, as reality.

Well, then, perhaps knowledge is *true* judgment, true belief? But we may hold random or ignorant views which merely happen to be true; we may guess or conjecture and be proven right through pure luck; yet lucky guesses are surely not the same as knowledge. Our own confidence in our beliefs is no good, for we may feel sure but be in error.

Perhaps, then, knowledge is true belief or true judgment plus an account, an explanation. That seems more like it. But no, Socrates spins us around again. How can we judge the truth of the account without also knowing the truth of the subject of the account? If the account is based on a distinction, for example, and if the distinction is comprehensible and persuasive, then we must already have knowledge of the thing we are explaining: otherwise the distinction would not enlighten us. Relying on an account traps us in circularity: we cannot have knowledge without an account, but we cannot have an account without knowledge.

"So, Theaetetus," says Socrates to the younger version of himself, "neither perception, nor true belief, nor the addition of an 'account' to true belief can be knowledge." Replies the young man, presumably confirmed in his belief that philosophy is dizzying, "Apparently not." And here the conversation ends abruptly in defeat, leavened only by Socrates's assurance that at least the two of them are clearer on what it is they do *not* know, and therefore will be humbler and more agreeable to their companions.

So much ratiocination, so much spadework, leading nowhere? Perhaps. And surely disappointing. "But tomorrow morning," says Socrates, "let us meet here again."[1] The conversation will continue. Not, tragically, for Socrates; he would soon be executed for impiety. But the conversation outlived him and continues to this day. At age eighteen, as a college freshman, I encountered *Theaetetus* with a jolt. I sensed that it asked an important question, yet it provided no answer. Instead, it was an exercise in relentless deconstruction, in gentle but ruthless analytical demolition. Plato's message came through in bold relief: this business about truth, about distinguishing reality from error—it is not easy, and if you think otherwise, go away!

And yet, as Plato instructs us, our analytical ruthlessness is not nihilism or a waste of time. It teaches rigor and humility, the foundations of the truth-seeking attitude. If Socrates could not on this occasion define or explain knowledge, he could nonetheless demonstrate its spirit. The most important words of the dialogue are those five words at the end. *Let us meet here again*: acquiring knowledge is a conversation, not a destination. It is a process, a journey—a journey we take together, not alone. Others are always involved. Knowledge is not just something I have; more fundamentally, it is something *we* have.

Here, implicitly at least, Plato anticipates the richest and most advanced insights of today's philosophy of science. Yet, in his grand political treatise, *The Republic*, Plato would take a very different view of knowledge than the one Socrates implies: the ideal regime invests an authoritative leader with the power to distinguish truth from falsehood. That governing model, whenever implemented, proved to be a wrong turn, one which contributed to centuries of human grief. Today, we can say that it was *Theaetetus* which pointed the way forward, even if more than two millennia would pass before the path it blazed was rediscovered.

In my own way, as a young man, I set out on Theaetetus's journey. After college I became a journalist and, as such, dedicated myself to finding out what is true and to telling stories which enlighten and instruct. Good journalism, like philosophy, and like science, begins with curiosity, with wonder. Then come the hypothesis, the thesis, the seemingly plausible account. Then come the efforts to test that account against the world, by asking still more questions; and then, often, comes the moment when the hypothesis lists or collapses and my head, like Theaetetus's, spins. And then, if I am lucky, out of the dizziness comes a stronger hypothesis, something closer to truth; or, if I am not as lucky, out of the dizziness comes a reminder to be humble in the face of reality's caprice.

However, my personal struggles to find the right questions and assemble mosaic tiles of information to tell the tale coherently—while necessary for journalism—are not in fact journalism. A crackpot, a loner, a conspiracy theorist will engage in the same steps, yet is not a journalist. I became a journalist by being forced outside of myself. From my very first steps into the world of journalism, first on my college newspaper, then as a summer intern at *National Journal* magazine in Washington, D.C., and then in the newsroom as a cub reporter for the *Winston-Salem Journal*, I was thrust into contact with the world outside my own head. Apart from the lonely process of writing a first draft, I could do nothing on my own. Facts were gathered from interviews and sources; analysis was checked with experts; every sentence was edited, copy-edited, and often fact-checked; tipsters suggested story ideas, sources waved me off bad leads, and challenges to my claims percolated in conversations within the newsroom and outside of it. The sense of having joined something much greater than myself, and of swearing allegiance to the exacting standards of a great tradition, made the enterprise of journalism appealing and compelling to me even on the days when the practice of journalism seemed grinding and routine (which was often).

There were some things, I learned, that we—*we*, as professionals—do: prize accuracy; seek a comment from a person before publishing something about her; prefer on-record information; consult multiple sources with varied viewpoints; abjure jargon, longwindedness, extravagance, and opinion (except in sports writing, which seemed to require all of the above). There were other things, I learned, that we do not do: pay for information, accept gifts from sources, betray confidentiality, tolerate meddling from the ad department. As a young journalist, I was being rebuilt, reshaped, into a worker ant in humanity's hive-mind, humans' most important and beneficent creation. Without realizing it at the time, I was being inducted into a community, the reality-based community—the same community into which Socrates was inducting Theaetetus so long ago. I was learning the Constitution of Knowledge.

An Epistemic Crisis

When Americans think about how we find truth amid a world full of discordant viewpoints, we usually turn to a metaphor, that of the marketplace of ideas. It is a good metaphor as far as it goes, yet woefully incomplete. It conjures up an image of ideas being traded by individuals in a kind of flea market, or an image of disembodied ideas clashing and competing in some ethereal realm of their own. But ideas in the marketplace do not talk directly to each other, and for the most part neither do individuals. Rather, our conversations are mediated through institutions like journals and newspapers and social-media platforms; and they rely on a dense network of norms and rules, like truthfulness and fact-checking; and they depend on the expertise of professionals, like peer reviewers and editors—and the entire system rests on a foundation of values: a shared understanding that there are right and wrong ways to make knowledge. Those values and rules and institutions do for knowledge what the U.S. Constitution does for politics: they create a governing structure, forcing social contestation onto peaceful and productive pathways. And so I call them, collectively, the Constitution of Knowledge.

The world I was trained for seems, in hindsight, a long way off, in some respects more unfamiliar than Socrates's Athens. In science, in journalism, in politics, and in daily life, truthfulness is for the most part a civic norm, not a legal requirement, and the twenty-first century put it under severe pressure. Most shockingly, a president of the United States gleefully shattered every known record for lying. One might be tempted to write off all politicians as liars, but no prominent figure in American politics had lied nearly as brazenly, wantonly, and prolifically.

Even more telling, perhaps, than his contemptuous attitude toward facts was his contemptuous attitude toward corrections. In 1690, the first newspaper in North America went to press. Called *Publick Occurrences*, it was soon stamped out by censorious authorities. Still, it made an impression, partly by declaring its mission on its front page:

That something may be done towards the Curing, or at least the Charming of that Spirit of Lying, which prevails amongst us, wherefore nothing shall be entered, but what we have reason to believe is true, repairing to the best fountains for our Information. And when there appears any material mistake in anything that is collected, it shall be corrected . . .[2]

The idea of accountability to truth, and thus of a responsibility to correct the record, was a threshold idea in the establishment of mainstream journalism, and it remains foundational today. In 2017 several leading journalists at CNN reported that a confidant of President Trump was linked to a dicey Russian hedge fund. The story turned out to be wrong. CNN retracted it, apologized for it, and forced out the journalists responsible for it after determining that they had breached CNN's standards. One response would have been to tweet out some statement like: "Kudos to CNN for caring enough about truth to correct its story and clean house. That's Real News!" What the president tweeted out, however, was this: "Wow, CNN had to retract big story on 'Russia,' with 3 employees forced to resign. What about all the other phony stories they do? FAKE NEWS!" And this: "So they caught Fake News CNN cold, but what about NBC, CBS & ABC? What about the failing @nytimes & @washingtonpost? They are all Fake News!" In the president's worldview, by holding itself to account, the network had proved not its integrity but its corruption—and, indeed, the corruption of the entire news industry.

In much the same spirit, in 2018 the president and the Republican National Committee touted something they called the "Fake News Awards." What the president and the committee did not note was that of the eleven supposedly fake news items, at least seven had been promptly corrected by the outlets which had published them. In other words, the president and the committee knew the reports were false because the outlets had said so. Two of the faulty reports, according to the *Washington Post*, had prompted suspensions or resignations (the CNN report was one of them). Two were merely tweets, also corrected. Another was an opinion piece. Apparently, scouring the mainstream media for fake news, the president and his political team could find nothing worse. (Perhaps they lacked time to glance at the acres of inaccuracies rolled out by conspiratorial right-wing outlets.)

In any case, the moral they drew was the same: correcting error is a sign not of integrity but of crookedness.

The president's behavior may have been compulsive, delusional, or pathological, to one extent or another. But it could not have been anything other than intentional. In 2013 someone using the handle @backupwraith tweeted: "I firmly believe that @realDonaldTrump is the most superior troll on the whole of twitter." Trump quoted the tweet with the comment: "A great compliment!" In 2018 CBS News's Lesley Stahl recounted asking Trump, during his presidential campaign, whether he planned to stop attacking the press. "He said, 'You know why I do it? I do it to discredit you all and demean you all, so when you write negative stories about me no one will believe you.'" The White House did not deny Stahl's account. Why would it? Trump and his troll army had, by their lights, every reason to be proud of what they were doing.

And they did know what they were doing. We know Trump knew, because he had warned us. In 2004, in an interview with NBC News's Chris Matthews, Trump was asked to reflect on the Republican presidential convention, which had just ended. In that year's presidential race, a challenge for Republicans was that their candidate, President George W. Bush, had safely sat out the Vietnam War in the Texas Air National Guard, whereas his opponent, Senator John Kerry, had won a Silver Star, a Bronze Star, and three Purple Hearts for valor in combat. A group called Swift Boat Veterans for Truth waged a successful propaganda campaign challenging Kerry's wartime record. That was the context in which the following exchange occurred:

Trump: I sat through the convention in New York. And they did a great job, the Republicans. But maybe the greatest spin I've ever seen on anything is, it's almost coming out that Bush is a war hero and Kerry isn't. I think that could be the greatest spin I've ever seen.

Matthews: Because?

Trump: Well, the whole thing with the Swift Boat group, which obviously is being done by Bush and Bush's people, happened to be brilliant. They've taken all of that war hero thing away from Kerry and they've almost given to it Bush. And Bush, frankly, was not serving. That we know.

> *Matthews:* . . . Let me ask you about perhaps what you might call
> unnecessary roughness in politics. This week, Dick Cheney, the
> vice president, a very tough guy, said that if we elect, the Ameri-
> can people elect Kerry, that we're basically going to face ourselves
> with the threat of a devastating [terrorist] attack. He is saying
> vote Democrat, you're going to get attacked.
> *Trump:* Well, it's a terrible statement unless he gets away with it.

A terrible statement unless he gets away with it. Trump was
hardly the first politician to lie. Yet as president, more than a decade
later, he went far beyond an ordinary political hit job like the Swift
Boat campaign. In the scale and brazenness of his lying, many people
sensed something different from ordinary political spin and exagger-
ation, something with more sinister aims and more disorienting consequences: something from the world of George Orwell's *Nineteen
Eighty-Four*: "The party told you to reject the evidence of your eyes
and ears. It was their final, most essential command." Trump and his
media echo chambers were normalizing lying in order to obliterate
the distinction, in the public realm, between truth and untruth. They
were practicing the hallowed (if infamous) art of disinformation.
They lied in trivial ways, when there was no point in lying except to
show contempt for truth, as when Trump claimed rain had not fallen
on his inauguration. They lied in grandiose and fantastic ways, as in
their months-long disinformation campaign claiming to have won
an election which Trump had demonstrably lost (a campaign which
ended only when he was impeached for inciting a violent insurrec-
tion). They lied without distinguishing between truth and falsehood
or between big lies and small lies, because their goal was to denude
the public's capacity to make any distinctions at all.

Observing events, an assortment of commentators and academics
thought they saw a threat to the underpinnings of the liberal order
itself, and not just from Trump and his political allies but from a
whole industry of trolls and foreign actors and even bots and algorithms. "In threatening to erode the forms of intellectual trust and
cooperation that are required for democratic life, and in making the
determination of 'truth' more and more obviously a consequence of
brute power alone, our current practices threaten democracy itself,"

wrote Sophia Rosenfeld, a historian at the University of Pennsylvania, in her book *Democracy and Truth: A Short History*. In reports and books with titles like "The Misinformation Age" and "Truth Decay" and "Post-Truth" and "The Death of Truth," scholars explored aspects of what all agreed was uncharted territory, at least in the United States.[3] Politicians and pundits—everyone from senators and two former secretaries of state to leaders of the intelligence and law-enforcement communities—sounded alarms that American civic life might be losing its grip on reality: its ability, that is, to tell truth from untruth or even believe there is a difference. "We have a risk of getting to a place where we don't have shared public facts," Ben Sasse, a Republican senator, said in a 2017 interview with CNN, voicing the prevalent concern. "A republic will not work if we don't have shared facts." Michael Hayden, a former director of the Central Intelligence Agency, sent a distress signal when he wrote (in the *New York Times*): "These are truly uncharted waters for the country. We have in the past argued over the values to be applied to objective reality, or occasionally over what constituted objective reality, but never the existence or relevance of objective reality itself." The battle lines, Hayden perceived, made for some strange bedfellows. "In this post-truth world, intelligence agencies are in the bunker with some unlikely mates: journalism, academia, the courts, law enforcement, and science—all of which, like intelligence gathering, are evidence-based."

An arcane multisyllabic word began cropping up in the public discourse. "At its heart . . . the current crisis belongs primarily to the realm of *epistemology*, or how we know what we know," wrote Rosenfeld (italics added). The esoteric term, previously a staple of philosophers but little known outside the ivory tower, had found a new mainstream application. In 2020, former President Barack Obama stated the matter starkly: "If we do not have the capacity to distinguish what's true from what's false, then by definition the marketplace of ideas doesn't work. And by definition our democracy doesn't work. We are entering into an epistemological crisis."[4]

A Chill Wind

The crisis had many elements, but two seemed central to its character. One was the deployment of disinformation on an unprecedented scale by Trump, his troll armies, foreign governments, conspiracy mongers, and a conservative media ecosystem which was increasingly detached from reality-based norms. That attack came predominantly, though not exclusively, from the right. Peculiarly, it received an assist from the left, in the form of an attack on epistemic liberalism which came to be known as cancel culture.

Canceling, like trolling, was not unique to one part of the ideological spectrum; many conservatives were politically canceled for opposing Trump. Still, it was predominantly the left which had the cultural power to police speech and weaponize shaming. "Young-adult books are being targeted in intense social-media call-outs, draggings, and pile-ons—sometimes before anybody's even read them," reported *New York* magazine's Kat Rosenfield in 2017.[5] One first-time novelist withdrew her book from publication under pressure from an online mob who had not actually read it.[6] A prominent television writer told me that he and his industry were routinely censoring themselves. His creative choices, he said, were constrained by unwritten rules; for example, female characters always had to be strong and secure. "You just learn to channel your imagination along certain paths," he said. "You feel the pressure. Everybody's aware of it. Social media is watching everything you do."

As a member of a sexual minority and a longtime gay rights (and free speech) advocate, I was especially discouraged to see an unrepresentative but outspoken minority of transgender activists resort to social intimidation. In Britain, reported *The Economist* in August 2019, "any discussion of transgender issues is explosive." In the United States, wrote Robby Soave in his 2019 book, *Panic Attack: Young Radicals in the Age of Trump*, "many of the loudest trans voices, particularly on social media, routinely decry all criticism of their activism as not just wrong but a form of assault." He quoted one professor as saying, "They do manage to terrify people into silence." Targets of such campaigns could become socially radioactive. They could lose their reputations and their jobs or businesses, and also many of their friendships and social connections. Socially and professionally, they could be, as the new term had it, canceled.

For sure, self-censorship is part of living together (we call it "courtesy")—but not when it impedes honest conversation and criticism in university intellectual life, where honest conversation and criticism are the whole point of being there. In the 2010s an unmistakable turn in that direction had happened. Jonathan Haidt, a prominent social psychologist at New York University (whose work is an inspiration for this book), said in an interview with the radio host Bob Zadek in 2018:

> In 2015, call-out culture spread much more rapidly around the country. I would say that it is everywhere to some extent. Students are much more defensive and much more afraid of disagreeing with the dominant view. The nature of college as a free place with free-flowing discussion, where you can be provocative and challenge the dominant people or ideas, is weaker than it was just four or five years ago.

Ordinarily, one might have hoped that coercive pressure to conform with particular viewpoints would meet resistance from academia, and sometimes it did. What was worrying, though, was that, at least as often, figures in the academic world led and justified canceling campaigns—and their most frightened targets were often their academic peers. "I'm in my mid-forties," a stranger named Holly emailed me, "and have always considered myself a liberal, but it's getting harder and harder to associate with this absurdity. I'm currently in grad school in Denver and I'm betting there are fewer places on earth more ridiculously left-wing than colleges right now. The terms seem to change by the week and it's completely exhausting. People don't want to say anything because everyone's so goddamn scared of offending someone."

Increasingly, when I visited campuses in recent years, I would be approached by students—frequently first-years, not yet acculturated to university life—who expressed dismay about limits on acceptable thought. Left-of-center students felt just as besieged as right-of-center students. One Princeton graduate told me he had made it a rule never to discuss race, gender, or sexuality on campus—period.

When I asked why, he replied, "Because it's all downside." His friend, a recent Harvard graduate, agreed.

Campus threats to freedom of expression were not new in the 2020s. University speech-codes had been on the books, and controversial, since the late 1980s. Off-campus threats to freedom of expression were even less new. My first newspaper boss liked to say that if the First Amendment were put to a plebiscite, it would lose. Chances are you have read quite a lot about those problems, and I have examined them in my own previous work, and so the object of this book is not to rehash what has already been hashed.

Something did seem new and different, though. In the late 1980s, when campus free speech became a national issue, challenges came predominantly from professors and bureaucrats championing speech codes and defending them with elaborate theoretical rationales. Although they did not give up, by the mid-2010s the complexion of the problem had changed. Both in academia and outside of it, the problem had come to look less like censorship and more like censoriousness, which is to say a combination of conformity and intimidation. Students said they worried less about speech codes than social pressure, mostly from their peers, not professors. In polls and in conversations, they reported being worried that one wrong comment might set off a firestorm of condemnation among peers or on social media, and they could never be sure what comment might be the trigger. They frequently told me that their professors, far from being "tenured radicals," generally tried to encourage honest classroom discussions— yet unorthodox students still shrank from speaking freely for fear of inviting hostility. A law student I know recounted how a white male student became the object of a call-out campaign after other students overheard him using the phrase "Do you understand what I'm saying?" in conversation with a female African American professor. (Fortunately for him, she came to his defense.) An Ivy League teacher told me, "I've found that if students have an opportunity to jump on someone, they usually take it." Sam Foer, an undergraduate I interviewed, transferred out of his private liberal arts college because white male students like him were ritually denounced on campus and online as Islamophobic, racist, misogynistic, and the like. "People who were genuine liberals were being eaten alive by the radical wing of this campus culture," he told me. If a student "so much as disagreed with a person of color, in such a way that a person of color could even manufacture an argument to call the other person racist, then they would do that. It instilled this feeling of being coerced into self-censorship: not being able to speak, even to have conversations, with our peers. That coupled with the treatment I was subject to, I just said, I'm out; it's not worth it."

Polls showed he was not alone in feeling "coerced into self-censorship." A poll conducted in 2017 for the Heterodox Academy project found that almost half of all students reported reluctance to discuss race and politics in the classroom; 41 percent were reluctant to discuss gender. A majority said they did not think their school frequently encouraged students to consider a wide variety of viewpoints and perspectives. Over the next three years, other polls suggested the temperature was only growing chillier. A poll for the Knight Foundation in 2019 found that "more than two-thirds (68 percent) of college students say their campus climate precludes students from expressing their true opinions because their classmates might find them offensive."[7] That result had become quite typical.

Faculty felt the chill, too. News stories abounded about incidents like one at Sarah Lawrence college: when a professor wrote a *New York Times* op-ed piece arguing that college administrators lacked ideological diversity, students mobilized to demand his firing (euphemized as "tenure review"), saying his presence on campus threatened their "safety and well-being." A professor I met, who taught sociology at a university widely regarded as conservative-leaning, told me, "Everyone is 'careful' on campus these days. Including me: I have not and will not discuss my research on affirmative action and diversity outside my own classroom." At one private university, a young neurobiologist told me she had dropped a module on autism from her course on brain development. A student had complained that the module might be interpreted as demeaning to the autistic. Her dean had dismissed the complaint, she told me. And, as I pointed out, dropping the material gave her no real protection because another complainant could just object to something else. Why, then, drop the module? Because, she said, she took the complaint as "strike one." She lacked tenure protections and could not afford a strike two or three. Even world-famous faculty with tenure silence themselves. In a lecture at Case Western Reserve University in 2018, Haidt, the psychologist, said: "I don't take any chances at NYU. I don't say anything controversial. I can be controversial with you, because you can't report me. You can't do anything to me if I say something that offends you. But if I'm at NYU, there's a sign in every bathroom telling students what number to call or what email to send to report me or anyone else who says something that they think is offensive. So I just don't take chances at NYU."

All downside.

Ironically, although canceling chilled dissent on the center and left, it was a godsend to trolls on the right. Political correctness, as they called it, helped raise the likes of Trump and Breitbart News and even Russian troll farms to new heights of influence. "For decades," wrote the political scientist Bill Schneider, "political correctness has been used to shut down debate. Activists on the left refuse to allow people to say things that might offend less privileged groups such as women, gays, African Americans, and immigrants. . . . White working-class men seethe whenever political correctness denigrates them as 'privileged.' They certainly don't feel 'privileged,' not after the economic devastation of the past decade. Their response? Defiance."[8]

Research confirmed what common sense suggested: in a land of free, independent-minded people, norm-policing backfires against the norm police. The policed may go mute in public, but resentment builds up in their hearts and homes, then bursts forth in the voting booth when activated by a demagogue. As one study found in 2017, "Temporarily priming PC [politically correct] norms significantly increased support for Donald Trump" (and not just among right-wingers: the study's participants were "largely politically moderate Americans").[9]

Donald Trump certainly agreed. "I think the big problem this country has is being politically correct," he said during his 2016 campaign. "I've been challenged by so many people, and I don't, frankly, have time for total political correctness. And to be honest with you, this country doesn't have time, either."

Maybe not much time, unless the traditional champions of the Constitution of Knowledge return to the fold.

The Strangest, Best Idea Ever

This book explains and defends the Constitution of Knowledge, liberalism's epistemic operating system: our social rules for turning disagreement into knowledge. The system did not assemble itself by some automatic social magic; it was the product of hard-fought battles and hard-won norms and institutions, and many people suffered and bled for it along the way. It is not self-maintaining; it relies on an array of sometimes delicate social settings and understandings, and those need to be understood, affirmed, and protected. By explicating the Constitution of Knowledge, and by exploring contemporary threats to it, I hope to arm its advocates with a clearer understanding of what they must protect, and why, and how.

The argument builds upon the framework I developed in my book on how free societies make knowledge, *Kindly Inquisitors: The New Attacks on Free Thought*. Those familiar with that book will find no fundamental rethink here, but they will find a change in the angle of view. In the earlier book, I teased out the implications of two rules on which the modern liberal epistemic order—what I call "liberal science"—is founded: *no final say* and *no personal authority*. I argued that wherever people adhere to those rules, they will form a community of error-seeking inquirers accountable to each other but never to any particular authority, and knowledge will arise from their hive-like, largely self-organizing activities. I used the term "liberal science" partly to emphasize that the system is, like capitalism and democracy, depersonalized and decentralized and rules-based; also because I needed a more inclusive term than just "science," which connotes hard sciences like physics, whereas "liberal science" includes the softer sciences and even humanities such as literary criticism and moral philosophy, plus mainstream journalism and aspects of jurisprudence and intelligence work: all the fields in which investigators use impersonal critical exchange to seek truth and hold each other accountable for accuracy.

Over the years, I came to believe that the framework of *Kindly Inquisitors*, while it had held up well, could be strengthened by paying more attention to the institutional and communitarian foundations of collective inquiry. The sudden rise of industrial-scale trolling and disinformation made the institutional defense seem urgent. In this book I have supplemented "liberal science" with the term "reality-based community," by which I mean the social network which adheres to liberal science's rules and norms. My hope is that "reality-based community" captures the notion that liberal science is no mere colloquy of individuals, each doing her own thing and occasionally interacting with others, like gas molecules in a balloon or bumper cars at the amusement park. The community's interactions are structured and elaborate and amount to much more than just the sum of its individuals' doings, and the essential enablers, connectors, and transmitters are *institutions*. Institutions propagate and enforce norms and rules, evaluate and certify credentials, set agendas and direct resources, enforce accountability, and train future generations to do all of those other things, and more. That is why, today, the institutions and norms of liberal science, not individuals, are the real targets of attack by nihilists and bullies.

But institutions and norms are hard to see. Unlike individuals, they do not star on television or YouTube, and they do not entertain or outrage us. When they work, they permeate the intellectual environment, providing context and policing boundaries and nudging behavior without drawing too much attention to themselves. Making them visible and bringing them to the foreground is hard. Where, I wondered, might one look for an understandable way to think about the rules and institutions which vet knowledge and produce facts? The answer, when it finally came to me, seemed obvious.

Modern liberalism—what the philosopher Karl Popper and subsequently others have called the open society—is defined by three social systems: economic, political, and epistemic. They handle social decisionmaking about resources, power, and truth. The epistemic system is often analogized to the economic system, through the metaphor of the marketplace of ideas. But the parallels between the epistemic and political systems, although less well developed, are in important respects more revealing.

This book, then, proceeds by way of an extended analogy: between the United States Constitution (not just the text of the Constitution on paper but the institutions and norms which embody the Constitution in action) and the Constitution of Knowledge, by which

I mean the rules which define liberal science and organize the reality-based community. Like all analogies, it can be taken too literally or too far, and in some respects I may have overworked the comparison. Still, the parallels are real and many, and even the differences are illuminating. Both constitutions are foundational to modern liberalism and instrumental in bringing the peace, prosperity, and freedom which liberal societies uniquely enjoy. Both have their taproots in the same stream of social thought; they even trace their pedigrees to some of the same people. Both are social compacts, agreements to follow certain rules and forgo certain claims because other group members will do the same. Both place coercion off-limits and require people to negotiate and reach agreement in order to make laws or knowledge. Both distribute decisionmaking across many competing and cooperating actors, using checks and balances to create networks of accountability. Both provide strong guarantees of individual rights, yet also, in exchange, require participants to meet challenging standards of behavior. Both work only because they combine formal rules and strictures with informal norms and implicit virtues. Both are embodied in institutions and require being understood and defended in institutional terms. Both are simultaneously resilient and fragile. Both are under unending attack from adversaries who never tire of trying new attacks when old ones fail.

The book begins by updating Plato's *Theaetetus* with a survey of the reasons humans make cognitive blunders, turn them into tribal disagreements, and wind up at war over knowledge. It then shows how generations of philosophers and scientists developed the modern epistemic order—a more gradual and organic constitutional founding than the one in Philadelphia in 1787, to be sure, but a founding nonetheless. With that as background, it explores the architecture of the Constitution of Knowledge—like the U.S. Constitution, a social mechanism to force conciliation—and the boundaries of the reality-based community.

In its second half, the book turns from history and theory to several contemporary challenges, beginning with the most unpleasant epistemic surprise of the twenty-first century: digital media have turned out to be better attuned to outrage and disinformation than to conversation and knowledge. Truth-friendly digital architectures are possible and indeed are already emerging, as digital platforms begin to take on institutional responsibilities to truth. Less fortunately, however, they—and we—are in for a fight against two insurgencies: the spread of viral disinformation and alternative realities, sometimes called troll culture, and the spread of enforced conformity and ideological blacklisting, sometimes called cancel culture. One is predominantly right-wing and populist, the other predominantly left-wing and elitist. One employs chaos and confusion, the other conformity and social coercion. But their goals are similar, and often, weirdly, they act as de facto allies.

What troll culture and cancel culture have in common is that they are techniques of what propaganda experts often call information warfare. Rather than using rational persuasion to seek truth, they manipulate the social and media environments for political advantage. They may appear marginal, disorganized, or unhinged, but they are aggressive, expansionary, and rooted in a sophisticated understanding of human cognitive and emotional vulnerabilities. They have captured commanding institutional heights, including (for four years) the White House and substantial parts of academia. They exploit the capabilities of digital technology to amplify their speed and reach. But they have also engendered encouraging pushback, as awareness of the methods they use and the dangers they pose has grown.

Woke to Reality

I am not an alarmist. To the contrary, I write this book in a spirit of hope and guarded optimism. In the digital-media world, impressive commitment and innovation are being brought to bear against disinformation attacks, and the enemy no longer has the advantage of surprise. In the academic world, deep reservoirs of scientific integrity remain present to be tapped. Today's challenges to the Constitution of Knowledge are comparatively tame by historical standards. The miracle is how robust free expression and liberal science have proved to be, despite unremitting attacks from every direction over hundreds of years. The idea that obnoxious, misguided, seditious, blasphemous, and bigoted expressions deserve not only to be tolerated but, of all things, protected is the single most counterintuitive social principle in all of human history. Every human instinct cries out against it, and every generation discovers fresh reasons to oppose it. It is saved from the scrapheap of self-evident absurdity only by the fact that it is also the single most *successful* social principle in all of human history. Those of us who favor it, and also our children, and also their children and *their* children, will need to get up every morning and explain and defend our counterintuitive social principle from scratch, and so we might as well embrace the task and perform it cheerfully.

By way of recompense, we can marvel at how well our seemingly ludicrous proposition has done. Somehow, despite its implausibility and its exacting rules and its complex institutions, the liberal epistemic order—the Constitution of Knowledge—has always found a way forward. But it relies, at bottom, on the full-hearted embrace and full-throated defense of its principles by ordinary members of the reality-based community—people like you and me and Sam Foer.

Foer left his liberal arts college. "I wanted a place where I could have intellectual conversations without that fear of being defamed," he told me. He transferred to a public university. There, after a summer internship at the Foundation for Individual Rights in Education (or FIRE, a civil liberties group), he launched an effort to revise the student handbook's speech policies, which had received FIRE's lowest free-speech rating. He organized a free-speech event and lobbied the university administration, where he found support. And he succeeded. The student handbook was rewritten. As of this writing, his school boasts FIRE's highest rating, a symbolic green light.

"For me," Foer said of the socially enforced conformity at his first college, "it inspired a political awakening, and it inspired serious concern for the future of education. In that sense, what I experienced there was a blessing. It was a blessing disguised as a curse. I wish I hadn't been subjected to that treatment, but truly it has inspired me to push back and keep the fight up.

"A lot of people," Foer continued, "back down in the face of resistance and say, 'My degree is more important to me than fighting to change these policies.' From what I've seen, it takes a person with the passion of a die-hard activist to make these kinds of changes."

Foer's passion is the spirit of the Constitution of Knowledge—the spirit this book seeks to defend and empower.

2

The State of Nature: Tribal Truth

Bias, groupthink, and the epistemic
war of all against all

In 2018 Americans waited anxiously for answers. A special prose-cutor, Robert Mueller, was digging into the activities of a president, Donald Trump. The president's future seemed to hang in the balance.

Well, some people waited anxiously. Others already knew the result. As a Trump supporter named Donna Kowalczyk told the journalist Ben Bradlee Jr., "I don't think there's anything to it. If they find something, they will have made it up."[1]

To say that she and I approached the question differently would be an understatement. As a professional journalist, I am evidence-based, dispassionate, and fair-minded. I decide after I have the facts, not before. At least, that is how I flatter myself.

But really, am I so different from Ms. Kowalczyk? Or am I merely a member of a different tribe, and as biased and blind to my biases as she or anyone else? And suppose, for argument's sake, Ms. Kowalczyk is in fact less evidence-based and dispassionate than I: whose way of thinking is more normal and natural? Whose way is more serviceable for most humans in most circumstances?

The answer: not mine.

"Reason Is the Slave of the Passions"

In the mid-1600s, the English philosopher Thomas Hobbes delivered a jolt from which political philosophy never entirely recovered. Aristotle had identified humans as political, or social, animals. But to what kind of politics and society are humans naturally inclined? As we might say today, what is human society's default setting—or, as philosophers framed the question centuries ago, what is the human "state of nature"? From Plato down through the Middle Ages, the predominant answer was that people are hierarchical: they settle into orderly patterns in which the wise or strong or godly or aristocratic rule over and protect the ignorant or weak or infidel or vulgar.

Hobbes demolished the Great Chain of Being. Around him raged the English civil war, a traumatic struggle which would haunt and shape political thinking for generations to come. No wonder he regarded the human animal as fundamentally self-interested and warlike. Left to themselves—as he argued in *Leviathan*, his masterpiece about state and society—people live not in orderly hierarchies but in a state of constant competition and rivalry, riven by personal and tribal struggles for power. The state of nature, Hobbes argued, is a state of war of all against all.

> In such condition there is no place for industry, because the fruit thereof is uncertain, and consequently no culture of the earth, no navigation nor the use of commodities that may be imported by sea, no commodious building, no instruments of moving and removing such things as require much force, no knowledge of the face of the earth, no account of time, no arts, no letters, no society, and which is worst of all, continual fear and danger of violent death, and the life of man, solitary, poor, nasty, brutish, and short.

Audaciously, Hobbes set himself the seemingly impossible task of using his pessimistic view of human nature not as an argument for anarchy but as a foundation for order. The task of bringing peace, he argued, could be performed only by "leviathan," a sovereign monarch invested by the people with irrevocable power to govern them. But who would govern the monarch? Who would rule the ruler? That question awaited an answer.

Something like the Hobbesian political earthquake happened in the epistemic realm, too. Ever since Plato, philosophers had been aware that the senses can deceive and belief can err. But they assumed that humans naturally incline toward truth and that reason, God's unique gift to our species, would guide us. Almost 300 years ago, the Scottish philosopher David Hume challenged that default assumption. In his *Treatise on Human Nature*, he issued one of the firmest and most famous declarations on the matter: "Reason is, and ought only to be, the slave of the passions, and can never pretend to any other office than to serve and obey them." Hume did not deny the utility of reason as a tool for thinking, but he believed that reason is like the navigator in the passenger seat, able to suggest directions but not to steer the car, and that our emotions and moral intuitions are in the driver's seat. In the last few decades, a blizzard of scientific research has settled the argument between Hume and the ancients. Hume won.

Back, again, to the state of nature, or what modern scholars call the environment of evolutionary adaptation: why did higher reasoning, the pride and joy of *Homo sapiens*, arise in the first place? Certainly, doing arithmetic, manipulating symbols, and communicating concepts are useful for survival; but all kinds of creatures survive and thrive and form sophisticated social groups without the help of symbolic reasoning.

Modern scholarship suggests that reasoning arose from a different imperative than raw survival: persuasion. People originally lived in small bands, or tribes. Survival depended on being able to win a secure place within the group for one's self and one's children. Being shunned, abandoned, or cast out could be fatal. In contrast, high status could bring resources and mating opportunities. One way to gain dominance might be physical, by killing or overpowering competitors; but that path invites rivals to form alliances and go to war.

The gift of persuasion has lower costs and higher returns. With it, we can persuade others to follow where we wish to go, to do what we prefer to do, to ally with us and protect us, and to provide us with aid and resources. Giving reasons, it turns out, is a good method of persuading others, and so those who are good at giving reasons can prosper.

But here is a potential snag: the implication is that evolution selects not for the ability to reason in a way which leads to truth, necessarily, but for the ability to reason in a way which *persuades*. Reason, writes the social psychologist Jonathan Haidt in his book *The Righteous Mind: Why Good People Are Divided by Politics and Religion,* "evolved not to help us find truth but to help us engage in arguments, persuasion, and manipulation in the context of discussions with other people." True, on simple empirical questions where mistakes can be deadly or easily exposed, such as where to find water or where the neighboring tribe is camped, our thinking is likely to be pretty realistic (or else we wouldn't be here). But on the more abstract moral and intellectual questions which so often preoccupy and divide us, reasoning, argues Haidt, is like a press secretary whose goal is to justify whatever position her boss has already taken. "Intuitions come first, strategic reasoning second," writes Haidt. Moreover, in conversations about matters which arouse strong moral reactions, "people care a great deal more about appearance and reputation than about reality." They care more about *looking* right than *being* right. "Our moral thinking," says Haidt, "is much more like a politician searching for votes than a scientist searching for truth."[2] Maybe Socrates would rather be right than popular, but most of us prefer to maintain our good standing with our tribe, a reasonable call when one considers that Socrates was executed by his fellow citizens.

Besides being useful for persuading others, the ability to construct reasons is useful for persuading ourselves. Persuading others is easier, after all, if we believe what we say. The old political saw holds that if you can fake sincerity, you've got it made; but that is not quite right, because the best way to seem sincere is to be sincere. Detecting trustworthiness is a basic life skill in small groups which depend on sharing and reciprocity, and so people have developed good bullshit detectors. The best way around other people's bullshit detectors is to believe what you say. If your social reputation and group identity depend upon believing something, then you will find a way to believe it. In fact, your brain will help you by readily accepting and recalling congenial information while working to bury and ignore uncongenial information.[3]

That is why intelligence is no defense against false belief. To the contrary, it makes us even better at rationalizing. Super-smart people, as Haidt notes in *The Righteous Mind*, are more skilled than others at finding arguments to justify their own points of view. But when they are asked to find arguments on the *opposite* side of a question, they do no better than anyone else. Brainpower makes people better press secretaries, but not necessarily better at open-minded, self-critical thinking.

Reason cannot be twisted infinitely, and we must not give up on it. Beyond a certain point, strategies like rationalizing self-interest and believing whatever we hear ourselves say are self-limiting. In the longer run, persuading ourselves and others to abandon reality poses its own social (and material) hazards. Eventually, people who are consistently wrong or deceptive or self-deceptive will see their credibility suffer. Reason may have evolved to serve the passions, but it develops its own agenda, too. Rationality persuades precisely because evidence and argument have persuasive pull; often, though not always, persuasive reasoning is also good reasoning. When someone we disagree with walks us through a chain of inference or shows us the math, we feel an uncomfortable internal dissonance, which sometimes—not always, to be sure, but sometimes—can lead us to question a conviction, mistrust a passion, even change our minds (a process we call "education").

What the research suggests, then, is not that reason never prevails, or even that it rarely prevails, but that it does not reliably prevail. Worse, it is likeliest to fail precisely when we need it most: namely, when we are most in thrall to passions which cloud our judgment. As Haidt told a *Reason* magazine interviewer in 2018, "The more passionately we feel about something, the more likely it is that our reasoning is warped and unreliable." Rational decisionmaking, based on carefully reckoning pros and cons, is more likely to break down when the options have strong emotional valences. "The emotional signals sent out by the alternatives themselves are so powerful that we neglect to consider the objective information that should help us to distinguish the pros and cons of the options in the first place," writes Joseph Árvai, an expert on risk and decisionmaking.

A study he conducted with Robyn S. Wilson provides an elegant example. Participants were shown data indicating that the harms of deer overpopulation, a problem whose emotional valence is low, were greater in a certain place than the harms of property crime, a problem whose emotional valance is high. How, the participants were then asked, would they allocate $100,000 in resources? Participants spent much more on crime—the viscerally alarming issue—and much less on deer than the objective data would warrant. "To test our ideas further," Árvai writes, "we repeated the experiment several times, each time making the damages from deer overpopulation even bigger, while holding those from property crime constant. No matter how big the difference in damages, we could not get people to take action on deer overpopulation. It was as though people simply couldn't get past the emotional tug of the problem—crime—no matter what empirical data we presented about it."[4]

As demagogues have demonstrated time and again, the tendency to react emotionally to emotionally charged issues is easy to exploit and manipulate: for example, by hyping nonexistent crime waves, statistically rare murders by immigrants, and "American carnage." Worse, even when emotion is swaying us, we *feel* we are reacting rationally. Voters who claim their decisions are based on candidates' stands on the issues "are probably making their selection based in large part on the emotional connections they forge with the candidates themselves," writes Árvai. In other words, when forming political loyalties, we rationalize backward from our emotions and intuitions—yet we will swear that we are reasoning forward from our policy views.

You're Biased, I'm Not

Theaetetus and Socrates puzzled over how it is that errors ever arise in the chain of human cognition. In light of recent research, the better question is: how is it that errors ever do *not* arise? Cognition suffers from all kinds of distortions. "A solid group of 100 or so [cognitive] biases has been repeatedly shown to exist, and can make a hash of our lives," writes Ben Yagoda in *The Atlantic*.[5] They include, just for example:

- optimism bias, the tendency to overestimate our chances of success,

- availability bias, a tendency to overestimate the likelihood of phenomena which stick in our minds (terrorist attacks; child kidnappings),

- familiarity bias (or repetition bias), a tendency to believe things which we hear often (in fact, even debunking a false claim, by repeating it, can make it more familiar and thus more believable),

- fluency bias, a tendency to believe statements which are easy to understand and assimilate (we are more likely to believe unaccented speakers, statements written in large, bold, or high-contrast fonts, aphorisms which rhyme, and statements accompanied by photos, even if the photos convey no relevant information),

- the illusion of asymmetric insight, which leads us to presume that we understand others' thinking and motives better than they understand ours,

- the gambler's fallacy, which leads us to expect that if a flipped coin comes up heads five times in a row, it is more likely to come up tails the sixth time,

- the anchoring effect, a tendency to over-emphasize the first piece of information offered,

- framing effects, a tendency to be influenced by the way content is presented to us,

- superiority bias, a tendency to overestimate how competent we are,

- source confusion, a tendency to misattribute where we learned information and how we know what we think we know, and

▪ perseverance bias, a tendency to hold onto beliefs despite disconfirming evidence.

To all of which can be added a meta-bias, because one of the things our biases do is blind us to our biases. "These and other cognitive biases not only sometimes rob us of our ability to think clearly, but inhibit our realization of when we are not doing so," writes the philosopher Lee McIntyre in his 2018 book, *Post-Truth*. Often we think we are most rational and feel we can be most certain when we are in fact most mistaken and most deceived.

People are biased for a reason: for early humans, not much changed from one day to the next, and survival often depended on reacting fast. Humans' response patterns evolved to suit our environment; our brains are tuned to make certain guesses or predictions. Those cognitive shortcuts save time, energy, and potentially lives. On the savanna, where underreacting to a danger can be deadly and statistical risk analyses are hard to come by, it makes sense to be guided by emotional responses to stimuli or threats; in small tribal groups, where survival requires relying on others for information and protection, it makes sense to trust statements we hear often from people around us. Even today, there is usually nothing wrong with using heuristics: that is, applying decisionmaking shortcuts based on intuitions and snap judgments and rules of thumb, some learned, some evolved. No one with a real-world time budget could process all of the available information about, say, every politician's stance on dozens of issues, let alone all the information about every product we buy or service we use or person we meet or group we encounter. Relying on shortcuts, such as what brands we have heard of or what party someone belongs to, is a necessary part of navigating daily life in a complicated world. Still, in a complex environment calling for sophisticated judgments, our biases often lead us astray, while desensitizing us to the possibility that we might be wrong.

And it is important to emphasize that precisely because our biases evolved to guide us in some directions and away from others, they do not result in randomly distributed errors. Rather, the errors lead us down predictable pathways, again and again. Terrorists, who are skilled psychologists, exploit our hard-wired overreaction to spectacular acts of violence, even though the numbers they kill are statistically trivial compared with everyday losses to things like car crashes and street crime.[6] Osama bin Laden explained the principle: "All that we have to do is to send two mujahedeen to the furthest point east to raise a piece of cloth on which is written 'al Qaeda' in order to make generals race there to cause America to suffer human, economic, and political losses."[7] Propagandists, also skilled psychologists, exploit repetition bias by repeating lies until they sound familiar, and by baiting the outraged targets of lies to repeat them even more. (As Adolf Hitler in *Mein Kampf* put it, propaganda "must confine itself to a few points and repeat them over and over. . . . [P]ersistence is the first and most important requirement for success.") Advertisers, who may be the best psychologists of all, are virtuosos at exploiting framing effects, using images and associations to influence our attitudes before the first word of the pitch has been uttered. Even when their manipulations are blatant (the flag waving in the opening frames of the political ad; the puppy cavorting with the happy senior in the ad for arthritis medicine), we cannot entirely resist them.

The literature on cognitive and perceptual bias is monumental, and surveying it is beyond my purview here.[8] For purposes of understanding why we need the Constitution of Knowledge, a few biases seem particularly important. One is *confirmation bias*, which operates primarily at the personal level, biasing the way we think—as does its close kin, motivated reasoning. Another is *conformity bias*, which operates more at the social level, biasing the way we interact—as does its close cousin, epistemic tribalism.

"Confirmation bias and motivated reasoning have been widely researched and explored in both political and nonpolitical contexts," write the RAND Corporation's Jennifer Kavanagh and Michael D. Rich in their 2018 report, *Truth Decay: An Initial Exploration of the Diminishing Role of Facts and Analysis in American Public Life*. The research would not please Socrates, who teaches us to be humble about our beliefs, to assume we are often wrong, and to seek out challenging information and opinions. Unfortunately, those are usually the last things we want to do. Instead, we seek out congenial beliefs, then look for evidence and arguments to defend them. The British psychologist Peter Wason, who coined the term "confirmation bias," found in experiments in the 1960s that people who were asked to guess the rule which was used to generate a string of numbers (such as 2, 4, 6) by proposing additional numbers would come up with a rule easily, but then test it by only offering additional numbers that confirmed their guess (such as 8, 10, 12). They hardly ever tested their guess by offering numbers which would *dis*confirm their theory, such as 7, 8, 9—which would have worked, because the rule was "increasing integers." Neglecting to seek disconfirmation is like seeing three black cats, hypothesizing that all cats are black, and then not bothering to look around for any non-black cats.

Other studies since then have confirmed the same tendency.[9] Kavanagh and Rich, of RAND, cite research finding that "people will choose search and decision methods that are most likely to lead to desired outcomes or conclusions, not to the best-informed ones." Confirming partisan beliefs delivers a dose of satisfaction by triggering a little hit of dopamine in the brain, according to Haidt. "Like rats that cannot stop pressing a button, partisans may be simply unable to stop believing weird things," he writes. "Extreme partisanship may be literally addictive."[10] By the same token, studies find that people are strongly averse toward seeking out, listening to, or even noticing information which challenges their beliefs. One study in 2017 found that two-thirds of subjects would pay money to avoid the discomfort of exposing themselves to the other side's political views.[11] "Over a third of Obama voters and more than half of Romney voters," reported *The Economist*, in its account of these experiments, "compared the experience of listening to the other side's voters to having a tooth pulled."[12]

Motivated reasoning and confirmation bias might not be so important if they were easy to identify and counteract. As we have seen, however, the same biases which distort our thinking in the first place also hide our biases from us, and make us disinclined to look for them and even more disinclined to acknowledge them. You are biased, but I definitely am not! As a result, finding and correcting mistakes is difficult and uncomfortable for all the same reasons that making mistakes is easy and natural. Intelligence, as we have seen, is not particularly helpful; motivated reasoning weaponizes it. Sometimes evidence and argument do the trick; but they work much better for questions whose answers we do not particularly care about. When we care about a proposition, changing our mind about it will be difficult. Contrary facts will be rationalized away, or their source discounted, or their implications rejected, or their veracity denied altogether. "Most forms of political persuasion seem to have little effect at all," writes the political scientist Brendan Nyhan.[13]

I spent two decades working to change people's minds about same-sex marriage. Appeals to reason and evidence, I found, could persuade, but only after people had moved to a persuadable place emotionally: by knowing gay people or couples, or by a change of heart among friends or family, or by receiving a signal from a trusted leader or authority that supporting same-sex marriage was OK. People's personal opinions, political identities, and peer-group norms all had to be nudged and cajoled simultaneously, which was a long, slow process—though impressively effective, in the end. One thing which never worked was telling people they were biased, or even showing them their biases. Other people's biases were visible, but never their own.

Believing Is Belonging

You might think that perverse stubbornness would be maladaptive from an evolutionary point of view. The reason it is not goes back to Aristotle: humans are social animals. What matters most from an evolutionary perspective is not that a person forms beliefs which are true; it is that she forms beliefs which lead to social success. In effect, what matters most is not what *I* believe or what *you* believe but what *we* believe.

The Yale University psychologist and law professor Dan Kahan has proposed a compelling model based on what he calls "identity-protective cognition." Once a belief becomes important to the way we think about ourselves or important to the group we identify with, changing it becomes very costly. Breaking with the group carries "the prospect of losing all manner of peer support," writes Kahan.[14] Moreover, most of the issues people disagree about in modern life are pretty abstract and distant from our personal lives. We can't afford to be wrong about whether a bear is chasing us, but being wrong about climate change or gun control will impose no personal cost on us at all, especially when compared to the cost of challenging the sacred beliefs of our group. From an individual point of view, using our cognitive firepower to defend our cherished beliefs makes good sense, even if defending them makes us less accurate about reality—as it demonstrably does. Research finds that partisan identification, for example, affects our memory, our unconscious judgments, even our perceptions. People are more likely to remember falsehoods which support their partisan identity, note Jay J. Van Bavel and Andrea Pereira. "There is even evidence that political affiliations may even shape the way we see the world."[15] Research has found, they report, "that Republicans judge the skin tone of political leaders—like Barack Obama—as darker than [do] Democrats." Bring people into a lab, tell them (randomly) they are members of either a blue team or a red team, then put them in a brain scanner (an fMRI machine) and ask them to evaluate whether photos of faces show real human beings or dolls; their brain activity confirms that they process images from their own "side" as looking more human than images from the other "side," even though they have never encountered a member of the other "team" and literally nothing is at stake. "Once you trip this wire, this trigger, this cue, that you are a part of 'us-versus-them,' " Van Bavel, who conducted the experiment, told *National Journal's* Brian Resnick in 2014, "it's almost like the whole brain becomes re-coordinated."[16]

Even at the most rational end of the cognitive spectrum, where painstaking logical analysis and mathematical calculation take place, identity and ideology filter and distort our thinking. Dan Kahan and three other researchers presented participants with a table of data labeled as showing either how skin cream affects a rash (an issue with no partisan valence) or how concealed-gun laws affect crime (an issue with high partisan valence). The participants were then asked to figure out, based on the data, whether the skin cream, or the concealed guns, helped or hurt. When people thought they were looking at skin cream, their interpretations of the data showed no ideological leanings. Not surprisingly, participants with better math skills did a better job of interpreting the data correctly. But when they thought they were looking at data on gun control, participants split on ideological lines. Each side erred in its own ideological direction—and more-numerate participants were the most ideologically biased, not the least biased.[17]

Think of it this way: humans are equipped with some of evolution's finest mental circuitry to protect us from changing our minds when doing so might alienate us from our group. We have hundreds of thousands of years of practice at believing whatever will keep us in good standing with our tribe, even if that requires denying, discounting, rationalizing, misperceiving, and ignoring the evidence in front of our nose. We see this talent put to work every day by others, and by ourselves. Just today, as I wrote these words, I noticed an example in a news article. Alleged mistreatment of asylum-seeking migrants by Border Patrol authorities had been in the papers, especially after a heartrending photo surfaced showing the bodies of a father and his young daughter lying face down in a river. The father's posture suggested he had died trying to save his daughter from drowning. The picture's authenticity was not in dispute. Nonetheless, someone commented on a Facebook page for current and former Border Patrol agents, "I HAVE NEVER SEEN FLOATERS LIKE THIS," adding, "could this be another edited photo. We've all seen the Dems and liberal parties do some pretty sick things." It can't be true! Far more likely that the other team made it up! When facts collide with beliefs which implicate our prestige or define our identity ("Border Patrol officers are caring people"), the facts tend to bend. During the Trump administration's Ukraine scandal, it was an undisputed fact—revealed in a written summary released by Trump himself—that the president had discussed Joe Biden by name in a phone call with the Ukrainian president. Nonetheless, a poll by the Monmouth University Polling Institute found that only 40 percent of Republicans believed Trump had mentioned Biden, and "his number goes up only to 50 percent among Republicans who have heard a lot about the call."[18] Given the identity challenges which the undisputed facts posed to Trump's defenders, perhaps what is surprising is not how many Republicans denied the facts but how few.

What kind of belief can be identity-defining, then? The answer turns out to be *any* kind of belief, provided the belief is important to the group. The belief can concern a moral question: "Human life begins at conception, and so abortion is murder." The belief can be metaphysical, mystical, religious: "God exists as three personifications of one being." The belief can be technical and empirical, something which in principle could be resolved easily by checking the facts. "Capital-gains taxes reduce revenue." "Illegal immigrants commit more crimes." "Unemployment is rising." It doesn't matter. If a belief performs the function of defining a group and knitting it together, it plays the social role of a sacred or religious belief (as Jonathan Haidt has explained, drawing on the great sociologist Emile Durkheim). When facts challenge the belief, the congregation will defend its faith by denying the facts.

Intergroup animosity need not be *about* anything, or at least not about anything at first. It can be "about" itself: about humans' need to feel part of a group, to defend and protect that group, to show solidarity with friends, and to engage in public displays of animosity toward foes. Once tribal lines have formed, there will be no shortage of ideologies for identity and conflicts to be "about." Lilliana Mason, a political scientist at the University of Maryland, has done research suggesting that identity is a stronger cause of political polarization than ideology, but the two are hard to tease apart, even in principle.[19] Distinguishing whether identity drives ideology or ideology drives identity is a chicken-and-egg problem. The larger point is that the two drive each other.

Credit Donna Kowalczyk with candor. She is the woman who said, of the prosecutors investigating the president, "If they find something, they will have made it up." She has made a commitment to the president and, she tells us, she has no intention of relinquishing it. She makes no bones about comporting the facts to her identity rather than the other way around. Not everyone is as honest.

Echo Chambers and Confirmation Loops

So human thinking is biased in many ways. The biases are non-random, which means they introduce systematic distortions into our thinking. Many of them exist to solidify the social allegiances upon which our ancestors' survival depended. Reason can overrule our biases, but usually not when our personal prestige or group identity is at stake. Group solidarity can amplify ideological conflicts and even create them.

Now add another element. What happens when individual biases, especially confirmation bias, interact with the group dynamics of conformity bias? The result is epistemic tribalism.

Our beliefs, our reasoning, even our perceptions are contagious, often regardless of whether our beliefs, reasoning, and perceptions are steering us toward truth or error. Cognition is influenced not only by our own biases but also by the biases of others we identify with. As Haidt has said, our minds "unite us into teams, divide us against other teams, and blind us to the truth."[20]

Again, in the conditions for which humans evolved, belief contagion was useful. Instead of learning everything from scratch, we looked to our community's beliefs and traditions. Most of the time, believing what others believed was a good idea, because our ancestors had had a long time to figure things out. And so conformity bias became a feature of our mental operating system. We need not consciously choose to follow the group; it just happens. "Most of cognition consists of intuitive thought that occurs below the surface of consciousness," write Steven Sloman and Philip Fernbach in their 2017 book, *The Knowledge Illusion: Why We Never Think Alone.* Human intelligence, they say, is less like a computer than a beehive. "To function, individuals rely not only on knowledge stored within our skulls but also on knowledge stored elsewhere: in our bodies, in the environment, and especially in other people." They continue: "Because our knowledge is enmeshed with that of others, the community shapes our beliefs and attitudes. It is so hard to reject an opinion shared by our peers that too often we don't even try to evaluate claims based on their merits. We let our group do our thinking for us." To state the point another way: we think with our tribes.

The effect of groups on the cognition of individuals has been thoroughly documented. In the mid-1930s, the psychologist Muzafer Sherif showed experimental participants what he said was a moving dot of light in a dark room. In a series of trials, he asked them to estimate how far the dot had moved. In reality, it had not moved at all; Sherif was exploiting a cognitive quirk called the autokinetic illusion. Whatever movement the participants perceived was entirely a function of what they *thought* they perceived. In some sessions, participants made their estimates alone, without others present; in others, they made their estimates in small groups. His finding: groups and individuals perceived differently. Alone, participants' estimates were all over the map. In groups, by contrast, participants' estimates were scattered at first but then, after several trials, the estimates quickly converged on a consensus. The consensus estimate was not negotiated, nor was it an average of individuals' estimates. It was a different view, a group view: its own thing, a product of unconscious interpersonal influence.

In other words, what people perceived, or believed they perceived, depended on whether they were observing as individuals or in groups. Sherif interpreted his result as showing that groups establish not just shared public claims but a shared perception of reality, even though individuals are not necessarily aware of doing so and will often insist they made up their mind on their own. Cognition is often a group process. It goes, so to speak, not from the eye to the brain and then to the group, but from the eye to the group and then to the brain.[21]

Even more famous is an experiment conducted in 1951 by the social psychologist Solomon Asch. He brought eight people together for what they were told was a vision test. The eight were presented with a straight line and asked which of three other straight lines were the same length as the first line. The lines were drawn to make the answer obvious: one of the three choices matched the target line perfectly; the other two were not even close. But seven of the eight people in the room were accomplices of the experimenter who all deliberately gave the same wrong answer, with six of them answering before the real experimental subject got a turn. In the trials, about three-fourths of subjects conformed to the group at least once, despite the clear evidence of their own eyes. About a third went along with the group in a majority of trials. (Whereas in a control-group setting, where answers were not rigged, subjects had no trouble getting the answer right.) Most of the subjects, after the experiment, said they had not believed their conforming answers but went along for fear of being ridiculed or deemed weird.[22]

Two points are of interest here. First, the confederates in Asch's experiments were total strangers to the subjects. Subjects had no particular reason to care what the confederates thought of them but still often felt obliged to conform. Imagine, then, how much greater is the pressure to conform when your friends and trusted social group all fall into line. Second, as we have seen, people are good at conforming their actual beliefs to their identities and tribes, and even if they disagree with the group, they pretend to conform. Wrong beliefs and wrong perceptions are contagious whether or not they are sincere, because dissidents tend to self-censor and act like believers. That is how entire societies, such as the Soviet Union, can be built on everyone's publicly pretending to believe what many privately know to be false. After a while, in a community where people are struggling to conform with each other, it can be very hard, even in principle, to know whether people are sincere or faking, or even which is which.

"Our ability to successfully evaluate evidence and form true beliefs has as much to do with our social conditions as our individual psychology," write the philosophers of science Cailin O'Connor and James Owen Weatherall in their 2019 book, *The Misinformation Age: How False Beliefs Spread*. Even when individuals try to keep their minds open and their thinking straight, the group can get trapped in a loop of mutual bias confirmation. Members believe they are checking with others and seeking good information, but actually they are repeating and amplifying each other's misapprehensions. The whole community becomes an echo chamber. "Agents who learn from others in their social network can fail to form true beliefs about the world, even when more than adequate evidence is available," O'Connor and Weatherall write. "In other words, individually rational agents can form groups that are not rational at all."

Confirmation loops, like market bubbles, can run far afield of reality before they finally break. The cycle is difficult to arrest, because for individuals in the group, group-think can be *rational* despite being *wrong*. We face powerful incentives to stay on good terms with our friends and community, and the personal costs of estrangement are high. The writer Megan Phelps-Roper described leaving the cultlike Westboro Baptist church as "losing everyone and everything and being left to a world that I had spent my whole life antagonizing."[23] For each of us as an individual, it makes sense to sing in harmony with the tribe, and to believe harmoniously, too. Like sensitive antennas, we monitor the views of our leaders and preachers, our in-group media outlets, and our friends and neighbors to detect what it is that people like us believe on any given day, and what it is that people like us do not believe. Then we adjust our beliefs to stay in tune. As individuals, we benefit from preserving our status and sense of self. Yet, as Yale's Kahan points out, if a whole community behaves this way, the collective effect is devastating: the whole community loses touch with reality.

Kahan calls this problem an "epistemic tragedy of the commons," adapting economists' term for behavior which is rewarding for individuals but self-defeating for communities. In markets, tragedies of the commons cause price bubbles, resource exhaustion, environmental depredations, and sometimes wholesale economic collapse. Something analogous can happen with epistemic tragedies of the commons, turning communities—even entire nations—into cults of personality or ideology which are on a collision course with reality, yet are unable to self-correct without self-destructing. Think of Jonestown or the Symbionese Liberation Army on a small scale, Nazi Germany or the Soviet Union on a large scale. In parts of the American South before the Civil War, secessionists constructed an elaborate echo chamber to make sure "wrong" opinions did not penetrate. In Charleston, South Carolina, a group of secessionist grandees who called themselves the Society of Earnest Men took it upon themselves to "paper the entire South" with inflammatory pamphlets: "circulate tens of thousands, or even hundreds of thousands, of copies in cities, towns, and villages from Richmond to New Orleans," as Paul Starobin writes in his account of Southern war mania. They also ginned up demonstrations: "men parading, flags waving, and trumpets blaring on visible behalf of secession to excite the public and invigorate revolutionary consciousness."[24] By conjuring the illusion of monolithic mass public support (and also by suppressing moderate voices), they created a paranoid alternative reality in which a vast Northern conspiracy sought to dominate and destroy the South. Bursting the bubble cost something like 600,000 lives. Smaller bubbles and echo chambers form all around us every day, and can blind even the most perceptive.

The Specter of Creed War

Mass alternative realities are common and resilient, and they tend to end badly. They also tend to be aggressive. Recall that we are quick to see others' biases but slow to see our own. Recall also the illusion of asymmetric insight, which leads us to suppose we understand others' worldviews and motives better than they understand ours. When we encounter groups whose worldviews are at odds with ours, we have trouble imagining they are operating in good faith. Can't they see what is in front of their noses? Why do they deny the obvious? In American politics, the belief that the other side must be evil, stupid, or willfully ignorant—or all of the above—has become a defining feature of partisan polarization. "Because people believe that they see the world around them objectively," write Van Bavel and Pereira, "members of other parties who disagree with them are seen as uninformed, irrational, or biased."[25]

And dangerous, too. In any human society, a foundational problem is how to resolve conflicts of belief. Some conflicts are trivial, but others, for whatever reason, are intractable. If a belief—even an arcane, abstract, or downright metaphysical notion like trinitarianism or transubstantiation—becomes identity-defining, any challenge to the dogma threatens the group. Alternative realities outside the bubble and dissidents inside the bubble sow confusion, inspire heresy and apostasy, split the tribe, corrupt the young. The very fact of disagreement implies that the group's sacraments and solidarity are in jeopardy.

How to cope with a threat to a group's sacred beliefs? Through most of human history, only a few methods have worked. Groups can isolate themselves and eject dissidents, hunkering down as many religious sects have done. But that method cuts them off from reality and stunts their collective intellect, condemning them to backwardness, insularity, and manipulation by their leaders. Over time, it leads to factional splits, and conflicts break out all over again. And losing touch with reality never works out well.

Or groups can prostrate themselves before a leader or institution, a priest or prince: some authority which rules by decree, deciding what it is that "we" believe. Authoritarianism was Plato's recommendation. He tried to sugarcoat it by supposing that the leader would be a wise, disinterested philosopher (presumably someone like himself), but history has shown that Orwell, not Plato, was right about authoritarian control of belief and expression—what today we call totalitarianism. Any threat to prevailing orthodoxy is a threat to the authority structure and, through it, the whole social order.

Orwell imagined a vast state which could project its manipulated version of reality without challenge, forever. But real life is not like that. The outside world keeps butting in, and internal dissent keeps cropping up, and reality keeps asserting itself. In self-defense, authoritarian regimes sooner or later turn aggressive, toward their own dissidents and eventually toward outsiders, too. They brand dissidents as traitors, seek to exclude them from power or social participation, boycott and deplatform them, dehumanize and cancel them. Eventually, they use violence, sometimes to the point of seeking to wipe out a political faction or ethnic group altogether. "When complete agreement could not otherwise be reached," wrote the American philosopher Charles Sanders Peirce in his great 1877 essay, *The Fixation of Belief*, "a general massacre of all who have not thought in a certain way has proved a very effective means of settling opinion in a country."

Creed war—violence and repression organized around ideas—is an all too familiar human trait. History's most searing example may be the long religious war between Catholics and Protestants during the Reformation. Conflicts broke out across Europe and lasted for more than a century, from the 1520s through the 1640s. The most severe stage, the Thirty Years War, was among the most destructive conflicts in history, with deaths thought to have run well into the millions. (Some scholars think the war may have killed a third of the population of Germany.) Many other conflicts have been creed wars in whole or in part: for example, the American Civil War, World War II, the Cold War, and the conflict with radical Islamism.

My point is not to categorize any particular conflict as creedal or non-creedal. Just the opposite: every conflict has creedal elements (even if the creeds are generated after the conflict begins), and any creedal difference can spark conflict. Ideas can be inflammatory and disagreement can be dangerous. The problem of maintaining peace in the face of ideological conflict is an existential challenge for every human society: no society can long exist without managing it. And when mechanisms to manage conflicts of belief break down, societies begin to behave more tribally. When that happens, creedal conflict and political conflict become indistinguishable.

One such time was the early twenty-first century, in the United States.

Americans were not at the fever pitch of the 1850s. No outright civil war was in the offing. But creed war can also take low-grade, simmering forms whose result is not violence but ungovernability. Signs of that kind of conflict abounded. Many religious conservatives believed they confronted a war on Christianity, by which they meant a relentless campaign by secular liberals to drive Christian belief and practice out of respectable society. Many secular liberals thought they faced a war on women, by which they meant a relentless campaign by religious conservatives to take physical control of women's bodies. The use of the term "war" was metaphorical, but only up to a point: both sides believed they were fighting for their continued existence as free people. More and more Americans believed that only one side could prevail and that the conflict could only end in the other side's elimination as a political force. Every election, every Supreme Court nomination, even every budget bill or tax bill was liable to become yet another battle to stave off the final catastrophe. The high stakes made compromise look at best futile, at worst suicidal. When compromise fails, ungovernability sets in.

Was America's political polarization ideological (that is, creedal) or partisan (that is, tribal)? The answer is both, and what's the difference? When creedal warfare takes hold, reality becomes a weapon in tribal conflict. Seemingly ordinary questions of fact turn into chasms of incommensurable conflict; instead of looking for ways to adjudicate their disagreements, groups escalate them in order to sustain in-group solidarity. In 2016 a poll by NBC News and SurveyMonkey asked Republicans and Democrats what should have been a straightforward empirical question. Barack Obama was born in the United States: agree or disagree? Only about a quarter of Republicans agreed, versus more than eight in ten Democrats. How much Republicans knew about politics and government made no difference at all.

"A greater factual understanding of the political system does not diminish Republicans' doubts about Obama's birthplace," the pollsters reported.[26] Reality had merged with identity. Where identity-defining beliefs are concerned, opinions are never just opinions and facts are never just facts. They are also markers of affiliation, like team colors and football cheers. Tribal differences and opinion differences reinforce each other in a spiral of polarization.

One way to view what political scientists call "affective polarization"—emotional hostility toward the other political party or group, as opposed to non-hostile disagreement over issues—is through a political lens: as a rise of extreme partisanship and dangerous political polarization. Which is perfectly valid. But another, equally valid, lens is epistemic. Through that lens, we see something which looks disconcertingly like a reversion to a Hobbesian epistemic order: a war of each tribal reality against each. Those realities compete but do not connect; they do not admit of stepwise, rational resolution on empirical grounds; rather, they end only when one side dominates the other, at least politically if not physically.

When a society's capacity to resolve disagreements diminishes, factions retreat to the isolation of their tribal bubbles and the authority of their tribal leaders. And when factions repair to insularity and authority, the society's capacity to resolve or dissolve disagreements diminishes further still. As we will see, smart disruptors understand this dynamic and aggravate it. In a war of all against all, charlatans, demagogues, and sociopaths thrive, roaming and pillaging like warlords in a stateless Hobbesian world.

A Path Past Hobbes

But here an obvious question arises. Given humans' innate tribal wiring; given our natural facility for hypocrisy and self-serving belief; given our many cognitive biases and our need to conform: how, then, could we possibly have created the advanced and generally peaceful world we occupy? How is it that the reality-based community not only exists but has gone from triumph to triumph? If anything is striking about the modern age in advanced democracies, it is how rare creed wars are, not how common.

In the discussion so far, I have omitted half the story. Hobbesian behavior is not the only kind of behavior we are equipped for. Humans are inherently biased and tribal, but we are also capable of outwitting our biases and tribes and thinking well. We do it a lot of the time. We are not doomed to be gullible, easily brainwashed suckers who are likely to believe whatever people tell us. In fact, as the cognitive scientist Hugo Mercier says in his book *Not Born Yesterday*, evolution has tuned us to be good at sorting through large amounts of information and rejecting what is wrong and harmful, when that is to our benefit; otherwise, we would never have made it this far.[27] If we go in for quackery or conspiracy theories, that is often because the personal cost of believing is low and the personal reward of believing is high. Believing that 9/11 was a government plot or that Barack Obama was not born in America does us no personal harm, but it can help us feel enmeshed in a special group of insiders with privileged information. Experiments show that a good way to help people think more rigorously and accurately is to pay them to get the right answer; when they have skin in the game, the personal cost of being wrong goes up.

Whether and where and how much of the time we think well thus depends not just on how biased we may be as individuals or even how we behave in unstructured groups; it also depends, crucially, on the design of the social environment in which we find ourselves. To phrase the point more bluntly: *It's the institutions, stupid.* And so the most interesting question is not how often humans get reality right or wrong in a laboratory or in small kinship-based tribes or in a hypothetical state of nature; it is how we can create a social environment which increases rightness and reduces wrongness.

Something has made it possible not only to defeat the Hobbesian paradigm but to reverse it, creating a virtuous cycle linking more and more people into a reality-based community, not just in America but worldwide. *Something* allowed us to surmount the myriad biases and impulses and group dynamics which deceive and distort. *Something* made it possible for humans to learn not just individually but on a species-wide scale. That *something* did not arise naturally, of its own accord. Like the U.S. Constitution, it was founded by visionaries and born of struggle.

3

Booting Reality:
The Rise of Networked Knowledge

*Outsourcing reality to a social network
is humankind's greatest innovation*

Thomas Hobbes's vision of society is dark. Peace and prosperity are possible, but only under the reign of an absolute sovereign who can forcibly impose order and suppress the war of all against all. But who will rule the sovereign? No one: necessarily, the sovereign reigns supreme, her power neither divided nor limited. Nor can the people change the form of government, or rebel against it; their grant of authority to the sovereign is irrevocable. As with Plato's philosopher-king, and then emperors and monarchs and popes for two millennia, the sovereign must be wise and good. And if she is not wise and good? Then we must live with her abuses, for the alternatives—anarchy and war—can only be worse. There can be room for some differences, but not for dissent on fundamental civic matters such as religion: "for words can be a crime," wrote Hobbes, "and can be punished without injury with whatever punishments the legislators wish—indeed, with the ultimate penalty."[1]

Two centuries after Hobbes, millions of idealists would be inspired by a brighter vision of humans' default social settings; at least, brighter superficially. In the mid-1700s, the French philosopher Jean-Jacques Rousseau argued that humans innately possess empathy and cooperation; inequality, oppression, and other depredations of civilization—not human nature—are the causes of social deformation. "Man is born free, but he is everywhere in chains," Rousseau famously declared. But that which can be deformed can also be reformed; people can learn to be pro-social and enlightened. To that end, governments should embody the "general will," a set of political preferences which people of good conscience agree (or should agree) represents individuals' and society's best interest (something like what some today call the public interest, or perhaps like what some call social justice). Still, once the general will is discovered and embodied in law, all must obey, for to defy the general will would be to defy their own best interests.

Rousseau is a controversial figure. Some see him as the forebear of today's progressives, championing social equality and personal emancipation; others, as a utopian social engineer who inspired the totalitarian impulses of Robespierre, Lenin, and Pol Pot (the murderous Cambodian dictator). Both views contain truth, but at a minimum his philosophy raised problems akin to the ones which backed Hobbes into an authoritarian corner. The idea of a single general will seems to allow room for only one legitimate ruler or viewpoint; how, then, can pluralism be accommodated? Who exactly can discern the general will when individuals disagree (as they are bound to do)? Once certain leaders or factions lay claim to the general will, how can their power be bounded? What if reformers decide to do a good deal of destroying and oppressing in order to enforce the transcendent public good, as so infamously happened in the French Revolution? Today, Rousseau's thinking remains influential: dangerously so among populists—of both the right and the left—who assert that they, and only they, speak for the will of the people; more benignly, but still often mischievously, among idealists and ideologues of many stripes who claim that their insights and doctrines empower them to speak for the public interest.

You're both wrong, came a reply to Hobbes and Rousseau. Who can be trusted to make political choices in a world of inherent conflict?

Where can authority be safely reposed? From the fires of European wars and revolutions came a group of thinkers and practitioners whom today we call liberals. In important respects, their vision was and remains astonishingly radical. A properly ordered society looks neither to the king nor the general will to discern the public good and establish legitimate government; instead, it looks to no one in particular.

Until the 1600s, the average annual rate of economic growth in human history was approximately zero, on a per capita basis. Economies developed haltingly and, by today's standards, minimally. Until about the same time, politics consisted of a long and bitter series of wars, revolutions, and coups, punctuating variously short or long periods of oppressive and corrupt rule. Regimes came and went, and borders were redrawn, and politics staggered from one empire, invader, or upheaval to the next. Until then, doctors and scholars knew barely more than the ancients had known—in some respects, less. The word "scientist" did not exist; nor did the concept of science, as we know it today. Knowledge existed, of course, and impressive kingdoms appeared, and new technologies emerged. But an objective observer would probably not have said that the Europe of the late medieval period was better organized or more advanced than, say, the Europe of the Roman empire at its height, a millennium earlier. In the year 1500 or so, alien visitors might reasonably have pegged *Homo sapiens* as a stuck species. "Come back in another 100,000 years," they might have concluded, "and maybe these goofballs will be interesting."[2]

And then it all changed.

Three Liberal Orders

Of course, there were breakthroughs and advances before the Industrial Revolution, the American Revolution, and the scientific revolution. What was lacking, though, was a social order capable of generating and then cumulating advances systematically. And systematic social orders require constitutions: formal, political ones, or informal, culturally embodied ones—but, in either case, systems of rules which channel human energies in pro-social directions.

All three of the great liberal social systems—economic, political, epistemic—are traceable to breakthroughs in the seventeenth and eighteenth centuries. All were pioneered by men who followed each other's writings and doings and who sometimes knew each other personally. They and their works were flawed with the inequities and blind spots of their eras (one of which is reflected in the fact that all of them were men). But the founders were not just blundering along; they self-consciously sought to create an alternative to the failed regimes of the past. The greatest of them—especially John Locke, Adam Smith, and James Madison, the big three of modern liberalism—were men of genius, whose acuity and sophistication remain astonishing even today.

The economic system has no formal constitution. It does have something like a founding document, in the form of Smith's *The Wealth of Nations*, plus Smith's equally important and closely connected, though until recently neglected, treatise on moral development and social behavior, his *Theory of Moral Sentiments*. Between them, Smith elaborated a sophisticated theory of human cooperation: where cooperation comes from, how to encourage and exploit it, how to wire it into societies' rules and institutions. Smith (like Rousseau) argued that Hobbes was wrong: humans are oriented toward cooperation as well as conflict. People, he argued, come into the world equipped with what he called sympathy, or fellow-feeling; "empathy" is the word we might use today.[3] We have a natural inclination to imagine how others see and feel, and to align our own perspectives and dispositions with theirs. (Modern neurology bears out Smith's claim: humans and other primates seem to possess systems of so-called mirror neurons, which help us intuit others' feelings and imitate their behaviors.) Also, humans come equipped with a desire to be trusted and respected by others. Through our desire for mutual esteem based on our empathetic intuitions, we can align our interests and form social bonds on a basis other than force or domination. True, humans are also greedy and ambitious; yet—here is Smith's most famous insight—a well-structured social order can harness those very traits to promote activity which benefits ourselves by benefiting others. If we get the rules right, millions of people of every imaginable skill and temperament and nationality can cooperate to build a fantastically complex device like a Prius or iPhone, all without the oversight or instruction of any central planner. *If* we get the rules right.

Smith's proposition seemed ridiculous, given that human history through his time was soaked in blood and oppression. His claim was redeemed only by the fact that it proved to be true. Although Smith did not invent markets, he notated the code which enabled a tribal primate, wired for personal relationships in small, usually related groups, to cooperate impersonally across unbounded networks of strangers, and to do so without any central authority organizing markets and issuing commands. Economic liberalism—market cooperation—is a species-transforming piece of social software, one which enables humans to function far above our designed capacity.

Political liberalism grapples with another version of the cooperation problem: can we make rules which channel self-interest, ambition, and bias to benefit society as a whole? Can we provide social stability without squelching social dynamism, and without submitting to a Hobbesian authority? Yet another version of the cooperation problem preoccupies epistemic liberalism: can people with sharp differences of opinion be induced to cooperate in building knowledge, again providing both stability and dynamism without recourse to authoritarianism?

Solving those problems requires a constitution, but in a broad sense of the word: not necessarily a piece of paper or a formal law, but a social operating system which seeks to elicit cooperation and resolve differences on the basis of rules, not personal authority or tribal affiliation or brute force. In that sense, the liberal economic, epistemic, and political systems all have constitutions, even if only the political constitution is written down. (Even then, as I emphasize throughout this book, the written U.S. Constitution is only words on paper; the real Constitution is a dense system of explicit and implicit social rules, many of which are not written down.)

Whether formal or not, all three liberal constitutions share a family resemblance. They all organize far-flung cooperation, distribute decisionmaking across social networks, and exploit network intelligence (where the system knows much more than its constitutive individuals), all with a minimum of centralized authority or control. They all emphasize impersonal rules over personal authority, open-ended processes over fixed outcomes, and consent over coercion. They all take as their starting point that individuals are by nature free and equal, and that freedom and equality are important and valuable. They are all extraordinarily successful, especially compared with the alternatives. Which is not to say they are perfect. Far from it. But they are much better than their competitors at adapting to change and at identifying and correcting mistakes: that is, at self-correcting. And they are much better at averting the destructive social conflict which Hobbes believed was the only alternative to authoritarian government.

For exactly that reason, all three liberal social systems—economic, political, and epistemic—can seem disquieting and unnatural. They allow for no ending points, no final arrival; no absolute certainty, no shelter from change. They place strains on local relationships and tribal ties. They can be harsh and unfair. They are difficult to understand and explain; indeed, they are deeply counterintuitive. They all depend on complex, intricately balanced rules, norms, institutions, and moral values, most of which did not arise organically but took centuries to construct. Acculturating people to all those rules and norms and institutions and moral values requires years of socialization and deep reservoirs of civic mutuality and trust. As a wag said: where developing the rule of law is concerned, the first five centuries are the hardest.

Investing abstract rules and impersonal institutions with the power to run our societies will never be easy or natural. That was why America's founders—Adams, Washington, Franklin, Madison, and others—all warned that no constitution is worth the paper it is written on if it is not also inscribed in people's hearts and grounded in public virtue. "Avarice, ambition, revenge, or gallantry would break the strongest cords of our Constitution as a whale goes through a net," John Adams said. "Our Constitution is designed only for a moral and religious people. It is wholly inadequate for any other." Or, as Benjamin Franklin even more famously said when a woman of Philadelphia asked him what kind of regime the deliberations of 1787 had produced: "A republic, if you can keep it."

The story of the founding of the American political order needs no retelling here. We all know its characters, documents, and dates. By contrast, the epistemic founding had no constitutional convention, no founding document, no date we commemorate. It emerged gradually, bit by bit. But there were founders, and foundations.

Locke's Political Revolution

The wars of religion wracked Europe not just for years but for generations. They spanned the whole continent plus England. They brought a mass uprising in central Europe, a revolution in England, civil wars in France, and clashes of what were then the world's mightiest armies. European wars mowed down not only combatants but large numbers of civilians, according to the historian Brad S. Gregory. "These more-than-religious wars were destructive, expensive, and inconclusive," Gregory writes. "By the middle of the seventeenth century they had drained and exhausted Europeans."[4] The wars left traumas and scars whose effects linger to this day.

Of course, many wars are long and scarring, but the religious wars were supposed to be *about* something. The contests between Catholics and Protestants, and also among Protestants (whose internecine disagreements rivaled their disagreements with Catholics), were about power and political advantage, as all wars are. But they also were about theology, priestly authority, biblical interpretation, ritual, and more, which is why, after all, they are called wars of religion.

Notice, in that context, the last word of Gregory's formulation: "These more-than-religious wars were destructive, expensive, and *inconclusive*." Politically, the wars ended in the mid-1600s with the Peace of Westphalia, which amounted to a nonaggression pact in which sovereigns agreed to stop interfering in each other's internal affairs and to tolerate minority religions. Epistemically, the outcome was similarly stalemated. "By the 1650s, theological experts [had] come no closer to reconciling their disagreements than they were in the 1520s," writes Gregory. "Conflicting claims about Christian truth were no more settled by 1648 than they had been in the 1520s."

Also unanswered was an even more important question: who should settle disagreements—religious, political, epistemic? Does authority over truth reside with the Catholic Church, with the Protestant laity, with heads of state, or elsewhere? In religious controversies, who is the boss? That was the question which triggered and defined the wars. Yet violence had failed to resolve it. To the contrary; the conflicts had proved the costly futility of relying on contending authorities and force of arms to resolve differences of opinion. The Hobbesian model had failed. "Weary Europeans started looking for alternatives," writes Gregory.

Among those seeking alternatives was an English thinker and writer named John Locke. Trained in medicine, he dabbled in politics and, for his trouble, found himself exiled to the Netherlands for five years, where he was steeped in the ideas of freethinkers like Baruch Spinoza and Pierre Bayle. Many thinkers and practitioners contributed to building modern liberalism, but if the source code were to be traced to just one man, he would have to be Locke. He stands unique among all the great thinkers in one respect: he was the germinal figure in the development of two branches of liberalism, political and epistemic.

In his politics, Locke was not a modern democrat (in his day, no one was). He accepted the authority of the British crown, and in his advocacy of toleration he drew the line at Catholicism and atheism. But he formulated three ideas which are foundational to political liberalism.

The first is the idea of natural rights: fundamental rules which apply to all persons from birth to death—rules which all other persons and also sovereigns and governments are bound to respect, and which are to be respected impersonally and reciprocally. Because they are natural, these rights inhere in human nature and are present in the state of nature. They provide a built-in limiting principle to the war of all against all. For Locke, the fundamental rights are life, liberty, and property (meaning not just material property but also what today we call autonomy: authority over one's own body and conscience). Because rights are inborn rather than earned by merit or conferred by social position, they inhere equally. Individuals are always equal in their fundamental rights, even as they differ in countless other ways.

A second foundational principle is rule by consent. Governments are not instituted by divine authority to rule the people; they are instituted by the people to enforce natural rights. To do their job, governments need to be granted broad authority, but if they exceed their authority or use it to violate the people's rights, they lose their claim to govern and may rightly be replaced. Government is sovereign within its grant of power, but the ultimate sovereignty belongs to the governed.

Third, toleration. Religious differences had torn Europe apart, in good measure because the combatants assumed that if one religion is true, then others must be false. Because false religions endanger souls and deceive societies, they seemed intolerable. Religious war had shown how costly intolerance could be in practice, but, even so, few thinkers questioned the principle that false belief was dangerous and should be stamped out. Hobbes, for example, believed that the state's stability depended on uniformity of religious belief, or at least uniformity of religious expression. Locke, by contrast, argued that force cannot save souls because it cannot change hearts, and even if it could, governments cannot be relied upon to discern religious truth. In any case, the person who worships wrongly does not injure others, and the state's business is not to save souls but to protect rights.

All of those ideas had precedents and echoes in other thinkers. Hobbes affirmed inalienable rights; the Levelers (an English reform movement of the 1640s) had staked a claim to popular sovereignty; John Milton and Roger Williams had argued for toleration. In Locke, however, we find pretty much the entire code, embedded for the first time in a worked-out theory. Natural rights, popular sovereignty, and toleration together make up something larger than the sum of the parts. Impersonal rules, neutrally applied; limited government, accountable to the people; pluralism of belief, and government which protects rather than persecutes dissent: the elements of modern liberalism are all there, although elaborating and applying them would be the work of centuries.

If Locke had ended his inquiries there, he would have earned his place as a giant. But he was not finished.

Locke's Epistemic Revolution

In the late 1500s, a successor of Theaetetus and Socrates looked at the state of the world and the state of knowledge and threw up his hands in disgust. Michel de Montaigne, a politician and lawyer who had become exhausted by the conflicts of politics and sophistries of law, shut himself in the tower of his family château, where he wrote probably the greatest body of essays in literary history (or, if not, tied with George Orwell's). Both profound and puckish, Montaigne's essays—still scintillating today—poked and prodded at received wisdom of all sorts, including, not least, the proposition that human beings could ever reliably know anything.

The wars of the Reformation and the Counter-reformation were burning through Europe, and to Montaigne, as to many others, they brought a profound sense of pessimism that any truth could be confidently asserted or any disagreement effectively resolved. In the longest and most influential of his essays, *Apology for Raymond Sebond*, he marched through the arguments which had humbled Theaetetus and Socrates, to which he added some of his own. Our judgment, he wrote, often leads us astray: "the slightest things in the world whirl it around."[5] Our senses do no better; they convey only impressions of things, variably and unreliably; for all we know, we might be dreaming or hallucinating right now. "As for the error and uncertainty of the operations of the senses, each man can furnish himself with as many examples as he pleases, so ordinary are the mistakes and deceptions that they offer us," he wrote. "The uncertainty of our senses makes everything they produce uncertain." True, we may *feel* certain of truth, but certainty is no guide. From his own experience of past error, Montaigne knew that his own convictions were untrustworthy, and by extension, the same must be true for everyone else's. "Since a wise man can be mistaken, and a hundred men, and many nations, yes, and human nature according to us is mistaken for many centuries about this or that, what assurance have we that sometimes it stops being mistaken, and that in this century it is not making a mistake?" As for the power of reason, it is the servant of what today we call confirmation bias, an idea Montaigne impressively anticipated. "Men's opinions are accepted in the train of ancient beliefs, by authority and on credit, as if they were religion and law. They accept as by rote what is commonly held about it. . . . On the contrary, everyone competes in plastering up and confirming this accepted belief, with all the power of their reason, which is a supple tool, pliable, and adaptable to any form. Thus the world is filled and soaked with twaddle and lies."

The implication of Montaigne's ruminations is that we can have the illusion of knowledge but never the real thing. "Not that it is impossible that some true knowledge may dwell in us: but if it does, it does so by accident. And since by the same road, the same manner and process, errors are received into our soul, it has no way to distinguish them or to pick out truth from falsehood." The social implication is just as bleak: people are doomed to eternal conflict over their beliefs. Because no two individuals see, hear, or believe the same thing, "we get into disputes at every turn." No wonder that "men are in agreement about nothing, I mean even the most gifted and ablest scholars, not even that the sky is over our head." Indeed, the very fact that so many people disagree about so many things implies that all claims to knowledge are unfounded, for amid the cacophony, why should we assume that anyone is ever right about anything? "By this variety and instability of opinions they [disputants] lead us as by the hand, tacitly, to this conclusion of their inconclusiveness."

Perhaps uncertainty and disputatiousness might be resolved by some all-knowing authority; but, demanded Montaigne, "Who shall be fit to judge these differences?" When the authorities themselves disagree, who will decide *their* disputes? (Here Montaigne reaches the epistemic version of the question which tripped up Hobbes, "Who will rule the rulers?") Besides, no one is immune to error and misperception, and no one is dispassionate. "We would need someone exempt from all these qualities [of bias and passion], so that with an unprejudiced judgment he might judge of these propositions as of things indifferent to him; and by that score we would need a judge that never was."

Montaigne's demolition of knowledge appears, at first blush, to reflect almost nihilistic despair. Yet there are seeds here of something more. Notice, in his discussion, the emphasis on disagreement. The problem of truth, Montaigne hinted, is a social problem: a problem about reaching, or failing to reach, a working consensus. The knowledge problem centers not on what you know or what I know, but on what *we* know.

Two generations after Montaigne, and two before Locke, the English philosopher Francis Bacon adopted some of Montaigne's skepticism but steered it in a different direction. Knowledge, he wrote in his work *Novum Organum*, in 1620, comes not from what truthseekers believe but what they do: make observations and perform experiments which eliminate wrong answers and point us toward right ones. Using this method, Bacon claimed, we can overcome the inherent flaws of our senses and cognition (what Bacon called Idols of the Tribe), the limits of our individual experiences and parochial viewpoints (Idols of the Cave), and the errors of received dogmas and superstitions (Idols of the Theater).

"Bacon was a bad scientist," the sociologist of science Joseph Ben-David has argued, "and in many details he was not a very good philosopher either. There was little connection between the rise of new astronomy and mathematical physics and Baconian principles; experimentation without theory and collection of empirical knowledge had produced few scientific results."[6] Yet in his own era Bacon was revered and his work was widely influential (and today he is still adjudged a seminal figure in the emergence of science). His real importance, and his appeal, lay in his method's implicit *social* promise. In an age of seemingly endless, fruitless creed wars, Bacon's experimental method suggested a conciliatory path: things people could do to reconcile their disagreements, taking their conflicts off the street and into the lab. Ben-David continued:

> By sticking to empirically verified facts (preferably by controlled experiment), the method enabled its practitioners to feel like members of the same "community," even in the absence of a commonly accepted theory. It was possible for scientists to go ahead with several competing views of the common subject matter and have the feeling of shared progress and eventual consensus. They no longer had to split into factions opposing each other on an increasingly wide and diffuse front, as the case had been before in philosophical conflicts.

Montaigne, Bacon, the religious wars, and of course much more than I can shoehorn into this schematized account were in the background when, in 1689, Locke published his *Essay Concerning Human Understanding.* Knowledge, he argued, is not innate; it is not something we are born with. Nor does it come from revelation, at least not when revelation is inconsistent with experience or existing knowledge. Nor can it come merely from general theories. Rather, knowledge comes from experience and particulars (what today we might call facts and data), which we can find only by looking outside ourselves: by investigating the world and comparing notes with each other. If our claims or hypotheses cannot be reduced to particulars and then checked against the experience and reason of ourselves and others, they are outside the boundaries of what today we call "science." Broad generalizations and abstract axioms, Locke said, are useful "in disputes, to stop the mouths of wranglers"—in other words, they make good debaters' points—"but [are] not of much use to the discovery of unknown truths, or to help the mind forwards in its search after knowledge." Without checking our beliefs, we can have knowledge of our own existence and God's, but not much more. Moreover, without empiricism, we merely enshrine our mistakes. "All men are liable to error, and most men are in many points, by passion or interest, under temptation to it," he wrote. "Good men are men still liable to mistakes and are sometimes warmly engaged in errors, which they take for divine truths, shining in their minds with the clearest light."

What Locke was doing, here, was expelling from intellectual respectability—from the epistemic rulebook—claims which, because they are not *checkable*, are not *adjudicable*. Those claims, not incidentally, would include most of the theological and metaphysical disputes over which the wars of religion were ostensibly fought. Locke saw how untestable certitudes sparked irreconcilable social disputes:

> The strength of our persuasions is no evidence at all of their own rectitude: . . . and men may be as positive and peremptory in error as in truth. How come else the untractable zealots in different and opposite parties? For if the light, which everyone thinks he has in his

mind, which in this case is nothing but the strength of his own persuasion, be an evidence that it is from God, contrary opinions have
the same title to be inspirations; and God will be not only the Father
of lights, but of opposite and contradictory lights, leading men contrary ways; and contradictory propositions will be divine truths, if
an ungrounded strength of assurance be an evidence that any proposition is a Divine Revelation.

Revealingly, to describe disputes which cannot be addressed empirically, Locke used the word "dangerous," at least when the disputes rise to the level of moral conflict (values questions, as we often
call them today). "Nothing can be so dangerous as principles thus
taken up without questioning or examination; especially if they be
such as concern morality, which influence men's lives, and give a bias
to all their actions."

Locke's empiricism, then, is a social principle, and he understood
it as such. It aims not just at knowledge but also at peace. Combined
with his principle of toleration, it would have required the religious
disputants of his day to seek paths toward resolving or dissolving
their disputes; or else to change the subject and talk about something
else—something they could resolve by finding facts and comparing
experiences, rather than by coming to blows over divine revelation.

The implicit requirement to consult and persuade, Locke hinted,
points toward a concept even more radical than his principle of toleration: the positive welcoming of intellectual diversity. "It would,
methinks, become all men to maintain peace, and the common offices of humanity, and friendship, in the diversity of opinions; since
we cannot reasonably expect that any one should readily and obse-
quiously quit his own opinion, and embrace ours, with a blind resignation to an authority which the understanding of man acknowledges
not." In a world of conflicting certitudes, we must accept and even
embrace pluralism. Here, in empiricism and pluralism, was an alternative to Hobbes's unpalatable dilemma of choosing between war
and authoritarianism.

Notice how Locke's empiricism dovetails with the political principles of natural rights and basic equality: because all people have
eyes and ears and minds, and because we must check and consult

with each other to find truth, the many, not just the few, are entitled to assert their own beliefs and contest others'. Epistemic rights, like political rights, belong to all of us; empiricism is the duty of all of us. No exceptions for priests, princes, or partisans.

Kill My Mistakes, Not Me

As the Enlightenment unfolded, philosophers, politicians, and citizens in Europe and North America moved rapidly to build on Locke's ideas. In autocratic France, Baron Montesquieu developed the idea of separate and competing power centers, with legislative, executive, and judicial authorities operating in their own spheres—a sharp departure from the prevalent unitary models of monarchism and theocracy. In England, John Trenchard and Thomas Gordon, writing under the pseudonym Cato, published a series of influential essays arguing for freedom of speech and conscience and for accountable republican government. In Britain's North American colonies, a printer and journalist named John Peter Zenger, who was prosecuted by the crown for seditious libel, beat the charge by arguing that truth is a defense even when criticizing the government. Political liberalism was developing organically and creating facts on the ground, a process which would soon culminate in a revolutionary breakthrough in North America.

In parallel, philosophers and practitioners laid groundwork for the Constitution of Knowledge. The Scottish philosopher David Hume, writing in the 1740s, completed the skeptical demolition of absolute certainty begun by Montaigne. In a tour de force of reasoning which stands unrefuted to this day, he showed that no prediction or causal attribution can ever be certain, even in principle; and that no invocation of miraculous or supernatural causes could ever be justified rationally, even in principle. If no naturalistic explanation can be true beyond any possibility of doubt, and if no supernatural explanation is within bounds, what basis for knowledge could there possibly be? That was Theaetetus's problem, and two millennia later it seemed as intractable as ever.

But what if knowledge does *not* require certainty? Indeed, what if knowledge is *incompatible* with certainty? In the nineteenth century, skepticism—the idea that if certainty is impossible, knowledge must be impossible—was elbowed aside by a related but quite different idea, that of fallibilism, a term coined by the American philosopher Charles Sanders Peirce. "On the whole," he wrote, "we cannot in any way reach perfect certitude nor exactitude. We can never be absolutely sure of anything," at least when any matter involves facts and statements about objective reality. "The scientific spirit," said Peirce, "requires a man to be at all times ready to dump his whole cartload of beliefs, the moment experience is against them."[7]

At first blush, that sounds little different from Montaigne, and no more hopeful. No certainty, ever? Dump whole cartloads of beliefs? But fallibilism bore a crucial difference from skepticism: whereas skeptics held that uncertainty is ubiquitous and so knowledge is impossible, fallibilists held that uncertainty is ubiquitous but knowledge is possible anyway. We can claim knowledge, but always provisionally, knowing we might be mistaken. For the skeptic, the job of knowledge-seekers is to search for truth, which, unfortunately, is unobtainable. For the fallibilist, the job is rather to search for error—and error is something we *can* find. We may not ever be able to achieve final confirmation of any empirical proposition, but we can achieve *dis*confirmation. No matter how many flying birds we see, we cannot positively say that all birds can fly; but as soon as we see a flightless bird, we know that *not* all birds can fly. And so we can claim knowledge, provided we always take seriously the idea that we might be wrong.

It fell to Karl Popper, the twentieth century's greatest philosopher of science, to unpack the powerful methodological implications of fallibilism. Science, he posited, in *The Logic of Scientific Discovery* and many other books and articles, may think of itself as looking for proof, or at least verification, but in fact its method is to seek falsification. True, individual scientists hunt for evidence that their hypotheses are true, but science as a system operates by subjecting hypotheses to criticism. By testing ideas experimentally, logically, and many other ways, science shoots down thousands, even millions, of hypotheses every day. The great advantage of scientific investigation is not that it frames hypotheses and then tries to confirm them (everyone does that), but that it floats and falsifies hypotheses on an industrial scale, something no other system can do.

If a frog has an incorrect hypothesis about how to catch flies in a certain environment, it corrects its hypothesis by dying, and generations may pass before frogs, as a species, remedy their error. That is an inefficient way of learning. Humans are better learners than frogs, for sure; still, for most of history, we had many ideas but no rapid, reliable way to test them. Instead of shooting down our beliefs, we sanctified them; instead of organizing our intellectual culture to look for error, we organized it to unify our tribes around dogmas. Finding and fixing mistakes often took generations, and often required bloodshed, and many mistakes were never fixed at all.

Liberal science, by contrast, separates the idea from the person. The critical method, Popper said, "consists in letting our hypotheses die in our stead." In other words, we kill our hypotheses instead of each other. No scientist pays with her life or liberty for a mistake, a fact which frees scientists to make fresh mistakes every day. And those mistakes, in turn, are the raw material for knowledge. Taking inspiration from biology, Popper propounded what he and his school called evolutionary epistemology. New hypotheses are akin to mutations: most will fail, but a few will succeed and drive adaptation. Once the mistakes are weeded out, what remains standing on any given day is knowledge.

Grounding knowledge not in verification but in falsification was both simple and radical. From the time of Socrates, philosophers had looked for knowledge in exalted places: revelations from the Creator, insights of wise philosopher kings, the discernment of metaphysical things-in-themselves, the pristine application of pure reason. In fact, Popper said, knowledge in all its glory, like the biosphere in all *its* glory, comes from that most unglamorous of all methods: trial and error. Science's genius is its ability to both make errors quickly and find errors quickly. It kicks the evolution of knowledge into warp drive.

In subsequent years, philosophers found many reasons to cavil with Popper (who died in 1994). In the real world, scientists use verification as a strategy all the time. They very often pursue and present evidence which confirms hypotheses, probably just as commonly as they present and welcome evidence which disconfirms. And what, exactly, is falsification? Popper could never define it very precisely, and working experimenters never could, either. In practice, falsification seemed to consist of whatever it is that convinces people a proposition is false: not exactly a helpful definition.

Yet Popper's core insight, that science is an error-seeking system, has held up. And its significance is amplified by the emergence of network epistemology, whose defining insight is that science is not a process. Science is a social network, but one of a particular and peculiar kind.

Through Anybody's Eyes

Charles Sanders Peirce's name (pronounced "purse") comes up often in this book, and for good reason: he is the greatest American philosopher you have probably never heard of. Born in 1839, he worked voluminously and brilliantly until his death in 1914, pioneering both the concept of fallibilism and the philosophical school which became known as pragmatism. Perhaps his most impressive contribution, however, was to lay the groundwork for network epistemology, which conceptualizes scientific knowledge not merely as the product of individual or even group effort but as an emergent property of interactions across a social network. His insights were so far ahead of his time that he died in obscurity, unable even to get a regular university professorship. To this day, only specialists know his name. A pity, because his achievement was amazing.

To begin with, he saw more clearly than anyone before him, and also more clearly than almost everyone today, that the concept of objective knowledge is inherently social. "It will appear," he wrote, "that individualism and falsity are one and the same. Meantime, we know that man is not whole as long as he is single, that he is essentially a possible member of society. Especially, one man's experience is nothing if it stands alone. If he sees what others cannot, we call it hallucination. It is not 'my' experience but 'our' experience that has to be thought of; and this 'us' has indefinite possibilities."[8]

Consider a shaggy-haired man furiously scribbling equations and theories in his room in Bern, Switzerland. Perhaps he is Albert Einstein, discovering new truths which will rearrange the whole universe. Or perhaps he is a madman, writing gibberish. Either way, he thinks he is a genius doing great science. Even in principle, however, he is not doing science as long as he works alone. Only when others look at his scribbles, evaluating and testing them, is science taking place. Knowledge can be made only when it can be validated by others.

But which others? Who specifically? Peirce's answer: anyone who checks. Which is to say, nobody in particular. The social network is the validator. "Unless truth be recognized as *public*—as that of which *any* person would come to be convinced if he carried his inquiry, his sincere search for immovable belief, far enough—then there will be nothing to prevent each one of us from adopting an utterly futile belief of his own which all the rest will disbelieve," he wrote.[9] The secret ingredient of scientific empiricism is not the performance of some experiment or the explication of some line of reasoning which seems compelling to you or me or any particular group. We must go out and check our claims in ways which ought to satisfy *any* reasonable person, including complete strangers whose attitude is disinterested or even skeptical. "The real, then," explained Peirce, "is that which, sooner or later, information and reasoning would finally result in, and which is therefore independent of the vagaries of me and you. Thus, the very origin of the conception of reality shows that this conception essentially involves the notion of a COMMU-NITY, without definite limits, and capable of a definite increase of knowledge."[10]

The capital letters are Peirce's, showing the emphasis he placed on the communal nature of knowledge. By definition, substituting the viewpoint of anyone for the viewpoint of someone (or even of everyone) is impossible for individuals, and it is also impossible for groups defined by shared dogmas. Only a certain sort of community, operating under certain rules, can attain objectivity as Peirce understood it. Notice, too, that Peirce described the community as being one "without definite limits." The reality-based community is no mere tribe, no cult, not even a nation. In principle, it includes all who are willing to be governed by its rules, and it is bounded only by the reach of those rules. Which to say that, in principle, it is not bounded at all. Although Peirce lacked the jargon we toss around today, what he was talking about is what we now call a social network.

Booting the Network

Constitutional democracy did not arise spontaneously, out of the blue. It needed formal organs like legislatures and courts, and informal organs like parties and political machines, and norms like rule of law and peaceful rotation in office. Market economies needed social arrangements like property rights and settlement systems and limited-liability corporations, and norms like observance of contracts and transparent accounting standards. The same is true of what would later become known as the marketplace of ideas: it was not self-organizing. It required the work of thousands of practitioners. Although they held no constitutional convention, they did establish the Constitution of Knowledge's conventions.

In the late 1700s, a Scottish natural philosopher named James Hutton published what he called a new theory of the earth. By no coincidence, he was a contemporary of Adam Smith and David Hume and a product of the same Scottish Enlightenment milieu. The debate he had entered was full of conjectures about how and when the world had come into being, most of which relied one way or another on stories in the Bible. One prominent theory claimed the earth was formed 6,000 years ago, devoid of all topography, with man as its occupant. Then God called forth the waters of the Noachian Flood, the earth cracked open to release immense volumes of water, and the cavities left behind collapsed to create oceans and mountains.

Hutton was not having it. He made two radical departures. One was methodological, concerning evidence: he insisted that no miracles were needed, or even allowed, in explaining the creation of the world; observable natural forces must suffice. No agencies may be employed "that are not natural to the globe, no action to be admitted except those of which we know the principle." The other was substantive, concerning time: because the geological forces which carve canyons or raise mountains are mostly slow, like the erosion of rock by water, the world must be extremely ancient, its origin no longer even discernable through the shroud of time. "We are not to suppose that there is any violent exertion of power, such as is required in order to produce a great event in little time; in nature, we find no deficiency in respect of time," Hutton wrote. For all practical purposes, geological time could be considered infinite. "Time, which measures every-thing in our idea, and is often deficient to our schemes, is to nature endless and as nothing."[11]

More an Enlightenment *philosophe* than a modern scientist, Hutton died an old man a couple of years after publishing his ideas in a 1795 magnum opus called *Theory of the Earth.* And, no, it did not revolutionize scientific understanding then and there; most people shrugged at his theory, some dismissed it as cranky, and a few lev-eled powerful criticisms. Still, Hutton's methodological and substan-tive radicalism (no miracles! practically infinite time!) did something more productive than winning quick assent: it helped spark, of all things, a creed war. Or rather, two creed wars. One was methodolog-ical: is it always against the rules to invoke supernatural forces, or for that matter to invoke natural but cataclysmic upheavals whose like are unknown today? The other was empirical: if natural forces did create the world, were they primarily aqueous, the result of flooding (presumably Noah's deluge), or volcanic, the result of eruptions?

In the empirical argument, so-called Neptunians and Vulcanists squared off. They debated seemingly quotidian subjects, such as the origin of granite (was it crystallized from water or disgorged from volcanos?). But, as so often happens when people divide into oppos-ing camps, the debate became polarized and tribal animosities sur-faced. Partisans took to hiding mineral samples which might support the other side; a play written by a Vulcanist was booed on opening night by an audience deliberately packed with Neptunians. As the British geologist Charles Lyell would write several decades later, in his 1835 *Principles of Geology,* "Ridicule and irony were weapons more frequently employed than argument by the rival sects, till at last the controversy was carried on with a degree of bitterness almost unprecedented in questions of physical science."

Notice Lyell's reference to sects. Naturalists were behaving like religious zealots, going at it hammer and tong in defense of their dogmas. Montaigne would have felt right at home. But his solution had been to give up on finding knowledge (which is to say, on reach-ing consensus), and that was not what happened. Instead, a back-lash formed. A younger generation, disgusted with the creed war, announced that they would reject theorizing altogether. Instead, they swore that they would talk only about facts. As one of them put it, "The science of geology is at present so completely in its infancy as to render hopeless any attempt at successful generalization, and may therefore be induced to persevere with patience in the accumulation of useful facts." "Theory" and even "hypothesis," to the younger generation, were dirty words. If anything, the backlash went too far; "the absolute rejection of theory," argued an essayist in 1823, "may be, and often is, carried to a blamable excess."[12]

Extreme though the recourse to empiricism may have been intellectually, it proved successful as a social strategy: that is, as a way to divert energy and attention to arguments which appealing to evidence could adjudicate. Over the first decades of the nineteenth century, the new, empirically minded breed of researchers roamed Britain and the continent, building troves of geological samples, archives of stratigraphic drawings, repositories of fossils. No less important, the founding of the Geological Society of London in 1807 provided a clearinghouse and social hub for a growing and increasingly self-conscious community of scholars. Peirce would have understood (and probably did understand) what the geologists of the early nineteenth century were really up to when they set out to dissolve their personal disagreements in impersonal evidence: not just fanning out to collect specimens or favoring facts over theories, but also building a community in which all agree to convince each other by following the same set of rules. They were creating Peirce's boundless, impersonal *we*.

The cumulating, community-building strategy worked. By the middle of the nineteenth century, the mass of evidence had tipped the empirical scales toward the Vulcanists, and what only a generation earlier had seemed an intractable clash of dogmas had become obsolete. Moreover, that the world was very old—the essential precondition for the entirety of modern natural science, including not just geology but biology and paleontology and cosmology—had become generally accepted (though dating the earth would have to await the discovery of radioactivity). Most important of all, when the dust settled, the methodological dispute had been resolved: miracles were unconstitutional. People who had once thought of themselves as natural philosophers embraced a still-recent coinage to describe themselves: geologists. With it came a transformation of what had been the preserve of speculative thinkers and biblical scholars into a social network of investigators, each contributing a small but meaningful quantum of facts to a new science.

Here was a social triumph for all to see. In the space of a couple of generations, the empirical, socially networked method had resolved a seemingly irreconcilable conflict. By contrast, creed wars had raged for centuries without resolving anything at all. The new social network brought unprecedented insight into the forces which shape the planet, but also, more immediately and usefully, it brought peace.

Geological controversies and disruptions would arise again—in the modern era, over tectonic theory and punctuated equilibrium and what killed the dinosaurs—and they would lead to hot and sometimes personal arguments. In *The Atlantic* in 2018, Bianca Bosker chronicled how one scientific dispute (over the dinosaurs' extinction) descended to insults and accusations likened by one researcher to the Thirty Years' War.[13] Vulcanists and Neptunians might have sympathized. Science as a whole may be unemotional and undogmatic, but many individual scientists are anything but. Still, even so fierce and bruising a controversy is waged mainly within the pages of journals and the halls of academic conferences—not on the streets or in a politburo. And it will be resolved in much the same way the original Neptunian-Vulcanist controversy was: by the accumulation of evidence and the gradual force of persuasion. Over time, as evidence and arguments accumulate, scientists figure out how to resolve impasses, or at least bypass them for the time being.

Before Hutton, arguments about geology had surfaced many interesting notions but made little progress. That was not because thinkers were stupid or dogmatic; it was because they lacked systematic ways to compile and test ideas and then build upon and reconcile those ideas. Isaac Newton was a genius, by any measure. But the world had seen geniuses before. And not all of Newton's insights were sound; far from being like a modern physicist, he was an alchemist and a mystic. What empowered Newton's genius? The world of alchemists, as the philosopher of science Noretta Koertge has noted, was "loose knit and closeted."[14] Their findings (such as they were) were held close and shared only with a few adepts, and so could not be falsified or developed. By contrast, Newton's great scientific ideas—as we think of them today—were injected into the environment of the budding Royal Society (the first scientific society, of which Newton was president) and Cambridge University (where he was a professor). There, his ideas could be tested, refined, and built upon to anchor what became the discipline we call physics and the community we identify as physicists.

In his book *The Scientific Attitude*, another philosopher of science, Lee McIntyre, adduces a more recent example of how reality-based networks boot up.[15] The nineteenth century was a time of momentous breakthroughs in the understanding of disease: Louis Pasteur and germ theory, Robert Koch and bacteriology, Joseph Lister and antiseptics. Yet throughout that century, and even into the early years of the twentieth, "For all its progress, medicine was not yet a science," writes McIntyre. All kinds of cranks claimed to be doctors; practices and training were haphazard and unscientific; practitioners based their work on hunches and anecdotes; folk medicine and lay healing were standard treatments; the number of drugs which actually worked could be counted on the fingers of two hands. Yet a few decades into the twentieth century, medicine was recognizably a science and breakthroughs came at a dizzying pace: penicillin and cortisone in the 1940s; streptomycin, open-heart surgery, and polio vaccine in the 1950s; kidney transplantation in the 1960s; chemotherapy, in vitro fertilization, and angioplasty in the 1970s; and much more. When a frightening new disease appeared in the early 1980s, identifying the human immunodeficiency virus took less than two years, and developing a life-saving treatment took less than two decades—a mobilization of intellectual resources whose scale and efficacy would beggar the imaginations of all earlier generations of humans. After a frightening new coronavirus appeared in late 2019, the mobilization was an order of magnitude faster still.

What enabled medicine's liftoff? McIntyre argues that the decisive change was social: the development of professional societies which linked practitioners, set standards, and provided accountability, thus allowing each researcher to coordinate and contend with all the others. The Federation of State Medical Boards and the American Medical Association set practice guidelines which acquired something akin to the force of law; medical schools instituted rigorous scientific curricula; professional journals and networks culled and disseminated the latest research; professional associations held doctors accountable for using up-to-date research. "Once physicians started to think of themselves as a profession rather than a band of individual practitioners, things began to happen," writes McIntyre. "They read one another's work. They scrutinized one another's practices. . . . As a growing majority of practitioners embraced the scientific attitude, the scrutiny of individual ideas became more common . . . and scientific medicine was born." Instead of relying on hunch and anecdote, researchers could scrutinize treatments, discard the ineffective ones, and develop the promising ones.

As many schoolchildren know, Alexander Fleming discovered penicillin accidentally in the late 1920s when he noticed that mold inhibited the growth of a bacteria culture which he had left near a window in his lab. What schoolchildren usually do not know is that, after investigating the mold, Fleming decided it was medically useless and shelved his research. Fortunately, he nonetheless published a paper on his findings. A decade later, two other researchers, Howard Florey and Ernst Chain, discovered Fleming's paper and developed penicillin into a useful treatment. "While it is easy to entertain students with the story that penicillin was discovered by accident," writes McIntyre, "it most assuredly was *not* an accident that this discovery was then developed into a powerful drug." The antibiotic breakthrough happened not on Fleming's windowsill but on the social network which developed his accident into knowledge.

Every reality-based discipline has its own founding story; what they have in common is the construction of social networks which do what even the most brilliant array of disconnected geniuses could not. From its founding in 1660, the Royal Society had encouraged travelers to send back accounts of what they found—and it encouraged dispassionate, organized methods of reporting, thereby building up a common body of facts and, just as important, a common concept of factuality.[16] It also commissioned and promoted translations. Methodological standardization, in turn, facilitated networking, which allowed scholars anywhere to evaluate and incorporate the work of scholars everywhere. "Not until scientists began to build on the work of their predecessors did 'science' come into existence," wrote the philosopher of science David L. Hull in his 1988 book, *Science as a Process*. "As they began to become organized into social groups, science changed its character. As cooperation among contemporaneous scientists emerged, competition between individual scientists became overlaid with additional levels of cooperation and competition."

The Globalization of Knowledge

Once the reality-based community began organizing, it bootstrapped itself with startling speed. The atomic theory, electromagnetism, germ theory, thermodynamics, radioactivity, evolutionary theory, genetics, relativity, quantum mechanics, and experimental psychology were just a few of the breakthroughs of the nineteenth century alone, give or take a few years. When James Hutton died, in 1797, the world was the recent creation of Noah's flood; by the early 1900s, geology and hydrology and paleontology and glaciology had traced the earth's history back hundreds of millions of years; scientists could peer back in time to view the dinosaurs' dominion and the glaciers' carving of the continents and the earth's cycles of climatic and atmospheric change; the earth's engines of vulcanism, radioactivity, and magnetism were understood, and plate tectonics was just around the corner. In James Hutton's day, naturalists thought of themselves as natural philosophers, clustering in small communities of adepts and engaging in frequently speculative arguments. Not until the 1830s was the term "scientist" coined, but by the end of the century it denoted a trained professional who was plugged into thousands of others through journals and universities and scientific organizations. They had their own rules and customs and resources and vocabulary.

The 1870s saw the opening of America's first recognizably modern research university, Johns Hopkins, replete with graduate and professional schools, state-of-the-art labs, and a mission to advance scientific research rather than to train farmers and ministers. The University of Chicago, founded in 1892, followed close behind. Older universities, such as Columbia, Yale, and Harvard, embraced the new model. In the twentieth century, America and other industrialized countries built universities and research infrastructure at a rapid pace. As they did so, they transformed the professor from a teacher who might dabble in research to a researcher who also teaches. "The professor was being professionalized," commented Frederick Rudolph, in his landmark history of the American university.[17]

Both driving and supporting the research infrastructure was the rapid proliferation of scientific and academic professional bodies and journals. In the United States alone, the eighteenth-century American Philosophical Society and the American Academy of Arts and Sciences were joined in the middle and late 1800s by the American Association for the Advancement of Science, the American Philological Association, the American Chemical Society, the Modern Language Association, the American Historical Association, the American Economic Association, the American Mathematical Society, the Geological Society of America, and then others too numerous to count. One of Johns Hopkins University's first actions was to launch the *American Journal of Mathematics*, which was followed by many other journals. By 1904 Columbia University alone was "churning out 35 serial publications," according to Rudolph. Books poured forth, too, as universities added their own presses.

Today the scale on which science and its offshoots organize is a marvel even to those who participate, and the pace is only accelerating. One count found about 24,000 academic journals in 2010, connecting researchers the world over.[18] According to the National Science Board's indicators, coauthorship has increased in "every broad field of science."[19] The percentage of publications produced with international collaboration rose by five percentage points, to almost 22 percent, in just the single decade of 2006–2016. In this century, developing countries have rapidly joined the network, and the network is becoming denser and better connected in developed countries. "Many more nations are represented in the global network over time, and by count, we can say that there are even more new participants from within existing nations who have joined global collaborations," write Caroline S. Wagner, Travis A. Whetsell, and Loet Leydesdorff in their 2017 study of collaboration in six disciplines.[20]

One can cite mountains of such data on the growing breadth and depth of the reality-based community—and on its growing capacity and efficacy, as well. In 2020, after a new and deadly coronavirus had suddenly emerged in China, the reality-based network brought people and resources to bear with unprecedented speed. Only ten days after the new virus was first reported, scientists released its genetic sequence. Only twelve days after that, scientists at the National Institutes of Health published an analysis of how the virus invaded human cells. Only twelve *hours* later, a Chinese team, using samples of the virus, showed that the NIH team was correct. "The pace is unmatched," one scientist told the *Washington Post*.[21] Primer.ai, a corporate website which tracked research on the virus, showed that the number of published papers grew from only one on January 21, 2020, to more than 100,000 a year later, with no end in sight. The amount of research available on COVID-19 more than doubled each month from March through August of 2020, an accumulation of knowledge whose rate of increase seemed to rival that of the virus itself.[22]

The Ultimate Social Network

So here, at last, in the epistemology of Locke and Peirce and Popper and in the ambitious network-building of practical inquirers, is an answer to the riddle of Theaetetus and Montaigne. In an uncertain world, where does objective knowledge come from? Not from the certitude of any individual, no matter her genius and insight; not from priestly or princely authority; not even from some freeze-dried, Baconian scientific method (set up experiment, turn crank, out pops truth). There is no one thing all researchers do or do not do. On any given day, even the highest-minded of researchers will frequently disagree on who is doing good science or "real" science and who is doing bad science or bending the rules. The boundaries of the reality-based community are never perfectly clear. What sets it apart is not that it is distinct from all other communities but that its members operate and interact on the basis of generally shared (if sometimes also disputed) values and rules; they embrace the authority of those values and rules, rather than the authority of any particular individual and tribe; and they hold each other accountable. That is why we can say (in jargon unavailable to Peirce) that they constitute a social network.

Since the early 1960s, philosophers of science have increasingly recognized the networked nature of the reality-based community, and in fact of knowledge itself. In his famous 1962 essay, "The Republic of Science," Michael Polanyi posited that "no single scientist has a sound understanding of more than a tiny fraction of the total domain of science." Every scientist has a core competency which overlaps with others' competencies, and those others will also have overlapping competencies,

> so that the whole of science will be covered by chains and networks of overlapping neighborhoods. Each link in these chains and networks will establish agreement between the valuations made by scientists overlooking the same overlapping fields, and so, from one overlapping neighborhood to the other, agreement will be established on the valuation of scientific merit throughout all the domains of science. . . . This network is the seat of scientific opinion. Scientific opinion is an opinion not held by any single human mind, but one which, split into thousands of fragments, is held by a multitude of individuals, each of whom endorses the others' opinion at second hand, by relying on the consensual chains which link him to all the others through a sequence of overlapping neighborhoods.[23]

Objectivity, factuality, rationality: they live not just within individuals' minds and practices but on the network, amid Polanyi's interlinked chains and overlapping neighborhoods. "Objectivity," wrote the philosopher Helen E. Longino in her influential 1990 book, *Science as Social Knowledge*, "is a characteristic of a community's practice of science rather than of an individual's."

As humans, we all outsource our interpretations of reality, and even our perceptions of reality, to our social groups and personal networks. Muzafer Sherif's and Solomon Asch's psychology experiments showed many decades ago how others influence what we think, say, and even see. But replacing a personal or tribal network, one which is small or local or familial or private or affiliative, with a liberal network, one which is large and global and impersonal and public and critical, changes the game. On the liberal network, reality can take forms which transcend ordinary people's experience altogether, to the point where only mathematics can describe them. (Think of superstring theory and high-dimensional space.) "What will become scientific knowledge is produced collectively through the clashing and meshing of a variety of points of view," wrote Longino. "As long as background beliefs can be articulated and subjected to criticism from the scientific community, they can be defended, modified, or abandoned in response to such criticism. As long as this kind of response is possible, the incorporation of hypotheses into the canon of scientific knowledge can be independent of *any* individual's subjective preferences."[24]

As the network transcends the contributions and even the cognitive grasp of any of its participants, it becomes a hive intelligence, a social mind. As Steven Sloman and Philip Fernbach write in their 2017 book, *The Knowledge Illusion: Why We Never Think Alone,*

> People are like bees and society a beehive: our intelligence resides not in individual brains but in the collective mind. To function, individuals rely not only on knowledge stored within our skulls but also on knowledge stored elsewhere: in our bodies, in the environment, and especially in other people. When you put it all together, human thought is incredibly impressive. But it is a product of a community, not of any individual alone.

Although geniuses like Newton and Einstein are always important, the distinctive attribute of the community is its ability to capitalize on ordinary minds and incremental discoveries. In a nice example, the geologist Andrew Scott has related how he benefited from some research by a Scot named Stan Wood. Wood was no professional; he was an ordinary fellow who got interested and started poking around, much like the amateur geologists who fanned out to hunt for fossils in early-nineteenth-century Britain. Wood, recounts Scott, in an interview with the online publication Fivebooks.com,

> had first found extraordinary fossils of early animals in a dry stone wall surrounding a football pitch during a halftime break of a match at which he was the referee! This led him to explore a nearby quarry and to involve what is now the National Scottish Museum. I love this story as it shows how anyone, professional or amateur, with a passion for fossils can find amazing things at any time of life. The ex-

cavation of the site became an international multidisciplinary affair and I was tasked at coordinating studies of the fossil plants and even named one Stanwoodia, after Stan.

A charming story. Stan Wood's sharp eyes and Andrew Scott's intellectual hospitality were admirable. But the magic ingredient which transformed Wood's fortunate discovery into knowledge was the larger network's ability to receive Wood's fossils, mobilize researchers to evaluate them, disseminate the findings to scholars everywhere, and then integrate the findings into a larger body of knowledge—in turn, triggering citations and research which pulse out over the whole network and cause adjustments large and small in the self-organizing spider's web we call reality. In a cultic or tribal or authoritarian social environment, fossils like Wood's might attract some attention, but not much else would happen. By engaging the eyes and brains of not only Wood and Scott but countless others, the network converts personal experience and belief into something much bigger than any of us—objective knowledge.

You and I Are More Biased than We Are

In networked rationality, we also find an answer to the problem of bias and misperception. Critics of science often argue that science must be biased because individual scientists, like all other humans, are biased. In fact, as the philosopher of science Thomas Kuhn argued in his 1962 book, *The Structure of Scientific Revolutions*, individual scientists sometimes are not even rational.

The answer is: *of course* scientists are biased. But that premise does not justify the conclusion that liberal science as a whole is biased. Although members of the reality-based community may be as blind to their own errors and biases as anybody else, they are not blind to the errors and biases of those with whom they disagree. What matters is not that individuals in the community be unbiased but that they have *different* biases, so that I see your mistakes and you see mine.

"Scientists check one another's numbers," Lee McIntyre writes in *The Scientific Attitude*. "They do not wait to find an error; they go out and look for one." Although individual scientists can be as irrational and stubborn as anyone else, *"science has made a community-wide effort to . . . make corrections"* (McIntyre's italics). He cites, as an example, an astronomer who published a breakthrough discovery, only to find an embarrassing mistake in his calculations. At an American Astronomical Society meeting, he "made no excuse for himself. He told the audience what he had found and then told them why he had been wrong, after which they gave him a standing ovation. It was 'the most honorable thing I've ever seen,' said one astronomer who was present. 'A good scientist is ruthlessly honest with him- or herself, and that's what you've just witnessed.'" Provided the network contains plenty of viewpoint diversity (a crucial proviso, as a later chapter will show), "science," writes McIntyre, "is more objective than the sum of its individual practitioners."[25]

In August 2019 in the journal *Current Biology*, a team of psychologists led by Jean Decety formally retracted an article they had published there four years prior. "An error in this article, our incorrect inclusion of country of origin as a covariate in many analyses, was pointed out in a correspondence from"—here followed the names of five other psychologists. "When we reanalyzed these data to correct this error," the statement continued, "we found that country of origin, rather than religious affiliation, is the primary predictor of several of the outcomes."[26] The original paper had clashed with another scholar's observations. That scholar had requested the original data, received it, found the mistake, and reported it in *Current Biology*, which published the finding of error and then, later, the formal retraction.

Notice what did not happen: Professor Decety and his team were not taken out and shot. They did not lose their livelihoods. They probably did not even lose any friends. In fact, they might have made a few new ones. Covering the incident, *The Economist* said it showed "both what is good and what is bad about the way the modern scientific method works. The good is that the error was exposed, and has been acknowledged by the paper's authors. The bad is that it took four years for the retraction to happen."[27] Actually, the journal had acknowledged the error after only a year. It waited longer to decide on a formal retraction, but retractions are a new development in science; traditionally, unless mistakes are the result of fraud, they are left to wither on the vine, uncited and unpursued, and everybody moves on. In any case, the larger point is that four years is the blink of an eye. Other epistemic regimes take four decades to correct their errors, or four centuries, or forever.

To be sure, wrong answers can linger too long because scientists are too biased or lazy to challenge them. One such wrong answer—the notion that homosexuality is a mental illness—harmed me and millions of other people by subjecting us to stigma, shame, and dangerous quack therapies (including electroshock and lobotomies). The shameful treatment of lesbian and gay people is an enduring stain on twentieth-century psychiatry; by the late 1950s, compelling evidence had surfaced that homosexuality was neither rare nor pathological, but the profession ignored it. Still, under pressure from evidence and activists, the American Psychiatric Association recognized reality in 1973 by depathologizing homosexuality—decades before society more broadly was ready to relinquish its irrational animus against homosexuals. ("The greatest mass cure in history," proclaimed Frank Kameny, a civil rights activist and trained scientist who had pressed for the change.) The advantage of the reality-based community is not that it catches every error immediately, but that it catches most errors eventually, and many errors very quickly. No other regime can make that claim, or come anywhere close.

The Big Three: Knowledge, Freedom, Peace

And so the best way to think of rationality and objectivity is not only as attributes of individuals but also, and primarily, as attributes of the reality-based community as a system, a network. As the psychologist Jonathan Haidt has written:

> We must be wary of any individual's ability to reason. We should see each individual as being limited, like a neuron. . . . A neuron by itself isn't very smart. But if you put neurons together in the right way you get a brain; you get an emergent system that is much smarter and more flexible than a single neuron. . . . If you put individuals together in the right way, such that some individuals can use their reasoning powers to disconfirm the claims of others, and all individuals feel

some common bond or shared fate that allows them to interact civilly, you can create a group that ends up producing good reasoning as an emergent property of the social system.[28]

Peirce, all those years ago, got it right. "It is not 'my' experience but 'our' experience that has to be thought of; and this 'us' has indefinite possibilities."

Liberal science is the greatest of all social networks. Only the global economy can challenge its scope and organizational capability, but capitalism has more defects and downsides. As for today's ballyhooed digital social networks, their organizational competence and productive output are piddling next to liberal science's. Or so I maintain. But when I praise liberal science so enthusiastically, by what standards do I judge it? A fair question, which deserves an explicit answer.

An epistemic regime—that is, a public system for adjudicating differences of belief and perception and for developing shared and warranted conclusions about truth—should provide three public goods.

First, *knowledge*. The system should be competent at distinguishing reality from non-reality, and at building on previous discoveries so that knowledge accumulates, thereby generating even more knowledge.

Second, *freedom*. The system should encourage rather than repress human autonomy, creativity, and empowerment. It should welcome and exploit human diversity, especially diversity of opinion, and it should not allow any person or faction to use force or intimidation to control what others say or believe.

Third, *peace*. The system should reward social conciliation, maximize the number of disagreements which are resolvable, and compartmentalize and marginalize disagreements when it cannot resolve them. It should inculcate intellectual values which abhor violence and bullying, and it should establish institutions and norms which tolerate and even embrace disagreement and doubt.

No one should expect any knowledge-producing system to be perfect, or close to it. Still, many centuries of history show that the liberal system—the reality-based community—comes closer to perfection than any other human social invention.

It has generated and accumulated and disseminated knowledge at a staggering rate. Every day, probably before breakfast, it adds more to the canon of knowledge than was accumulated in the 200,000 years of human history prior to Galileo's time. According to a benchmark estimate made in the early 1960s by Derek J. de Solla Price and updated in 2010 by Peder Olesen Larsen and Markus von Ins, the number of scientific journals—a commonly used indicator of the scale and scope of science—has doubled approximately every fifteen years.[29] Many are in disciplines, such as database management and artificial intelligence, which did not even exist a few decades ago. There is no reason to think the pace will slow.

The system has also fostered intellectual freedom and viewpoint diversity on a scale unimaginable to our ancestors. Although some countries with productive research communities are authoritarian (China, to name an obvious example), it is no coincidence that most of the world's cutting-edge innovating and thinking happen where critical exchange and intellectual imagination roam free. As Michael Polanyi pointed out two generations ago, authorities may be able to jail particular thinkers or block particular investigations, and they may thereby be able to distort the progress of knowledge; but the reality-based community, by its very nature, is much too large, too decentralized, and too fluid to be shaped or controlled. "You can kill or mutilate the advance of science," wrote Polanyi, in "The Republic of Science," but "you cannot shape it. For it can advance only by essentially unpredictable steps, pursuing problems of its own." In fact, anyone who calls for particular viewpoints to be privileged or for particular ideas to be censored is, by definition, not doing science. Moreover, as the reality-based community organizes more researchers and more teams across more countries—as developing countries and new recruits join the network—controlling and dominating the community only become harder.

Finally, liberal science has relegated violent creed wars to the history books. That is not to deny that bitter and polarized disputes can happen, as in the aforementioned feud over dinosaur extinction. In American political discourse more broadly, ideological conflict is increasingly taking on aspects of creedal conflict between contending realities. But creedal conflict is invariably more volatile and dangerous where the Constitution of Knowledge is not in force. Where the Constitution of Knowledge prevails, you will not find rival bands of scientists or journalists or lawyers calling for each other's books to be censored and bodies to be burned.

But what is the Constitution of Knowledge, exactly? What are its rules and boundaries? Who are its participants? So far I have alluded to them. It is time to define them.

4

The Constitution of Knowledge

The operating system of the reality-based community

In Steven Spielberg's classic 1977 science-fiction movie, *Close Encounters of the Third Kind*, an alien spacecraft releases abductees to an amazed crowd of scientists. "They haven't even aged," an awed scientist remarks to a colleague, adding, "Einstein was right." Nodding skyward, the colleague replies: "Einstein was probably one of *them*." James Madison, too, was probably a space alien. Otherwise, his dazzling political genius is hard to explain.

The United States Constitution and the Constitution of Knowledge differ in many respects, but in the end what they do is the same: they compel and organize social negotiation. Each forces competing people and factions toward compromise, or at least accommodation, in order to achieve something they want to accomplish, whether to pass a law or claim knowledge. In doing so, each answers a fundamental challenge for any large and diverse and contentious society: how to provide dynamic stability? How can you make the system resilient and innovative while also preventing it from spinning out of control or breaking apart? How can the system change and adapt without losing continuity? How can it be self-guided but not self-destructive, open to many factions and viewpoints, yet captured by none?

As we have seen, the liberal revolution's breakthrough was to discover the power of social organization without centralized control. With the right incentives, big social networks like markets and liberal science can organize cooperation on a global scale. But what, exactly, are the right incentives? What should the rules look like? Among all the humans who have tackled that question, Madison stands apart, and his insight, though primarily political, illuminates the realm of knowledge, too.

He was short and slight, soft-spoken and uncharismatic. Born in 1751, he was sickly and bookish as a boy, but at Princeton he proved a quick study, completing his bachelor's degree in only two years and then continuing his education under the tutelage of Princeton's president. Gravitating toward politics, he was a delegate at age twenty-six to the convention which drafted Virginia's first constitution; constitution-writing was a business he never subsequently abandoned. After the revolution, as it became clear that the fledgling country's Articles of Confederation were weak and unstable, he led the campaign to replace them, for which he prepared himself by reading everything there was to read about republican governments past and present. When the Constitutional Convention convened in 1787, he took center stage, still only thirty-six. Later, as one of three authors of the *Federalist Papers*, he wrote the user manual for the U.S. Constitution; as a leader of the first Congress, he drafted and shepherded the Bill of Rights; with Thomas Jefferson, he founded one of the country's first two political parties (its descendant, the Democratic Party, is the oldest political party in the world); as president, he saw the Constitution through its first wartime test. With Jefferson, he pioneered the implementation of religious liberty and separation of church and state. Enough, yet? Because one could go on.

There is no national Madison Memorial, which seems ungrateful; then again, it has been said of Madison, "If you want to see his monument, look around." He lacked the majesty of George Washington, the charisma of Jefferson and Alexander Hamilton, the charm of

Benjamin Franklin. What set him apart was a grasp of political systems as intricate, self-adjusting, constantly changing social machines. He more than anyone else translated the philosophical principles of Locke and the French philosopher Baron de Montesquieu, among others, into a working political order; and he did so with no successful precedent to consult. History could show him only a long record of failures, both democratic and authoritarian.

The Constitution which he (helped, of course, by others) designed was flawed, most deeply in the legal sanction it gave to slavery, but also in its unworkable conception of the vice presidency (which sparked a succession crisis in 1801), its failure to foresee political parties (Madison reviled them but went on to help found one), its lack of explicit protections for basic rights (which Madison was forced to rectify), and its many ambiguities (which future generations would wrangle over). It was more a broad framework than a detailed blueprint. America's Constitution only begins with the written document. The rest originated with the culture of freedom which American colonists imported from England, and then it was worked out over generations as the branches of government took shape, as politicians and courts established precedents, as constitutional norms wove themselves into the country's civic fabric, as slavery and civil war and Jim Crow and wartime internments and Watergate tested whether the Constitution meant what it said.

From where Americans sit today, the Constitution's success seems preordained. To Madison and his contemporaries, the Constitution was the longest of long shots. They understood that America's republic cannot be legitimate if it is not democratic, but they also understood that democracy, at least pure democracy, is an inherently unstable form of government, prone to manipulation and overthrow by parochial interests, passionate minorities, and dangerous demagogues. As *Federalist* No. 55 warned, "In all very numerous assemblies, of whatever characters composed, passion never fails to wrest the scepter from reason. Had every Athenian citizen been a Socrates, every Athenian assembly would still have been a mob." Madison understood that any truly representative democracy must allow factions to form and promote their various causes, but he also understood that unchecked factionalism would make the polity ungovernable.

He understood that the new government somehow had to find an elusive sweet spot between being dysfunctionally weak and oppressively strong. ("In framing a government which is to be administered by men over men," he famously wrote in *Federalist* No. 51, "the great difficulty lies in this: you must first enable the government to control the governed; and in the next place oblige it to control itself." Good luck with that!) He understood that politics is naturally attractive to the ambitious, who will seek self-advancement and domination; but he also understood that ambition is too strong a force to be contained indefinitely by mere "parchment barriers."

The Genius of Compromise

One might think it would take a space alien to meet all of those challenges. Each one is formidable by itself; together, they seem overwhelming. The Constitution, like the proverbial bicycle or bumblebee, should never have worked. So what went right?

Madison, although trained as a lawyer, had the great advantage of being not only a profound student of government but a working politician: a member of the Virginia legislature and the U.S. Congress, then later secretary of state, and then president. He had the gift of always seeing the Constitution as being about the everyday activity of politics, not just words on paper. He was a *dynamic* thinker. That is the respect, I believe, in which he stands out as unique among his contemporaries and even among ours. As a working politician, he thought about the way political forces act and interact over time; and when he foresaw them acting dangerously, he thought about using them to counteract each other—a very sophisticated notion. Given the right incentives and institutional arrangements, the system could harness the only force capable of containing and channeling ambition: namely, ambition itself. In perhaps the most important two sentences ever written about the Constitution, Madison said (again in *Federalist* No. 51): "The provision for defense must in this, as in all other cases, be made commensurate to the danger of attack. Ambition must be made to counteract ambition."

A few decades earlier, Montesquieu had suggested dividing power in order to contain it; in 1780, when John Adams drafted the Massachusetts constitution, he divided its powers among three branches. From them, Madison adopted the principle of separated, competing powers, and he placed it at the heart of the U.S. Constitution; but, more than his predecessors (and more than most people even today), he saw dividing power not just as a way of constraining ambition but also as a way to promote cooperation and compromise by channeling ambition dynamically. Power would be divided vertically among levels of government (federal, state, local), and horizontally among branches of government (legislative, executive, judicial). Each level would have some areas of preeminence, but all would have opportunities to check and sometimes veto each other. Like Montesquieu, Madison understood that forcing multiple power centers to compete could prevent tyranny. But also, paralleling his near-contemporary Adam Smith, he saw that competition could be an engine converting the anarchic energy of diversity into the coordinated motion of cooperation. The essential ingredient, Madison saw, was compromise.

Although the Constitution does many things, at its core it is a mechanism for forcing compromise. Congress can legislate, but the president can veto and the courts can overturn. Congress can override vetoes and the president can make new court appointments, but Congress can reject them—and so on. By design, no one actor can do much without the concurrence of others; and all, in turn, are checked by the periodic intervention of the electorate. Those formal checks and balances, though, are just the beginning. The Constitution forces compromise not merely between the branches, levels, and institutions of government but also within each of them, and within each of the political factions which populate them. Members of the majority in each chamber of Congress must negotiate with one another to garner votes, and members of the minority must negotiate with one another about whether to cooperate with the majority or obstruct it. Even individual politicians balance competing roles, playing the loyal partisan foot soldier one day and the self-interested political entrepreneur the next. Politics in Madison's system is a constant struggle for balance. Absent a rare (and usually unsustainable) supermajority, there is simply not much which any single faction, interest, or branch of government can do. Effective action in this system is nothing but a series of forced compromises.

Why arrange things in such an apparently chaotic and contentious way? Why should every little thing involve negotiation and coalition building? There are two reasons, only one of which is well appreciated today.

The negative advantage, so to speak, of forcing compromise is to guard against tyranny by any one actor or faction. Requiring compromise contains ambition, as Madison wrote in *Federalist* No. 51, and in fact it is the only way to do so. Less widely appreciated, but just as important, is a positive advantage: more than just containing ambition, compromise also harnesses it and puts it to work.

The founders had no way to know what sorts of problems the government they were designing might confront in the future. They faced an apparently insuperable dilemma: how to provide enough stability to make the system durable while also ensuring enough flexibility to let it adjust to new circumstances. Periodic elections, of course, introduce change. But what happens between elections? What happens when electoral results are ambiguous or produce deadlock?

The Madisonian answer was to build constant adjustment into the system itself. Forcing actors to bargain and contend and collaborate slows precipitous change by requiring multiple checkpoints, but it also, just as importantly, *ensures* change by requiring constant negotiations between shifting constellations of actors. To break deadlocks, actors need to make new arguments, try new ideas, recruit new supporters, find new allies, and take new steps to mollify old allies. The search for sweeteners and workarounds and allies rewards innovation and ingenuity. Compromise, in Madison's scheme, is thus a positive dynamic force, not merely a negative restraining force.

In today's polarized climate, people tend to think of compromise as, at best, a necessary evil: a baby-splitting process which bends principles and impedes progress, leaving everyone unhappy. That is unfortunate, because Madison's view is much closer to the truth. Compromise is a positive good: a balance wheel which keeps the government moving forward instead of toppling, and a source of constant pressure for innovation and adaptation and inclusion. Compromise, in other words, is Madison's answer to the seemingly impossible conundrum of how a democracy can be both dynamic and stable.

No one is saying that compromise is admirable in every instance.

The cliché about compromising, that whether it is good or bad depends on the compromise, is obviously true. But particular compromises which individuals justifiably dislike are nonetheless part of an ongoing process of negotiation which fosters peace and stability and adaptation over time.

By the same token, the Madisonian system does not assume, expect, or even desire that every person should be a deal-cutting moderate. In fact, it assumes the opposite: that people are naturally inclined to hold strong beliefs and usually enter into negotiations reluctantly. They compromise not because they want to but because they have to, and their firm convictions ensure that multiple views receive energetic advocacy. Political zeal is to Madison's political system what the profit motive is to Adam Smith's economic system and what strong opinions are to Locke's epistemic system: an energy source. Like all energies, ambition and zeal can be destructive; compromise contains, channels, and exploits them.

So that, in (very) brief, is Madison's plan: a system which forces anyone who wants power or influence to persuade others, thereby harnessing personal ambition to stimulate dynamism and organize cooperation. The Constitution of Knowledge works the same way, except the product is not governance but reality.

What Reality Really Is

So far, I have referred to reality and objective reality and the reality-based community without quite specifying what I mean. Now is the time to fill that gap.

The question "What is reality?" may seem either too metaphysical to answer meaningfully or too obvious to need answering. When most people speak colloquially of reality, they mean the world as it really is, the world "out there," the world independent of human perception and cognition, the world as we would perceive it if we perceived correctly. Surely that is what we feel reality to be, subjectively. Colloquially, people also use the terms "real" and "reality" to convey certainty or confidence that things are the way they are. Reality, in common parlance, is that which is reliable and intractable and cannot be wished away: the rock we stub our toe on, the abrupt encounter with the ground when we fall. As Theaetetus and Socrates pointed out, however, such colloquial definitions are not very helpful. The whole problem is that humans have no direct access to an objective world independent of our minds and senses, and subjective certainty is no guarantee of truth. (More like the opposite, because certitude is so often misleading.)

Faced with those problems and others, philosophers and practitioners changed their approach. Instead of thinking about reality metaphysically, as an external if unknowable "world out there," they think of it epistemically, as that of which we have objective knowledge. More specifically, they think of reality as a set of propositions (or claims, or statements) which have been validated in some way, and which have thereby been shown to be at least conditionally true—true, that is, unless debunked. Some propositions reflect reality as we perceive it in everyday life ("The sky is blue"). Others, like the equations on a quantum physicist's blackboard, are incomprehensible to intuition. Many fall somewhere in between.

Propositions turn out to have some interesting properties. They are infinite in number and so never scarce, but true propositions are precious and comparatively rare. Even so, the quantity of validated propositions—of statements considered to be part of the canon of knowledge—far exceeds the grasp of any human individual or even any large group of individuals. Propositions are not material objects, but neither are they purely ephemeral, especially if they are true. Karl Popper claimed they exist neither in the realm of material things nor the realm of subjective feelings and perceptions, but in a third realm of their own, "the world of objective contents of thoughts." Popper compared human knowledge to the webs spun by spiders or the honey produced by bees: "exosomatic organs" which animals build outside their bodies. In a similar fashion, humans create knowledge—validated propositions—and store their knowledge in books and equations and libraries and databases, where it exists independently of our minds and bodies and could be discovered and used by an alien species millions of years from now even if humanity were extinct. Propositions have no volition and can do nothing on their own. Yet once they are acquired by the reality-based network, they can interact with each other across the network: the modification, acceptance, or rejection of one proposition can force adjustments to many others. Although the network is a human creation and all its participants are people, it far exceeds the comprehension of its creators, and it undergoes a version of natural selection, driven by its own dynamics. The reality-based network behaves like an ecosystem, producing a body of validated propositions whose composition humans can influence but not control.

That is objective reality, insofar as we can know reality. The totality of those propositions is as close as we come to objective truth.

Now, you must have noticed that a phrase I used a few paragraphs ago, "validated in some way," hides a cheat. In epistemology, the whole question is, validated in *what* way? As we have seen, the epistemic and social consequences of validation using, say, a tribal oracle versus an authoritarian government versus social error-seeking are different. And the systems are in many ways incompatible with each other. If we care about knowledge, freedom, and peace, then we need to stake a strong claim: anyone can believe anything, but liberal science—open-ended, depersonalized checking by an error-seeking social network—is the only legitimate validator of knowledge, at least in the reality-based community. Other communities, of course, can do all kinds of other things. But they cannot make social decisions about objective reality.

That is a very bold, very broad, very tough claim, and it goes down very badly with lots of people and communities who feel ignored or oppressed by the Constitution of Knowledge: creationists, Christian Scientists, homeopaths, astrologists, flat-earthers, anti-vaxxers, birthers, 9/11 truthers, postmodern professors, political partisans, QAnon followers, and adherents of any number of other belief systems and religions. It also sits uncomfortably with the populist and dogmatic tempers of our time. But, like the U.S. Constitution's claim to exclusivity in governing ("unconstitutional" means "illegal," period), the Constitution of Knowledge's claim to exclusivity is its sine qua non. Defending that claim is no small task, and so we need to understand the logic which supports it.

Rules For Reality

Say you believe something (X) to be true, and you believe that its acceptance as true by others is important or at least warranted. X might be that the earth revolves around the sun, that God is a trinity, that an embryo is a human being, that human activity is causing climate change, that vaccination saves lives, that Joe Biden was lawfully elected president, or some other consequential proposition. The specific proposition does not matter. What does matter is that the only way to validate it is to submit it to the reality-based community. Otherwise, you could win dominance for your proposition by, say, brute force, threatening and jailing and torturing and killing those who see things differently—as we have seen, a standard method down through history. Or you and your like-minded friends could go off and talk only to each other, in which case you would have founded a cult—which is lawful but socially divisive and epistemically worthless. Or you could engage in a social-media campaign to shame and intimidate those who disagree with you—a very common method these days, but one which stifles debate and throttles knowledge (and harms a lot of people).

What the reality-based community does is something else again. In my book *Kindly Inquisitors*, I argue that liberal science's distinctive qualities derive from two core rules, and that any public conversation which obeys those two rules will display the distinguishing characteristics of liberal science. The rules are

- *The fallibilist rule: No one gets the final say. You may claim that a statement is established as knowledge only if it can be debunked, in principle, and only insofar as it withstands attempts to debunk it.* That is, you are entitled to claim that a statement is objectively true only insofar as it is both checkable and has stood up to checking, and not otherwise. In practice, of course, determining whether a particular statement stands up to checking is sometimes hard, and we have to argue about it. But what counts is the way the rule directs us to behave: you must assume your own and everyone else's fallibility and you must hunt for your own and others' errors, even if you are confident you are right. Otherwise, you are not reality-based.

- *The empirical rule: No one has personal authority. You may claim that a statement has been established as knowledge only insofar as the method used to check it gives the same result regardless of the identity of the checker, and regardless of the source of the statement.* Whatever you do to check a proposition must be something that anyone can do, at least in principle, and get the same result. Also, no one proposing a hypothesis gets a free pass simply because of who she is or what group she belongs to. Who you are does not count; the rules apply to everybody and persons are interchangeable. If your method is valid only for you or your affinity group or people who believe as you do, then you are not reality-based.

Both rules have very profound social implications. "No final say" insists that to be knowledge, a statement must be checked; and it also says that knowledge is always provisional, standing only as long as it withstands checking. In practice, it embodies the fallibilist principle that everyone can always be wrong, which implies that no one can claim to have settled any debate for good. Which in turn implies that no authority or activist can legitimately shut down inquiry or debate. Anyone who does try to shut down inquiry or debate, or anyone who tries to preordain the outcome of an inquiry or a debate, is by definition removing herself from the knowledge-making business. No ideologue, moralist, or authority can claim the last word. All anyone can do is participate in the conversation, like everyone else.

"No personal authority" takes a second step by defining what properly counts as checking. We tend to think of empiricism as a practical principle grounded in observation: if you want to find out something, go out and look. Fair enough; but for me or you or any other single individual to go out and look helps not at all in overcoming the multitude of biases and misperceptions which deceive us. The point, as the American philosopher Charles Sanders Peirce emphasized, is not that I look or you look but that *we* look; and then we compare, contest, and justify our views. Crucially, then, the empirical rule is a social principle which forces us into the same conversation—a requirement that all of us, however different our viewpoints, agree to discuss what is in principle only one reality.

To see this, imagine a strange thermometer. Three of us observe it at the same time and place. When I read it, it says 61 degrees; when you read it, it says 88; when someone else reads it, it says 104. Who is right? Each of us could try to settle the dispute by claiming oracular authority or murdering the other two, or maybe we could make the problem go away by agreeing we have witnessed a miracle. But the empirical rule prohibits any of those moves. It requires us to come up with some account which reconciles our different readings. We might ask whether the thermometer is really measuring characteristics of the observers, not the outside temperature. We might look for some optical illusion or atmospheric phenomenon to explain the discrepancy. We might investigate whether we are all interpreting the scale differently. Anyhow, whatever explanation we come up with should work for all of us and anyone else who views the thermometer. It thus requires us to relate our multiple viewpoints to only one reality. It forces us into a common conversation and then forces our conversation toward a common conclusion. It requires that propositions be *contestable*: subject to systematic, organized comparison and criticism from diverse points of view.[1] It prevents situations where, intellectually speaking, one person is playing checkers and the other is playing tennis and both are claiming to have won.

By extension, the empirical rule also dictates what does *not* count as checking: claims to authority by dint of a personally or tribally privileged perspective. In principle, persons and groups are interchangeable. If I claim access to divine revelation, or if I claim the support of miracles which only believers can witness, or if I claim that my class or race or historically dominant status or historically oppressed status allows me to know and say things which others cannot, then I am breaking the empirical rule by exempting my views from contestability by others.

Though seemingly simple, the two rules define a style of social learning which prohibits a lot of the rhetorical moves we see every day. Claiming that a conversation is too dangerous or blasphemous or oppressive or traumatizing to tolerate will almost always break the fallibilist rule. Claims which begin "as a Jew," or "as a queer," or for that matter "as minister of information" or "as Pope" or "as head of the Supreme Soviet," can be valid if they provide useful information about context or credentials; but if they claim to settle an argument by appealing to personal or tribal authority, rather than earned authority, they violate the empirical rule.

That distinction is worth emphasizing. "No personal authority" says nothing against expertise. In fact, by denying personal authority, it acts as a spur to earned authority. Whatever you do to become an expert must be something that others also could do. You may have a Ph.D., but I could get one. And whatever you do as an expert must likewise be something others could do. If an experiment works for Yale's Sterling Professor of Social and Natural Science, it should also work for the lowly undergraduate who replicates it. The views of experts can earn provisional deference, but they are still expected to withstand challenge.

"No personal authority" also says nothing against trying to understand where people are coming from. If we are debating same-sex marriage, I may mention my experience as a gay person, and my experience may (I hope) be relevant. In fact, good scientific practice requires researchers to disclose their personal equities so as to surface conflicts of interest. But statements about personal standing and interest inform the conversation; they do not control it, dominate it, or end it. The rule acknowledges, and to an extent accepts, that people's (and groups') social positions and histories matter (how could they not?); but it asks its adherents not to burrow into their social identities, and not to play them as rhetorical trump cards, but to bring them to the larger project of knowledge-building and thereby transcend them.

Make no mistake, the rules are at least as demanding as they are permissive. By protecting criticism and dethroning authority, both rules protect freedom of expression. But both also impose stringent obligations on anyone who purports to advance knowledge. You have to check your own claims and subject them to contestation from others; you have to tolerate the competing claims of others; you have to accept that your own certainty counts for nothing; you have to forswear claiming that your god, your experience, your intuition, or your group is epistemically privileged; you have to defend the exclusive legitimacy of liberal science even (in fact, especially) when you think it is wrong or unfair.

Sometimes hardest of all, you are obliged to be thick-skinned and to tolerate the emotional bruising which is unavoidable in a contentious intellectual culture. If you feel offended or traumatized by something someone else has to say, of course you can object or protest or suggest a better way to talk, and very often you should; but you cannot expect or demand to shut down the conversation. After all, you might be wrong, and they might be right. *No final say; no personal authority.*

The Marketplace of Persuasion

I do not mean to suggest that any two rules—or any roomful of rules—could begin to capture the variety of ways in which scholars and statisticians and journalists and other modern reality-builders work to advance knowledge every day. But if an epistemic community follows the fallibilist and empirical rules, what it is doing will look like liberal science. And that is because what its members are doing will look like organized social persuasion.

In 1919, dissenting in the case of *Abrams* v. *United States* (in which the government censored antiwar leafleting), Supreme Court Associate Justice Oliver Wendell Holmes Jr. wrote that "the best test of truth is the power of the thought to get itself accepted in the competition of the market." In the 1950s Justice William O. Douglas took the analogy further with the phrase "marketplace of ideas." It is a wonderful metaphor. It draws upon pro-free-speech arguments from Milton and Mill to the present day, and it makes them instantly intuitive in today's consumerist world. Ideas are like cereals in the grocery store, and we are like shoppers, and competition drives the market toward more and better products! Nice.

But ideas do not sell, exchange, or compete all by themselves, and so the metaphor leaves out something important: the mechanism of exchange, which is not purchase or barter but persuasion, because that is what you must ultimately do to make knowledge. In that respect, the political marketplace provides the better metaphor. The U.S. Constitution forces political factions and their agendas into nonstop negotiations, requiring multiple factions to agree in order to make law. Similarly, the Constitution of Knowledge forces epistemic factions and their beliefs into nonstop negotiations, requiring multiple factions to agree in order to make knowledge. You cannot silence others (no final say) or dominate them (no personal authority). If ultimately you cannot convince others that you are right, as, say, neither Neptunians nor Vulcanists could do in early nineteenth-century Britain, then you need to try some other proposition or some other approach, as those two factions ultimately did. You will need to figure out what kind of demonstration might be persuasive. Others need to do the same. As dogmatic or authoritarian as your own intellectual temperament might be, if you are reality-based, you are in the business of seeking noncoercive ways to adjudicate disputes about reality.

You are, therefore, in the business of contending, persuading, compromising—similar to the dynamic, creative, option-expanding form of compromise which Madison envisioned for politics. In the search for support, you will expose your ideas to peer review and public debate, and critics will suggest questions and experiments and alternatives; in seeking to recruit others to your view, you will refine your ideas, adapt them, incorporate amendments, meet objections, and try out other ideas. You will be forced to adjust your thinking and your strategy, and as the process is repeated millions of times a day across the reality-based network, the whole system becomes a dynamic web of mutual persuasion: critical persuasion, so to speak, a social process of continuously comparing notes and spotting errors and proposing solutions.

Critical persuasion is not the same as political compromise, of course. Physicists did not sit across a bargaining table and make a deal over Planck's constant. Neptunians and Vulcanists did not convene a summit and decide on modern geology. But persuasion is analogous to compromise in that negotiators must ultimately reach accommodations—settle on something—in order to make a new law or establish new knowledge. Just as checks and balances make the U.S. Constitution simultaneously stable and adaptable, so public checking makes the Constitution of Knowledge simultaneously stable and adaptable. Members of the reality-based community can polish their reputations and win professorships and prizes by establishing some idea of their own, debunking someone else's idea, achieving a new synthesis, devising a new question, or developing a new method to resolve an old question. They can demonstrate their bona fides and locate their own ideas in the larger matrix of knowledge by earning citations and citing the work of others, showing how their ideas build on and depart from prior work, and giving credit where credit is due while expecting others to do the same. Each individual, by proposing and persuading and connecting and correcting, seeks to develop a contribution and find the right place for it.

The phrase I used just now, "critical persuasion," may sound odd. Isn't criticizing someone normally the opposite of trying to persuade her? A moment's clarification is helpful. Like many under the influence of Popper, I often refer to the network as "critical," in the sense that it seeks truth by finding error. But taking the term too literally (as sometimes Popper and other falsificationists have done) is misleading. Sometimes community members will try to shoot down each other's hypotheses, but they also can and do endorse each other's work, adopt and adapt it, propose friendly amendments, form mutually supportive alliances. In my own career, I have spent more time agreeing with other people than disagreeing with them. When I do criticize someone, it is often after first stipulating the grounds on which we agree. The goal of the system is to disconfirm, but that can be done not only by critiquing a proposition but also by supporting a better alternative.

In any given discussion, the network will form fluid, shifting nodes of agreement and disagreement, support and antagonism, alliances and arguments. What is required of traders in the marketplace of persuasion is not that they always attack others' ideas (or their own), but that they accept the legitimacy of criticism and hold themselves accountable to it. They accept that there can be no other pathway to knowledge except by exposing their own beliefs to propositions and viewpoints which are different from their own. Provided individuals follow the fallibilist and empirical rules and hold themselves and each other accountable, and provided their viewpoints are many and diverse, the network will correct errors, even if many individuals cling to their mistakes.

A Social Funnel

Put a global network of intelligent, industrious minds to work in the marketplace of persuasion, promise them glory if they can find an error or establish a fact, and the system operates as a kind of epistemic funnel. At the wide end, millions of people float millions of hypotheses every day. Only a fraction of the ideas will seem sufficiently plausible or interesting or fruitful to be acquired by the network, or even to get noticed. Once acquired, a hypothesis passes through one screen after another: testing, editing, peer review, conference presentation, publication, and then—for the lucky few ideas deemed important—citation or replication. Only a precious few make it to the narrow end of the funnel; there, after a process which can take years or even decades, a kind of social valve admits the surviving propositions into the canon of knowledge by granting them prestige and recognition, indicated with designations like "generally accepted" or "well confirmed." People who successfully bring a proposition into the canon are rewarded with publication, professorships, promotions, and prizes. Those who follow the rules without scoring a breakthrough receive honorable mention and try again. Those who flout the rules are simply ignored; usually their ideas are not acquired by the network to begin with.

The two ends of the funnel operate very differently—almost antithetically. At the big end, the community collects as many interesting hypotheses and arguments as it can find; in its search for new input, it allows just about anyone to say just about anything. Its guiding principle is freedom: free speech, free expression, diversity, pluralism. Its interest is in stimulating new ideas, new agendas, new perspectives. If the intake end of the system squelches ideas or silences speakers, it risks losing valuable insights and allowing errors to go unnoticed. The fallibilist rule, "No final say," keeps the funnel open.

But as the network acquires an idea, the empirical rule, "No personal authority," begins its relentless winnowing. The vast majority of hypotheses are rejected out of hand or not even examined to begin with, and the few which are acquired face withering professional scrutiny. At its wide front end, then, the funnel is pluralistic; the more ideas, and the more different ideas, the better. But as it narrows, hypotheses pass through increasingly stringent stages of expert review. Think of medical research, for example, and the process of developing a new drug or device or treatment. The big end of the funnel screens millions of molecules, but reaching the small end often requires hundreds of trained professionals spending thousands of hours and hundreds of millions of dollars.

Civil libertarians, take note: free speech is necessary to make the reality-based community work, and that is why the Constitution of Knowledge (like the U.S. Constitution) so uncompromisingly defends it. But free speech is not sufficient. It provides raw materials in the form of ideas and criticism, but those raw materials are merely the inchoate potential for knowledge until rule-based social checking goes to work. Nor does the Constitution of Knowledge afford any guarantee that all speech will get attention or respect. In fact, the reality-based community ignores most of what most people say. The number of testable propositions may be infinite, but the time and resources of the reality-based community are finite and precious. The Constitution of Knowledge, like the U.S. Constitution, requires its adherents to follow elaborate norms and procedures if they want the community's attention, and the community's power to set its own agenda is its single most potent lever for influence. If you want to express yourself, great. But if you want to create knowledge, be prepared to jump through hoops and sweat and suffer. The sign over the door says, "This will be difficult!"

If you want to be reality-based, you need to accept and defend the whole Constitution of Knowledge, not just the easy parts: you need to accept and defend the rules and responsibilities it imposes as resolutely as the rights and liberties it confers. Defending freedom is often challenging, but unfortunately, in our anti-institutional age, defending rules is even harder; and the rules, as we will see, have enemies.

How to Organize Everything

Here is a problem, though, with the funnel metaphor. The boundaries of the reality-based community are fuzzy and frothy, not hard and distinct, and the same is true of knowledge itself. What has and has not been validated? Who qualifies as an expert reviewer? Who is doing good science or journalism, who is doing bad science or journalism, and who is not doing science or journalism at all? Distinguishing science from pseudoscience and real news from fake news and knowledge from opinion will never be cut and dried. Among philosophers of science, a debate over what kind of thing is and is not science, the so-called demarcation problem, has been going on for a long time without resolution, which makes philosophers unhappy.

In fact, however, efforts to define who is or is not a scientist or what science does or does not do miss the point. The beauty of the reality-based community is that it can acquire all kinds of propositions and organize all sorts of arguments, and it can do all kinds of things to resolve those arguments, so long as its methods satisfy the fallibilist and empirical rules. In the real world, checking does not need to mean falsifying a factual statement in some precise, authoritative way. It means finding a replicable, impersonal way to persuade people with other viewpoints that a proposition is true or false. The reality-based community is thus not limited to handling factual disputes. It can work its will on any kind of proposition which its members and rules can figure out how to adjudicate, and it can drive many kinds of conversation toward consensus. As I wrote in *Kindly Inquisitors*,

> "Checking" can mean performing crisply definitive experiments. But even in the hardest of the sciences, the means of testing include not just lab experimentation but thought experimentation, logical analysis, consistency with established facts, consistency with personal experience, facial plausibility, proponents' and opponents' credibility, ideas' aesthetic appeal (many physicists have regarded beauty as a sign of truth), and the residual X factor we call persuasiveness. All of that and more qualifies as checking, as long as no one has final say and no one gets personal authority.

As a result, the reality-based community can get at least some traction on almost any claim which its members choose to discuss, provided always that they follow the rules. Some propositions, to be sure, are comparatively easy to validate, since the terms are well defined and the test is uncontroversial: "*Hamlet* is Shakespeare's longest play," for example, would be accepted as a meaningful, scientific statement by even the strictest logical positivist (just count the words!). The same logical positivist, by contrast, would reject "*Hamlet* is Shakespeare's greatest play" as an aesthetic opinion and therefore unscientific and unqualified to count as knowledge. In the real world, though, the second proposition is much more interesting than the first, and it has been meaningfully and fruitfully discussed by generations of scholars who marshal arguments, cite evidence, and compare contending judgments. How often is *Hamlet* performed? How widely is its poetry quoted? How many other writers has it influenced? How innovative are its themes and structure? How was it received by critics? How do audiences react to it? How closely does it comport with literary standards dating back to Aristotle? There are all kinds of ways the community can get a purchase on the "greatest" assertion.

Nobody expects one conclusive experiment to settle such moral and aesthetic conversations definitively, but the same social dynamic applies as in chemistry and physics: participants in the marketplace of persuasion cast about for impersonal arguments which will sway others. Over time, elements of consensus develop and settle out: for instance, that *Hamlet* is a greater work than *Pericles, Prince of Tyre*—a proposition which, although not strictly factual, is so close to being settled that disputing it seems facetious. Meanwhile, as the critical conversation unfolds, it develops accepted standards and methods and vocabularies, so that even if checkers do not agree on particular propositions, they agree on what it is they are discussing and how to discuss it productively. In that respect, the conversation about *Hamlet* can *organize* the search for knowledge even when it fails to *produce* knowledge.

In this way, the reality-based community can advance not only empirical knowledge but aesthetic knowledge and even moral knowledge. The result may not always be a body of hard facts or technological innovations, but it rightfully qualifies as progress toward truth. Again, from *Kindly Inquisitors*:

> Moral knowledge, like other knowledge, is not definitive; but it is directional. Nothing is guaranteed among ornery humans, but, gener-

ally and over longer spans, you can look at a tape of a liberal society's moral development and know which way it is running: usually toward less social violence, more social participation, and a wider circle of dignity and toleration. And if you see a society which is stuck and not making this kind of moral progress, you can guess that it is not very liberal and that authorities or taboos or other causes of what Peirce called "fixation of belief" have stunted or suppressed public criticism.

Francis Bacon and his followers said that scientific inquiry is characterized by experimentation; logical positivists, that it is characterized by verification; Karl Popper and his followers, by falsification. All of them were right some of the time, but not always. The better generalization, perhaps the only one broad enough to capture most of what reality-based inquirers do, is that liberal science is characterized by orderly, decentralized, and impersonal social adjudication. Can the marketplace of persuasion reach some sort of stable conclusion about a proposition, or tackle it in an organized, consensual way? If so, the proposition is grist for the reality-based community, whether or not a clear consensus is reached.

The point is not that a pair of magical rules can settle any disagreement. Rather, the point is that the reality-based network includes the hard sciences but covers much, much more territory than just the hard sciences. In fact, science, as conventionally defined, makes up only a fraction of the reality-based community. The reason the reality-based community is good at preventing creed wars is that its purview is not limited to factual disputes.

I dwell on this point at some length for a reason: today's attacks on the reality-based community concentrate their fire mostly away from hard, experimental sciences like chemistry and physics. The attackers know they would break their spears against astronomy or geology, and they know the "softer" parts of the community are more vulnerable. So it is especially important to remember: politicizing an academic discipline like sociology or literary criticism, or spreading propaganda to discredit and drown out fact-based journalism, or shading an intelligence assessment to please the president, or lying to a judge: each of those is every bit as much an attack on the Constitution of Knowledge as is, say, banning the teaching of evolution or propagating fake science about vaccines. The reality-based community is defined not by its particular disciplines or findings but by its rules and values, and an attack on those rules and values in any one part of the community is an attack on them in every part.

Scholarship ... Journalism ... Government ... Law

Enough generalities. When I talk about the reality-based community, whom do I mean?

First, the world of professional scholarship, science, and research: the universe of people who develop specialties and expertise, gather evidence, form hypotheses, survey the existing literature, engage in critical exchange, conduct peer review, publish findings, compare and replicate findings, credit and cite others' work, populate conferences, edit journals and books, develop methodologies, set and enforce research standards, and train other people to do all of those things. Many of these people are in academia, but some are in think tanks, companies, nonprofits, and consultancies. One way to spot them is that reality-based researchers who are told in advance what their findings must be, or who are not allowed to follow the evidence where it leads, know they are not doing their job and feel uncomfortable about that. They may disagree on a lot of things, but they regard lying and making stuff up as a firing offense.

Second, the world of reality-based ("mainstream") journalism: the universe of people who gather facts, cultivate sources, organize investigations, sift documents, triangulate viewpoints, develop stories, check stories, edit stories, decide to publish or not publish stories, decide whether to follow or debunk stories published elsewhere, evaluate mistakes and publish corrections, and train other people to do all of those things. Many of these people are in news organizations, but some of them work in publishing houses, online platforms, and independently. One way to spot them is that reality-based journalists who are told in advance what their stories must say, or who are told to disregard what their sources are telling them, know they are not doing their job and feel uncomfortable about that. They may disagree on a lot of things, but they regard lying and making stuff up as a firing offense.

Third, the world of government agencies which gather intelligence, perform research, compile statistics, and develop regulations. In the intelligence community, these are people who develop specialties and expertise, cultivate sources, collect and assess information, weigh their confidence in their assessments, evaluate competing assessments (sometimes going as far as to stand up "red teams" to provide alternative viewpoints), publish their assessments for their clients, conduct post-mortem reviews to understand their errors, and train others to do all of those things. Intelligence work, writes Michael Hayden, a former director of both the Central Intelligence Agency and the National Security Agency, reflects "threatened Enlightenment values: gathering, evaluating and analyzing information, and then disseminating conclusions for use, study, or refutation."[2] A former CIA officer stated the ethic this way: "It is pounded into you: to be in the CIA, you have to be as objective as possible. Your personal beliefs don't have a place in dealing with facts objectively."[3] Inscribed near the front entrance of the CIA's headquarters in McLean, Virginia, is a famous verse from John 8: "And ye shall know the truth and the truth shall make you free."

Also within the reality-based parts of the government are agencies which gather statistics and conduct research: the Bureau of Labor Statistics, the National Oceanic and Atmospheric Administration, the Centers for Disease Control, the Agriculture Department's Economic Research Service, the Government Accountability Office, the Congressional Budget Office, and many more. Most of them operate under safeguards, both procedural and cultural, designed to maintain objectivity and insulate research output from political influence. When, in 2019, President Donald Trump deliberately falsified a hurricane forecast and leaned on the National Weather Service to do the same, it was national news; when officials seemed to do the president's bidding by repudiating the correct forecast, former leaders of the weather agency rallied to condemn the interference. "Scientific integrity at a science agency matters," a former head of the National Oceanic and Atmospheric Administration said.[4] That was the Constitution of Knowledge speaking.

Not to be overlooked are the reality-based regulators. A landmark achievement in making the government face facts was the enactment of the 1946 Administrative Procedure Act. It and subsequent rules require agencies to publish proposed regulations, subject them to public comment and criticism, justify them with objective evidence and analysis, and make sure the evidence and analysis can stand up in court. That process, not at all coincidentally, resembles the impersonal public checking which knowledge itself must undergo, and the discipline it imposes prevents regulatory mistakes and abuses every day. As I write this paragraph, I notice that a federal judge has voided a regulation on grounds that the Trump administration's justification "is flatly untrue," which "makes the agency's decision to promulgate the rule arbitrary and capricious."[5] Among safeguards against tyranny, the reality-basing of government rulemaking ranks high on the list.

Fourth, the world of law and jurisprudence: the universe of lawyers and judges and legal scholars who develop specialties and expertise, gather facts, survey case law and precedent, build cases and claims, cite evidence in support of their claims, argue with other professionals, render and justify judgments, publish judgments, hold themselves and each other accountable through layers of appeal, build and respect a cumulating body of precedent, set and enforce professional standards, and train others to do all of those things. Lawyers who distort facts or case law, or judges who are told in advance how to rule, know they are not doing their job and feel uncomfortable about that. They may disagree on a lot of things, but they regard lying and making stuff up as a firing offense. That was why, in 2014, a man who had fabricated articles in his previous career as a journalist was denied admission to the California bar. In issuing the denial, the state's supreme court said that his "deceit" was a form of "misconduct [which] bore directly on his character in matters that are critical to the practice of law."[6] The historian Barbara J. Shapiro argues that the very concept of *fact* originated in the realm of law and spread from there into the sciences and journalism.[7]

Common Cores

By no means do those four categories exhaust the taxonomy. Reality-based professionals work in many places, doing many kinds of things, each with unique attributes. There are reality-based professionals in museums, in libraries, in schools, and more. The many distinctions between the many different sectors of the reality-based community are worth a book, but that would be some other book. More important in understanding the Constitution of Knowledge are certain commitments which they have in common:

Fallibilism. Paying lip service to the fallibilist rule—the ethos that any of us might be wrong—is easy. Taking fallibilism seriously, and using it as an organizing principle for our lives and careers, is not easy at all. Being open to criticism requires humility and forbearance and toleration. Scientists, journalists, lawyers, and intelligence analysts all accept fallibilism and empiricism in principle, even when they behave pigheadedly (as happens with humans).

Objectivity. People and organizations also share a commitment to the empirical rule, the requirement that individuals should be interchangeable. They reject subjectivism; nothing is true merely because you feel it is true, or because your boss or priest or tribe feels it to be true. They reject perspectivism; nothing is true because it represents some person's or group's point of view or lived experience. Throughout the reality-based community, objectivity and interchangeability are closely linked. The law, for example, is full of what are called reasonable-person standards: what would some generic, sensible person do or think in this situation? In court, evidence must bear scrutiny from both (or many) sides; in investigations, police and prosecutors are supposed to use standardized methods and disclose their evidence.

Exclusivity. Members of the community share not just a commitment to the idea of objective reality but also an understanding that outside of that commitment lies anarchy, a zone of chaos where reality splinters and truth loses its grip. Recall Peirce's warning: "Unless truth be recognized as *public*—as that of which *any* person would come to be convinced if he carried his inquiry, his sincere search for immovable belief, far enough—then there will be nothing to prevent each one of us from adopting an utterly futile belief of his own which all the rest will disbelieve." The Constitution of Knowledge requires a commitment to one objective reality, accessible only through the Constitution's rules.

Disconfirmation. The system does all sorts of things, but it is tuned for what Greg Lukianoff and Jonathan Haidt in their 2018 book, *The Coddling of the American Mind,* call "institutionalized disconfirmation." Individuals, of course, work hard to confirm their own viewpoints, and try hard to persuade others. But they understand that their claims will and must be challenged; they anticipate those challenges and respond; they subject their scholarship to peer review and replication, their journalism to editing and fact-checking, their legal briefs to adversarial lawyers, their intelligence to red-team review. Individuals may feel as certain as they like; but as long as they follow the rules, the system as a whole will be in the business of disconfirming.

Accountability. Being wrong is undesirable, but it is also inevitable. We want people to feel safe making mistakes; otherwise they will not venture new hypotheses. On the other hand, we want to encourage them not to make mistakes; otherwise they will be slipshod. So we need just the right amount and kind of accountability—not too much or too little, not too harsh or too lenient. How do we thread that needle?

The answer is with multiple layers of accountability, of which the first and most important is internal: epistemic conscience. Sometimes scientists bury unfavorable data, prosecutors hide evidence, journalists cherry-pick quotes. What is important is that those failings be recognized as just that: failings. No reputable scientist or journalist or prosecutor, if exposed, says, "Sure, I made up fake evidence and hid the real thing. It worked! You should try it!" She expresses shame, and hopefully feels it, too. Epistemically, she tries to be law-abiding, and she expects others to do the same. It would never occur to members of the reality-based community to shoehorn more than 100 false or misleading claims into a single two-hour speech, as Donald Trump did on March 2, 2019.[8] The whole idea of spewing lies strikes them as bizarre and sociopathic (which it is).

In cases of outright misconduct, those who break the rules are called out and sanctioned, or at least should be; their papers or prizes may be withdrawn, their careers impeded, their reputations damaged. Sometimes, in extreme cases, when the violation is consequential and clearly committed in bad faith, they may lose their professional credentials or be fired. More often, however, accountability takes a simpler, subtler, and softer form: those who err lose the argument. In other words, they fail to persuade, and their views fall by the wayside. The marvel of this soft form of accountability—accountability to the marketplace of persuasion—is that the consequences are serious but not severe. Losing an argument is painful, but everyone lives to move on to the next question.

However, most of what the reality-based community does to deter wrongness is to encourage rightness. The community prefers carrots to sticks. Scholarly citations, follow-up stories by other journalists, inclusions in the President's Daily Brief, the opportunity to set a legal precedent: those and other positive incentives are the coins of the realm in the reality-based community.

Remember Theaetetus? He and Socrates suggest a further important respect in which accountability undergirds the reality-based community: community members hold each other accountable by, literally, giving accounts. To make a successful claim to knowledge, you cannot just pull rank or make an assertion. You must explain why your idea is better than other contenders. Scientists, historians, literary critics, reporters, editorialists, lawyers, judges, regulators—all spend most of their time every day justifying their own claims and weighing others' claims. Perhaps, as Socrates and Theaetetus concluded, providing an account is not sufficient to establish knowledge, but it is necessary; those who refuse to provide an account, or say they don't need to provide one, are self-banished.

Pluralism. The reality-based community not only accepts viewpoint diversity, it positively depends upon viewpoint diversity. The big end of the funnel requires maximum freedom to propose, to critique, to challenge, to defend; otherwise confirmation bias and conformity bias reign supreme. Which is not to say that individuals in the community always welcome competing ideas; if they did, they would not be human. But it is to say that they accept the legitimacy of competing ideas. "Shut up," they understand, is never an explanation.

Civility. Even the most accomplished reality-based professionals— among them some of the world's great scientists—can be as spiteful and dogmatic as any other merely human creature. But they do need to keep the conversation going, which is hard amid feuds and naked hostility. What is especially impressive about the reality-based community is how comparatively rare personal attacks are, and how commonly decorum prevails. Community members develop and follow elaborate protocols which encourage them to argue calmly and depersonalize their rhetoric—protocols which it is in their interest to observe. In the marketplace of persuasion, incivility is self-marginalizing. If you are obnoxious, you will have a harder time making converts. Collaborators will avoid you. Conference invitations will dry up. Editors will warn each other not to work with you. Judges will roll their eyes at you. If you are a genius or politically connected, you can get away with more; but, over time, cooperators usually prevail.

Professionalism. Earned credentials count. To develop a track record and reputation, you need to study and practice for years, often decades. To stay abreast of your field, you need to specialize. To reach your field's influencers, you need to be connected to the network. To organize resources and join teams, you need to be connected to institutions (universities, medical boards, scientific societies, media outlets, journalism schools, law firms, bar associations, government agencies, pharmaceutical corporations). To influence the agenda, you need credibility. Even to communicate, you will likely have to master a distinctive jargon. If you want to join the reality-based community, prepare to spend decades learning the ropes—and, with rare exceptions, becoming a professional. As such, you will be accountable to other professionals, and you will share with them a sense of integrity: a deeply instilled understanding that there are right and wrong ways to do things, and that cutting corners betrays your professional mission. Because the reality-building project is cumulative (professionals need to know what is already known), and because it is networked (professionals need to know what other professionals are working on), it is inherently biased toward specialization and expertise. There is always room for amateurs to contribute, but they cannot get very far without consulting with institutions and experts. In other words, the reality-based community is fundamentally a professional network, and its members are overwhelmingly professionals seeking to persuade other professionals.

Institutionalism. It is also, just as fundamentally, an institutional network. Think about only some of the tasks it needs to perform, day in and day out: incentivize millions of individuals to follow the rules and behave accountably; archive and retrieve vast stores of precedent and specialized knowledge; connect people within and across disciplines so they can interact productively; prioritize research agendas and allocate resources; establish norms of conduct and rules of the road; recruit, acculturate, and train the next generation. Only institutions—universities and scientific and medical organizations, law schools and bar associations, media organizations and journalism schools, government research and intelligence agencies, and the like—can do that work. Institutions are the network's connecting nodes. Which is why, as we will see, enemies of the reality-based community are in the business of demolishing, discrediting, and circumventing institutions.

No bullshitting. In recent years, epistemologists have felt obliged to think about what it means to behave without any sincere regard for truth, to the point where "bullshitting" has become a term of art in philosophy. Whereas the liar expresses a certain appreciation for truth by trying to conceal or deny it, the bullshitter "does not care whether the things he says describe reality correctly," as the philosopher Harry Frankfurt wrote in his famous 1986 essay, "On Bullshit" (later expanded into a book). "He just picks them out, or makes them up, to suit his purpose." Lying obviously violates the Constitution of Knowledge, but bullshitting can be even more damaging. "Genuine inquirers may come to false conclusions or be led astray by misleading evidence or arguments," writes the epistemologist Susan Haack. "But an honest inquirer won't suppress unfavorable evidence or awkward arguments, nor try to hide behind affected obscurity when things go badly; so, even when he fails, he won't make others' work more difficult." By contrast, bullshitters "are apt to waste their intelligence and ingenuity in suppressing unfavorable evidence or awkward arguments, or in devising impressively obscure formulations."[9]

I am not claiming that every good scholar or journalist needs to believe she possesses the truth, or even needs to believe that objective truth exists. (Some serious thinkers have argued powerfully against objectivity.) I am saying there are ways she should and should not behave in public interactions with others. Truth, as Karl Popper said, is a regulative principle. Like north, it is a direction, an orientation, not a destination. When we join the reality-based community—when we sign up for the years of training, the exacting research, the criticism and lost arguments—we resolve to conduct ourselves as if reality were out there and objectivity were possible, even while acknowledging that reality is elusive and perfect objectivity is impossible. From the axiom that truth is elusive but that searching for it regulates and organizes our community, a prime directive follows. Charles Sanders Peirce memorably stated it:

> Upon this first, and in one sense this sole, rule of reason, that in order to learn you must desire to learn, and in so desiring not be satisfied with what you already incline to think, there follows one corollary which itself deserves to be inscribed upon every wall of the city of philosophy:
>
> Do not block the way of inquiry.[10]

To be reality-based, in other words, is to identify with and serve the mission of *learning*. If liberty is the core value of the political constitution, then learning is the core value of the epistemic one.

Long ago, Socrates made much the same point. Learning, he implied, is a process, not an outcome; a conversation, not a destination; and it begins with, and cannot flourish without, the desire to learn. Recall his admonition to Theaetetus: "This sense of wonder is the mark of the philosopher. Philosophy indeed has no other origin."

Convergent Constitutions

Conjoined by the spirit of inquiry, the members of the reality-based community, whatever their branch or specialty, share a common citizenship. There are countless bias-confirming communities, each, as Peirce said, dedicated to its own fixed picture of reality, its members bonded by their dogmas. But there is only one reality-based community. Granted, it is bubbling with disagreement and difference; its far-flung members and sectors operate with a high degree of independence from each other; at any given moment, even the most erudite members of the community are aware of only a tiny fraction of what is going on across the network. Yet each member can in principle persuade or criticize any other. Every so often, distant nodes connect and intellectual electricity flows, as when an academic historian briefs an intelligence analyst or a lawyer tips off a journalist. As in an ecosystem or a market economy, each participant and niche may feel or appear separate from most of the others, but all interact across the network, often without particularly realizing it. For generations, scholars have spoken of the fundamental unity of the sciences, meaning the hard sciences; they should speak, more broadly, of the fundamental unity of the entire reality-based community. The uniting thread is not a common research method or a common body of opinions but a common commitment: to the Constitution of Knowledge.

In that respect, the Constitution of Knowledge resembles the U.S. Constitution. They share other important resemblances, too.

Both fundamentally are mechanisms of public decisionmaking and social adjudication. We all think of the U.S. Constitution that way because it is explicitly designed to force compromise. Less obviously, but just as centrally, the Constitution of Knowledge does the same thing, and in a similar way: by blocking coercion and requiring persuasion, thereby forcing negotiation.

Both thus assert their monopoly on legitimate decisionmaking, cutting off other pathways—to political power, to epistemic power. You cannot pass a federal law except through the operation of Congress or its designee, or join Congress except through election, or ignore a court order; you cannot make knowledge except through the marketplace of persuasion and its multiple layers of checking and vetting.

Both are fundamentally liberal inasmuch as they specify a process, not an outcome. Thomas Jefferson favored a small, limited government suited to an agrarian republic of small landholders; Alexander Hamilton favored a larger, more ambitious government, suited to a globally trading commercial republic. Who won the argument? James Madison, who pitted Jefferson and Hamilton against each other. In his Constitution, Jefferson's and Hamilton's visions continually contend, and the outcome on any day matters less than that the argument should never be finally settled, ensuring that the system remains dynamic and adaptive. Similarly, the Constitution of Knowledge allows for no resting point, no stasis, no fixed definition of its boundaries or methods. It allows only for constant negotiation across the network, a process of contestation and resolution, leading to new questions and controversies as older ones are settled.

Improbably, but demonstrably, both systems use their turbulence as a source of stability. The U.S. Constitution is almost halfway through its third century, and despite some severe challenges it has managed to survive and adapt better than Madison himself likely expected. (He knew that the historical record did not bode well for democracies' survival.) Likewise, the reality-based community has maintained recognizable continuity since before Madison's day, despite—actually, because of—its endless contentious churning.

The vital ingredient for both systems' stability? Both are built to institutionalize self-correction. The U.S. Constitution's internal balance-wheels and limits—regular elections, enforceable rights, rivalries between branches and levels of government—seek to ensure that if one faction fails or errs, another can displace it. Republicans and Democrats rotate through power, states take action when the federal government stalls, and presidents remediate the defects of their predecessors. The reality-based community is explicitly based on self-correction. Though the system makes plenty of mistakes, it is much less likely to get stuck with them for a long time than is any competitor.

For all their dynamism, both systems, the political and the epistemic, gain stability by being biased toward continuity and respect for precedent. Both are in that sense not only liberal but conservative. Politicians may promise to make a clean sweep and start fresh when elected, but the Constitution is designed to make radical promises difficult to keep. Laws accumulate on the books, programs develop constituencies, institutions maintain traditions; with rare exceptions, by Madison's design (at odds with Jefferson's preference for periodic revolutions), change is incremental and difficult—sometimes, as I have argued elsewhere, too difficult—yet ensures that the political system rolls rather than lurches.[11] By the same token, liberal science operates cumulatively, like a giant social crossword puzzle, each advance filling in a new detail which may require revising an old detail, but none replacing the whole grid.[12] Even the occasional revolutionary scientific idea—what Thomas Kuhn called a paradigm shift, something with the dramatic impact of heliocentrism or evolution or gene theory or relativity—is judged successful mainly by the extent to which it solves an old puzzle and then is absorbed into the everyday research of countless community members. Both systems, political and epistemic, are cumulative and constructive, and therefore conservative, in the sense that they conserve what they can of the old while seeking to incorporate and adapt to the new. Individuals can be radical; the system is not.

Both systems rely on another buffer against radicalism: they are participatory but not populist. In fact, they positively depend on professionalism, expertise, and specialization. At the wide end of the political and epistemic funnels, all are welcome to vote and volunteer and donate, and to offer ideas and evidence and arguments. But for action to happen—for a proposal to become law, for an idea to become knowledge—a whole series of intermediaries and institutions must intervene, and every step requires that professionals persuade other professionals.

And both constitutional orders, although mediated, distribute authority across the network, which makes them unusually resistant to takeover by authoritarians or factions. Madison designed the Constitution to disperse power within and outside of government. The reality-based community is even more resistant than the political system to authoritarianism and personality cults; there is no center, no head, no command structure. Particular parts of the government, or particular intellectual disciplines and cultures, can fall victim to corruption or capture; and that is a serious problem. But a system which distributes decisionmaking, blocks action except through persuasion, and stays open to new people and ideas cannot be dominated for long.

I could cite many other parallels, but will skip to what may be the most important. Both constitutions rest, ultimately, on versions of what the American founders thought of as republican virtue: habits and norms like lawfulness, truthfulness, self-restraint, and forbearance. If anything could ruin the American constitutional experiment, they believed, a failure of republican virtue would be the most likely culprit. They understood that the people would be tempted to exercise their constitutional rights without shouldering their constitutional responsibilities. That was why Adams and Franklin and Madison and the other Founders warned that democracy was only fit for a virtuous public. "As there is a degree of depravity in mankind which requires a certain degree of circumspection and distrust, so there are other qualities in human nature which justify a certain portion of esteem and confidence," wrote Madison in *Federalist* No. 55. "Republican government presupposes the existence of these qualities in a higher degree than any other form." If the people or their factions seek to win by lying, breaking the law, fostering extremism and demagoguery, or wiping out the other side, then no constitution will endure, however strong it might look on paper.

Similarly, the Constitution of Knowledge presupposes both rights and responsibilities—and, as between the two, the rights are the easier to grasp and defend. The rights include believing as one chooses, expressing one's opinions, criticizing and speaking out, and even offending within broad boundaries. Of all epistemic orders, only liberal science is premised on free inquiry and intellectual pluralism. Yet the responsibilities are heavy and tempting to shirk. We can believe as we like privately, but in making public policy, we must privilege the reality-based community's judgments about facts. We can say what we think, and even give offense; but we also need to be thick-skinned, resisting the urge to *take* offense. We can call out what we think are others' errors, but we should not criminalize error by jailing the errant, or firing them, or throwing them off campus. We can question and criticize to our heart's content, but we also must endure being questioned and criticized ourselves. We can feel certain that we are right and defend our beliefs uncompromisingly, but we also try to practice forbearance and humility, accepting that we might always be wrong. We can bullshit as much as we like in the barber shop or beauty salon, but not in law or journalism or academia; if we wish to be part of the reality-based community, we behave as if truth exists and evidence matters, and preferably we feel that way, too. Above all, we accede to the unique sovereignty of critical persuasion in establishing knowledge, and we accept no shortcuts. Failing to persuade means losing the argument, period. You cannot prevail by majority vote, by being divinely inspired, by being historically oppressed, by having justice on your side, by silencing the other side, or any other way.

Those are the republican virtues of the republic of science—and they require just as much discipline and commitment as do the republican virtues of politics. If we internalize and institutionalize them, then the Constitution of Knowledge performs the same kind of social magic as the U.S. Constitution. It makes pluralism a source of stability and conflict a source of dynamism. It enables social cooperation on an otherwise impossible scale. It provides a degree of personal freedom which no other system can match (or tries to). It fences out authoritarians who would impose their will. It enlists millions of independent minds to advance knowledge and make social choices. It converts the heat of disagreement into the light of progress.

Reality Is a Part-Time Job

But wait. Time to acknowledge some limits. Having praised the Constitution of Knowledge to the skies, having claimed it can make almost any kind of hypothesis socially adjudicable, and having insisted that it be arbiter of public knowledge, I need to say a word about what it does not do: run your life, rule the world, or control your brain.

Science is a great thing, but scientism—the idea that science does or should govern every domain of life—is a mistake, and the Constitution of Knowledge does not imply it. In fact, it implies the opposite. The reality-based community is *a* community—not *the* community. And because it is a liberal community, it embraces limits on its own authority. There is room, in liberal societies and in liberal science properly understood, for tradition, identity, rootedness. There is room to be our own personal, spiritual, embodied selves, each with our own lived experience and subjective outlook. There is room for me to understand myself as a privileged white male, as a formerly oppressed homosexual, as a secularized Jew, as a child of the 1970s and the American Southwest. That we are (in principle) interchangeable when debating objective reality does not mean we need to dissolve ourselves in a disembodied public conversation and go about as nameless, atomized ciphers. All that the Constitution of Knowledge says is, "Do this here. Do other things in other places. And yes, by all means, do both."

Francis Collins, the director of the U.S. National Institutes of Health, is one of the most distinguished biologists of his era. He goes to work every day to advance medical knowledge. He is also a devout Christian. To an atheist like me, Collins is a puzzle. He would never fund NIH research on exorcism as a treatment for glioblastoma, or tell a cancer patient to try prayer instead of chemotherapy. Science's whole professional outlook is based on the rejection of supernatural powers and miracles. Yet he believes that a supernatural being exists and had a son who died and was resurrected. He believes that science and Christianity are reconcilable, and wrote an entire book making that case.[13] Religion rests on faith, not on empirical probabilities. Yet he experiences no discontinuity.

So is someone like Collins a hypocrite? Not at all. He is human, and humans, including scientists (the majority of whom believe in a higher being), spend much of our lives in bias-confirming communities: social affinity groups where we seek not to test each other's beliefs but to affirm them. Every time a biologist sets aside her research to go to mass and take communion, she leaves the reality-based community and enters a community of faith and fellowship. She is not betraying science when she does religion, or betraying religion when she does science; she is acting differently in different communities and reaping the rewards of both. A person who applied the Constitution of Knowledge to every daily situation would be Sherlock Holmes or Mr. Spock: an otherworldly fictional character. In fact, when I compare Francis Collins's worldview with my own, I think mine is the more impoverished. He has access to two epistemic realms; I, only one.

Some militant secularists insist that faith and science are bound to be enemies: that, in effect, the Constitution of Knowledge cannot tolerate rivals. But that rigid view is wrong. The Constitution of Knowledge needs supremacy in the realm of public knowledge, but not in the realm of private belief. It decides what appears in academic journals, newspapers, school textbooks, university curricula, government reports, legal briefs, intelligence briefs. It requires reality-based professionals to follow its rules in their professional lives. But it does not require each of us to go around all the time behaving like a scientist or reporter, and if it did, it would fail. Fortunately, it does not need everyone to be truth-seeking; it can make do with most people's being truth-*friendly*.

By analogy, the U.S. Constitution sets the rules for America's national government, but it does not lay down the rules for running our families, teaching our children, organizing our communities, or doing our jobs; it merely asks us to behave in ways which support rather than undermine the Constitution's ability to do *its* job. To be sure, as the Founders so strongly emphasized, it only works in a society which upholds its legal authority and embraces its principles. It needs ordinary people to respect norms like rule of law, due process, orderly rotation in power, compromise, and the rest. But the U.S. Constitution's purpose is to create a legal frame within which individuals can freely and safely live all kinds of lives. In the same way, the Constitution of Knowledge creates an epistemic frame within which individuals can freely and safely hold many kinds of personal beliefs.

Notice what that frame does not require: unanimity about anything in particular. In chapter 1, I quoted Ben Sasse, a Republican senator, as saying: "We have a risk of getting to a place where we don't have shared public facts. A republic will not work if we don't have shared facts." Well, yes, but also no. Yes, people need to have some factual literacy, enough to uphold a commitment to common institutions; and those institutions need to privilege knowledge over mere belief. But if liberal science needed shared public facts, it would be doomed, because there aren't many.

According to Kurt Andersen in his 2017 book, *Fantasyland: How America Went Haywire: A 500-Year History*, two-thirds of Americans believe angels and demons are active in the world.

> A third believe that our earliest ancestors were humans just like humans today; that the government has, in league with the pharmaceutical industry, hidden evidence of "natural" cancer cures; that extraterrestrials have recently visited (or now reside on) earth. A quarter believe vaccines cause autism and that Donald Trump won the popular vote in the 2016 general election. A quarter believe that our previous president was (or is?) the Antichrist. A quarter believe in witches. Remarkably, no more than one in five Americans believe the Bible consists mainly of legends and fables—around the same number who believe that "the media or the government adds secret mind-controlling technology to television broadcast signals" and that U.S. officials were complicit in the 9/11 attacks.

Gallup polls conducted since 1999 find that three-fourths of Americans believe in paranormal events, almost a third believe in ghosts, and almost a fifth believe the sun revolves around the earth.[14] A 2015 poll by the Pew Research Center found that almost a third reject evolution, believing instead that humans and other living things have existed in their present form since the beginning of time. Examples of public misinformation can be multiplied ad infinitum, and the public's ignorance of many basic facts is equally impressive.

The reality-based community, then, cannot depend on individuals to know the facts (though it has an easier time if they do), and it certainly cannot depend on them to agree on the facts (which would be stultifying). What it does require is an elite consensus, and preferably also something approaching a public consensus, on the method of *establishing* facts. People need not and cannot all agree that the same things are true, but a critical mass needs to agree on what we do to distinguish truth from falsehood, and more important, on who does it. In other words, a liberal epistemic order requires not shared facts but a shared commitment to the Constitution of Knowledge. More specifically, it needs four kinds of assent:

- general acceptance of reality-based epistemic rules (the Constitution of Knowledge) and professionals and institutions which uphold them (the reality-based community);

- general consent to public decisionmaking systems which are reality-based (Christian Science and homeopathy may be believed by millions, but they cannot run the Food and Drug Administration);

- enough public trust in the reality-based community to legitimize its privileged epistemic standing; and

- enough public respect for the Constitution of Knowledge's underlying values to support norms like freedom of expression, intellectual pluralism, commitment to learning, and respect for factuality and truthfulness.

All four, as we will see, are under attack. In fact, they always have been. The Constitution of Knowledge has always been controversial and it has always faced challenges. But the nature of the challenges continually evolves, requiring defenses to evolve, too. In the next chapters, we examine the latest challenges, beginning with the technological earthquake which enabled them.

5

Disinformation Technology:
The Challenge of Digital Media

Making the online world truth-friendly
is difficult but doable

The Declaration of Independence is history's greatest summons to liberty and the Constitution is history's greatest governing document, so no wonder people forget the misshapen stepchild in between. In 1781, with the Revolutionary War still under way, the thirteen original states adopted the Articles of Confederation, granting the central government a modicum of power while reserving most authority for themselves. Lacking the power to tax, the Continental Congress had to beg the states for revenue, which they preferred not to provide. The states could print money, and they did so with abandon, causing runaway inflation. The states could run their own trade policies, which led to protectionism and trade wars. They even feuded over river navigation.

By 1786, the war was won but the Confederation was teetering. Among those who looked on with alarm was the young James Madison. Also alarmed was a farmer and businessman (and retired general) named George Washington, who had no love for inflation and instability. The Articles, they saw, were too rigid and weak to cope with governing. Having only just won independence from Britain, however, the states were in no mood to step aside. And so Madison, with Washington's quiet support, did some maneuvering, his specialty. Encouraged by the two Virginians' prodding, the Virginia legislature called for a multistate convention on harmonizing state commercial regulations. That seemed boring and harmless, and the convention attracted only twelve delegates, who met in a tavern in Annapolis. But the delegates were all Federalists, supporters of a stronger central government, and they included Madison and another Washington intimate named Alexander Hamilton. The Annapolis convention met for only a few days before deciding that it couldn't decide and issuing a call for a bigger convention with a bigger mission: to "devise such further provisions as shall appear . . . necessary to render the constitution of the federal government adequate to the exigencies of the Union." In Philadelphia in 1787, the Constitutional Convention's delegates immediately exceeded their remit by deciding to scrap the Articles and start over.

Though the Articles of Confederation are all but forgotten, give them their due. Without their failure, the Constitution might never have been adopted. And notice the pivot they provided: from liberty to order. The Constitution was designed to constrain the government and so protect civil liberties, to be sure, but it was born of a fear that the government was too weak, not too strong. "You must first enable the government to control the governed; and in the next place oblige it to control itself," wrote Madison, in *Federalist* No. 51. Notice the sequence: you must first empower the government sufficiently, and only then constrain it.

The challenge in 1787 was to design institutions to fill a dangerously anarchic space. The challenge of the digital era is analogous. The Constitution of Knowledge is embodied in a set of norms and institutions which were pushed to their limits by new technology. Even worse, design flaws and perverse incentives in the digital information environment ("digital media," as I will call it for short) actively favored epistemic anarchy. Weirdly, more than two centuries after the meeting in that Maryland tavern, the reality-based community found itself confronting an equivalent of the Articles of Confederation.

Checks and Valences

Suddenly, disseminating information is orders of magnitude cheaper and faster than ever before. Established information gatekeepers have been swept aside. Fake news, political propaganda, and personal provocations proliferate. No one knows how to stem the chaos. We must be talking about the internet? Actually, no.

"The printing press, as it spread across Europe beginning with Gutenberg's invention in the fifteenth century, revolutionized the public sphere as radically as the internet and the personal computer have revolutionized the public sphere in our time," the historian Niall Ferguson said in a 2018 interview with the podcaster Sam Harris. Movable type made replicating a book something like 300 times cheaper, according to Tom Wheeler, a former chairman of the Federal Communications Commission, in his 2019 book, *From Gutenberg to Google: The History of Our Future*. No wonder that within half a century of movable type's invention, printers had been established in every major European city. In the first fifty years after the invention of movable type, notes Wheeler, "more books were printed than had been produced in a millennium."

Just as suddenly, ordinary people had access to a far wider range of ideas—some of them false and dangerous. One of the first uses of the new technology was for what today we call conspiracy theories or fake news: a tract called *Malleus Maleficarum* ("Hammer of Witches") swept across Europe after its publication in the late 1400s, claiming that witches lurked everywhere and inspiring panics and tens of thousands of murders. The printing press gave wings to Martin Luther's radical dissent and spread religious controversy, and war, across Europe. As late as 1750, an appalled Jean-Jacques Rousseau commented, "If we consider the horrible disorders that printing has already produced in Europe, and if we judge the future in light of the progress this evil makes every day, we can easily predict that sovereigns will not delay in making as much effort to banish this awful art from their states as they made to establish it."[1]

We know how the previous information disruption turned out: at length, a new equilibrium took hold and publishing became a mostly reputable enterprise. Most—certainly not all, but most—of what you saw in print or on TV was likely to be true. ("I saw it in the newspaper," people would say when I was growing up.) Information technology developed what one might think of as a *positive epistemic valence*: in general, it channeled information in ways which favored reality over nonreality. One could publish or broadcast misinformation, of course. Lots of people did. But misinformation injected into the scholarly and media networks would normally wither away for want of evidence or plausibility or interest.

That was not always the case. Establishing positive epistemic valence was a long, sometimes difficult process. Universities had to fight for independence from corporations, religious groups, legislatures, and other outside forces seeking to influence what was studied and taught. Perhaps even more striking was the struggle to base journalism on truth.

In America's founding era, journalism was notoriously partisan and unreliable. Almost anyone could open a newspaper, and almost anyone did. Standards were low to nonexistent. "Editors and promoters, however much they proclaimed their loyalty to truth, more often than not were motivated by partisan political goals and commercial interests in the sensational," writes the historian Barbara J. Shapiro.[2] Newspapers did not scruple to publish what today we call fake news. In 1835 the New York *Sun* published bogus reports of life on the moon; in 1844 it published a fake story—by one Edgar Allan Poe—about a transatlantic hot-air-balloon journey. Fake news was not always harmless. Benjamin Franklin complained that "tearing your private character to flitters" could be done by anyone with a printing press. Press freedom, he groused, had come to mean "the liberty of affronting, calumniating, and defaming one another." At the Constitutional Convention, Elbridge Gerry, a prominent politician, observed bitterly that the people "are daily misled into the most baneful measures and opinions, by the false reports circulated by designing men, and which no one on the spot can refute."[3] Pamphleteers were even more scurrilous. "In the decades immediately before and after the American Revolution," write Cailin O'Connor and James Owen Weatherall in their 2019 book, *The Misinformation Age: How*

False Beliefs Spread, "partisans on all sides attacked their opponents through vicious pamphlets that were often filled with highly questionable accusations and downright lies."

In the latter half of the nineteenth century, urbanization and breakthroughs in printing technology transformed small presses into mighty urban newspapers, capable of reaching millions every day at the crack of dawn and generating previously unimaginable advertising revenues. Still, newsrooms remained rowdy fraternities following ad hoc rules. Reporting was more a trade than a profession, and coverage was as likely to focus on gossip or sensation as on what today we think of as newsworthy public events. "Faking was a rampant journalistic practice during the final quarter of the nineteenth century," writes Randall S. Sumpter in his 2018 history of journalism ethics.[4] In his memoir of life as a young reporter at the turn of the twentieth century, the American journalist H. L. Mencken nostalgically recounts how he and other reporters made up fake scoops to beat a competitor. They thought it was hilarious. Publishers would do anything to attract audiences, up to and including printing rumors, fake news, and wildly sensationalized articles which helped incite a war with Spain.

As the century turned, however, journalistic practices began to coalesce into informal codes of conduct. In 1893 the University of Pennsylvania's business school introduced the first journalism curriculum taught by a news professional; fifteen years later the University of Missouri founded the first separate school of journalism.[5] The American Society of Newspaper Editors was founded in 1922, and its first order of business was to promulgate an ethics code. "By every consideration of good faith a newspaper is constrained to be truthful," the code said. "It is not to be excused for lack of thoroughness or accuracy within its control." The code called for distinguishing between news and opinion, and for soliciting a response from anyone whose "reputation or moral character" might be impugned in print. News judgment should respect privacy: "A newspaper should not involve private rights or feeling without sure warrant of public right as distinguished from public curiosity." And—here a formulation which would make Locke, Peirce, and Popper smile—"it is the privilege, as it is the duty, of a newspaper to make prompt and complete correction of its own serious mistakes of fact or opinion, whatever their origin." Those two words, "the privilege," speak volumes; to news professionals, correcting error should be a point of pride, a distinguishing and defining feature of the culture.

I am a product of that culture. Beginning at my college newspaper in the late 1970s and then in my first job at a local paper in North Carolina, I had it drummed into me that accuracy matters, that real people would be hurt if I made mistakes, that I had a duty to seek comment from those I wrote about, that I should conduct interviews on-record whenever possible, that uncorroborated sources are suspect, that when I was wrong I should own up to it and file a correction. In journalism schools and mainstream newsrooms, reporters are still taught those values. "If you have a very small staff, checking what somebody said with a bunch of different sources is not always doable," a young reporter at a small-town newspaper told me. "But those principles are at the forefront of what we do every day. They're in the conversations we have about things we're working on. In the newsroom, we talk about those things with editors. When we get something wrong, we make sure the record is set straight. Particularly when you work for a small newspaper and you're the news source of record for that community, it's exceptionally important. We don't want to get it wrong the first time, but when we do, we have to own up to it."

In 2019 Harvard's student newspaper, the *Crimson*, earned itself a student boycott and a vote of condemnation by the Undergraduate Council for seeking a comment from the U.S. Immigration and Customs Enforcement agency about an "Abolish ICE" rally on campus. I felt proud of the paper when it issued a firm response to claims that its coverage had caused "feelings of unsafety": "Fundamental journalistic values obligate the *Crimson* to allow all subjects of a story a chance to comment. . . . For this story and all others, the *Crimson* strives to adhere to the highest standards of journalistic ethics and integrity." That was the voice, not just of one student editor, but of 100 years of reality-based professionalism.[6]

What the institutionalization of modern, fact-based journalism did was to create a system of nodes—professional newsrooms— which can choose whether to accept information and pass it on. The reality-based community is a network of such nodes: publishers, peer reviewers, universities, agencies, courts, regulators, and many, many more. I like to imagine the system's institutional nodes as filtering and pumping stations through which propositions flow. Each station acquires and evaluates propositions, compares them with stored knowledge, hunts for error, then filters out some propositions and distributes the survivors to other stations, which do the same.

Importantly, they form a network, not a hierarchy. No single gatekeeper can decide which hypotheses enter the system, and there are infinitely many pathways through it. If one journal or media organization rejects your claim, you can try another, and another. Still, if each node is doing its job, the system as a whole will acquire a strongly positive epistemic valence. A poorly supported claim might have a 50 percent chance of passing through one filter, but then a one in four chance of passing two filters and only a one in eight chance of passing three. Eventually—usually quickly—it dies out. A strongly supported claim will fare better, and if it is widely accepted it will disseminate across the network and enter the knowledge base. Working together, the pumps and filters channel information toward truth.

Flipping the Pumps

Now imagine running them in reverse.

Suppose some mischievous demon were to hack into the control center one night and reverse the pumps and filters. Instead of straining out error, they pass it along. In fact, instead of slowing the dissemination of false and misleading claims, they accelerate it. Instead of marginalizing ad hominem attacks, they encourage them. Instead of privileging expertise, they favor amateurism. Instead of validating claims, they share claims. Instead of trafficking in communication, they traffic in display. Instead of identifying sources, they disguise them. Instead of rewarding people who persuade others, they reward those who publicize themselves. If that were how the filtering and pumping stations worked, the system would acquire a *negative* epistemic valence. It would actively disadvantage truth. It would be not an information technology but misinformation technology.

No one saw anything like that coming. We—I certainly include myself—expected digital technology to broaden and deepen the marketplace of ideas. There would be more hypotheses, more checkers, more access to expertise. How could that not be a leap forward for truth? At worst, we assumed, the digital ecosystem would be neutral. It might not necessarily tilt toward reality, but neither would it systematically tilt against reality.

Unfortunately, we forgot that staying in touch with reality depends on rules and institutions. We forgot that overcoming our cognitive and tribal biases depends on privileging those rules and institutions, not flattening them into featureless, formless "platforms." In other words, we forgot that *information* technology is very different from *knowledge* technology. Information can be simply emitted, but knowledge, the product of a rich social interaction, must be achieved. Converting information into knowledge requires getting some important incentives and design choices right. Unfortunately, digital media got them wrong.

The commercial internet was born with an epistemic defect: its business model was primarily advertising-driven and therefore valued attention first and foremost. Traditional media companies relied partly (often heavily) on ad revenue, to be sure, but they attracted advertisers by building audiences of regular users and paying consumers, and many were rooted in communities where they were known and trusted, and so they tended to build constituencies to whom they felt reputationally and financially accountable. The gutter press and fly-by-night media also existed, but they were the exception rather than the rule, at least in the modern era. Digital media, by contrast, had hardly any paying customers and lured advertisers with fleeting "impressions" and "engagement," launching a no-holds-barred race to attract eyeballs. Digital media companies could use granular metrics to slice and sort their audiences, but those statistics were very different from accountable relationships with users and communities and sponsors.

The whole system was thus optimized to assemble a responsive audience for whatever information someone wanted to put in front of people, with only incidental regard (if any) for that information's accuracy. The metrics and algorithms and optimization tools were sensitive to popularity but indifferent to truth. The computational engines were indifferent even to meaning, since they had no under-standing of the content they were disseminating. They were exclu-sively, but relentlessly, aware of clicks and page views. A search or browsing session might turn up information or misinformation, de-pending on what people were clicking on. How-to videos about re-pairing your toilet were usually pretty reliable; information about vaccines and claims about controversial political issues, not so much. But whatever; the user would sort it out.

Now, the digital era was hardly the first time a new and ostensibly neutral information medium tilted against truth in practice. As we have seen, the scramble to attract eyeballs drove American journal-ism into surreal realms of half-truth and fake news in the nineteenth century, a problem which required several decades of institutional reform to iron out. Digital technology, with its capacity to dissemi-nate information instantaneously and at almost no cost, raised simi-lar problems, but to one or two higher orders of magnitude.

Normally, if an information-technology system is as likely to de-liver false results as true results, or cannot distinguish between the two, we say it is broken. If we are then told that the fault lies with the user, for failing to figure out on her own what is true or false, we reply that error-prone humans need help. We need our information systems to steer us away from error and bias, which was what the institutions and standards of modern science and journalism were set up to do. Digital media's built-in business model of treating all information like advertisements pretty much guaranteed an attention-seeking race to the bottom. That would have been challenging enough; but the digital information ecology compounded the problem by developing characteristics which were not just blind to misinformation but am-plified it.

Outrage Addiction

First, it hacked our brains.

In 2013 a young public relations executive posted a tasteless racial joke on Twitter, intending, she later said, to satirize racism and white privilege. "Going to Africa. Hope I don't get AIDS. Just kidding.

I'm white!" She had only 170 Twitter followers. "No one replied, which didn't surprise her," reported the *New York Times*.[7] Then she boarded an eleven-hour flight to South Africa.

While she was in the air, someone tipped an editor at a tech-industry blog, who tweeted out her post with a cluck of disapproval. Other reporters picked it up. At that point, outraged tweets began to cascade, targeting the woman's Twitter account mercilessly. ("You racist ass bitch.") The tweetstorm attracted more media attention. Celebrities piled on. After a woman in Miami started the hashtag #Has-JustineLandedYet, the episode turned into a reality entertainment show. On social media, scores of fake accounts were created under the woman's name. Meanwhile, the pile-on itself became a story. When the woman disembarked, she was world famous, and not in a good way. Her name had been tweeted more than 30,000 times, and the hashtag almost 100,000 times.[8] Shortly afterward, she was fired. Several years later, she still had not completely reassembled her life.

The episode became emblematic of what would later become known as call-out culture, or cancel culture, a subject I will say more about later. But the episode also illustrated the propensity of digital media to amplify outrage, impulsivity, and ad hominem attacks: what Jeffrey M. Berry and Sarah Sobieraj have dubbed the outrage industry in their 2014 book of the same name. "The genre has several distinctive attributes but is most easily recognizable by the rhetoric that defines it, with its hallmark venom, vilification of opponents, and hyperbolic reinterpretations of current events," they write.[9]

At first, such venomous behavior may seem puzzling. After all, in ordinary life, most people are courteous most of the time. And the internet seemed to offer new tools for communicating and connecting, which would seem to be inducements to civility. But digital media turned out to be an even better tool for *display*, which, as the psychologist Jonathan Haidt has pointed out, is very different from communication.

"We are obsessed with our reputations," Haidt told me. "Social media has such profound effects on so many social systems because it creates a form of community in which we're ostensibly talking to each other, but we're really signaling virtue to people we care about."

When I join others in a shaming campaign against you and bomb your Twitter account with imprecations, my tweets may take the form of communications *to* you, but in fact they are *about* you— and, especially, about *me*. What I am really doing is trying to impress my peer group with my virtue, cleverness, and loyalty. By joining the shaming campaign, and better yet by leading it, I can raise my status. You have the misfortune of being a useful object in my quest.

In 2009 social media took a turn which was practically designed to encourage virtue signaling and pile-ons. Twitter debuted the "retweet" button, and Facebook the "like" button, and then Twitter copied the "like" button, and soon their equivalents were standard features all over the web. Those functions, combined with the share feature, allowed people to spread any item of content instantly and unreflectively to their entire social grid. That proved to be a game-changer. "We might have just handed a four-year-old a loaded weapon," Chris Wetherell, who had built the retweet function at Twitter, later said. "That's what I think we actually did."[10]

Thanks to the dynamics of social media, I can participate in group outrage at little or no personal cost or risk. I can hide behind anonymity. Or, if named, I can "hide in a crowd," as the neuroscientist Molly Crockett has put it. You and I likely do not have a prior relationship or travel in the same circles, and so I probably will never encounter you face to face. I might not even give a thought to the job you might lose or the ostracism you may suffer, because empathy and accountability are disabled by outrage and anonymity. "Social networks [thus] massively amplify the reputational benefits of outrage expression," writes Crockett.[11]

If I do pause to consider how you might suffer by being shamed or smeared, I am likely to dismiss your suffering as deserved. After all, what I am expressing is not ordinary interpersonal anger, a face-to-face emotion which allows for interaction and can lead to reconciliation or new understandings. I and my tribe are expressing outrage, which, Haidt explains, has a peculiar attraction. Outrage is not one-on-one, personal anger so much as shared anger, a social emotion. "Shared anger bonds you together," he told me. "If you're outraged at President Trump and sharing that with other people, that's pleasant."

We, the in-group, bond over our common conviction that *you*, the object of our outrage, are a threat or traitor to *us*. Even if you meant well, you should have known better, and in any case your shaming serves as a warning to others. Even if you are not evil—in fact, even if you meant well—you are a justified casualty. In an article in *The Critic* in 2020, Marie Le Conte explained social-media objectification vividly:

> It's hard to describe what it feels like, being the main character on Twitter. People tweet at you, at first to criticize what you said, then insulting you for what you said, then trying to find other things you said to criticize and insult you for, then moving on to discussing your appearance, what you may be like in bed, and anything else they can think of. They also tweet about you, which is more disconcerting if you aren't a celebrity, which I am not. They are no longer talking to you but about you to each other; it's a book club and you're the book.[12]

One way to think of social display is as moral grandstanding, "the use of public moral discourse for self-promotion and status attainment," as Joshua Grubbs and four colleagues put it. In experimental research, they found that, as one might expect, moral grandstanding is associated "with a general desire to improve one's status or rank," and also, specifically, with narcissistic traits associated with status-seeking (and also, to a lesser extent, with a desire to display dominance—in other words, with bullying).[13] In a social environment where accountability and empathy are in short supply, we should expect recurrent waves of moral grandstanding, expressed as self-aggrandizing condemnations and bullying personal attacks. In *The Outrage Industry*, Berry and Sobieraj usefully describe grandstanding as a kind of outrage fandom, comparable to fans yelling chants and displaying team colors at a sports match: "We find that outrage-based political opinion programs create safe political spaces for fans. In these contexts, fans experience none of the discomfort we associate with face-to-face political conversation."[14]

The characteristics of moral grandstanding propel a still stranger dynamic. Staying aloof from online outrage, shaming, and moral posturing is difficult even for those who try. There is evidence, says Haidt, that "getting likes and expressing outrage give a hit of dopamine." If so, "it can be a hard-to-break behavior pattern: habituating." Moreover, although expressing or recycling outrage is trivially easy online, writes Crockett, "Positive feedback for these responses (likes, shares, and so on) is delivered at unpredictable times—a pattern of reinforcement well known to promote habit formation."

And what if you fail to express outrage? The social costs of being left off the bandwagon can be high. Expressing outrage, says Haidt, "is both pleasurable and socially necessary—meaning it's expected of you." Even if you do not actually feel outrage, you had best express it.

Herein lies the secret of trolling—that is, of getting famous (or at least notorious) by provoking outrage. In 2019 *The Economist* reported on the Boston Straight Pride parade, which attracted about 200 people. One marcher told a reporter, "I'm only here to make the left look ridiculous, to draw them out and expose their true colors." The thousand or so counter-protesters knew they were being manipulated, but the alternative—failing to show solidarity with their comrades—seemed intolerable. As one counter-demonstrator said, "I know they want to go home and say, 'I triggered a snowflake,' but it's a stronger message to oppose them. To do nothing is to say it's OK."[15]

Haidt likens trolling to terrorism, inasmuch as they both exploit the emotional dynamics of outrage, baiting us to overreact. Rationally, we may understand that rising to the bait makes the trolls (or terrorists) more visible and influential. But emotion rules. In 2018, when a gaggle of white nationalists planned a rally in the District of Columbia, I watched on Facebook as people piled in to pledge they would show up to counter-protest. "Here and in," wrote one person. "Massive denunciation of hate and reaffirmation of life is an energizing and powerful thing." Another said, "If I am here I'll take them on, too." Another: "I will meet you at the corner of Hell Yeah and F*** These Guys." The result would be to give a small band of pathetic haters more of the exposure and conflict they sought, but the desire to push back—and to be seen pushing back—was natural and, for many, irresistible.

No wonder the audience for what Berry and Sobieraj classify as outrage-based media has "grown exponentially." Its audiences, they write, "feel included in a like-minded community, have their lifestyles and viewpoints validated, and walk away armed with ammunition for any who might challenge them."[16]

A Billion Private Realities

Second, digital media splintered reality.

The main idea of the Constitution of Knowledge, as we have seen, is that reality is what *we* know, not what you or I know. No purely personal belief can be knowledge, no matter how much merit you or I might think it possesses. Recall Charles Sanders Peirce's dictum: "It will appear that individualism and falsity are one and the same." And: "Unless truth be recognized as *public*—as that of which *any* person would come to be convinced if he carried his inquiry, his sincere search for immovable belief, far enough—then there will be nothing to prevent each one of us from adopting an utterly futile belief of his own which all the rest will disbelieve."

A corollary is that members of the reality-based community accept that, despite their diversity, they are all exploring aspects of one reality. The Constitution of Knowledge does not require them to see the world the same way or to agree on facts. In fact, it only works where people see the world differently and disagree on facts, so that they can test their ideas and surmount their biases. Its unique capacity, however, is to force individual differences toward social convergence. It does so by requiring persuasion, which in turn requires that we try to account for our differences by comparing them. Research papers begin by surveying earlier research and showing how the authors' findings fit in. Legal briefs analyze precedents and the other side's claims and lay out the distinctions and disagreements. Journalists compare their stories with competitors' to calibrate their own coverage. Although disagreements can persist for decades or even indefinitely (try asking historians why World War I broke out), consensus is likely to form at least over what it is we disagree about, and on a way of talking constructively about our disagreements, and on what kind of conversation or experiment might resolve the disagreement. Even when the reality-based community cannot resolve disagreements, it organizes them so that we are talking about the same thing, or striving to. It provides contestability, the capacity to put diverse propositions and viewpoints in productive contention. We disagree often and vigorously, but we work together to agree, at least, on what we disagree about.

Consider, in that context, how digital technology can fine-tune appeals to outrage and target them to the most receptive audiences. It can tailor news feeds and messaging to individuals. Each of us can have a personalized outrage diet, fed to us by clickbait media and partisan activists and state-sponsored troll farms, all assisted by automated software which watches every click and learns how to trigger us. A system like that can push us away from comparing notes with others who see reality differently. We might not even be exposed to other people's viewpoints. What are others saying? What are our differences? What is it we're even disagreeing about? We might not know. We might not want or need to know. Even stranger: our own information diet can be influenced by software which cannot tell us what it is choosing to show us, because *it* does not know. It learns what we click on and what other people similar to us click on, then builds a virtual avatar of us, then feeds us whatever our avatar wants more of. Literally no one understands why we see what we see; and literally no one knows exactly what anyone else is seeing.

The Constitution of Knowledge seeks to force every subjective world, every social bubble, into contact and conversation with other subjective worlds and social bubbles, creating a reality-based *community*. By contrast, digital media drive information consumers toward solipsism: the "Daily Me," as some have called it. As the political scientist David C. Barker has said, the marketplace of ideas was supplanted by something more like a marketplace of realities. He and Morgan Marietta in their 2019 book, *One Nation, Two Realities: Dueling Facts in American Democracy*, use the term "dueling fact perceptions" to describe partisan and polarized versions of reality. "The result is a further retreat into like-minded bubbles, creating more distance and distrust, fostering greater polarization."

Scholars have returned mixed findings about the prevalence of filter bubbles in social media. The polarizing and filtering effects of partisan television and talk radio are better documented and larger than the bubble-making effects of social media, according to Barker. But social media are harder to study, precisely because no two people ever see the same reality. The Constitution of Knowledge is designed to force disagreements toward comparison and resolution, insisting on contestability and building one reality out of many; digital media was designed to do just the opposite, undermining contestability and splintering one reality into many. Worse, it did so in ways we could not detect, let alone correct for. Weirdly, not even the machines knew what their algorithms were doing.

Accelerating Untruth

Third, digital media ran liberal science in reverse. It inverted the social incentives which the reality-based community depends on.

Instead of slowing down information by reviewing and testing it before passing it along, digital media rewarded instantaneity and impulsivity. The Constitution of Knowledge checks before transmitting. It squelches bad information by filtering it out and slowing it down. By contrast, digital networks disseminate information at the speed of light and without regard to quality. They have given new substance to the old saying that a lie circles the world before truth gets its boots on.

In 2018 a study by three researchers with the Massachusetts Institute of Technology Media Lab compared the speed with which both true and false rumors diffused online. "We found that falsehood diffused significantly farther, faster, deeper, and more broadly than the truth in all categories of information," the researchers reported. "It took the truth about six times as long as falsehood to reach 1,500 people." Falsehoods on Twitter, they found, were 70 percent more likely to be retweeted than truth, "even when controlling for the account age, activity level, and number of followers and followees of the original tweeter."[17]

Instead of encouraging dispassion, digital media rewarded emotion. The MIT researchers were not sure why false reports outran true ones on digital networks, but they suspected it was because false rumors seem more novel and inspire more disgust than true ones. Surprise and outrage are viral emotions, and especially potent when combined. A 2017 study by five researchers (mostly psychologists) found that the presence of "moral-emotional words"—hot-button language—increased posts' transmission on Twitter by approximately 20 percent per word. Multiply that advantage by only a few reposts, and inflammatory misinformation leaves boring reality far behind. Moreover, the hot-button posts, the researchers found, accelerated even faster within like-minded political networks, encouraging "echo chambers [which] may exacerbate ideological polarization."[18]

Instead of marginalizing ad hominem attacks, digital media promoted them. The Constitution of Knowledge depersonalizes persuasion by attacking the hypothesis, not the person. In the reality-based community you can challenge someone's credentials or track record, but your challenge needs to be measured, evidence-based, and impersonal—and your reputation will suffer if your challenge is abusive. By contrast, in the outrage industry, smearing and trolling are easy and effective ways to capture attention. Even if conversations start out civilly, they degenerate rapidly to name-calling.

Instead of encouraging reputational accountability, digital media hid behind anonymity. Academics and journalists and other reality-based professionals put their names on their work and spend years establishing their reliability. By contrast, the outrage economy thrives amid anonymity and deceptive identities. Anonymity (though not so much deception) has its upside, at least when it circumvents government censorship or social retaliation. But it is a boon to fraud, trolling, and shitposting—and it is paradise for bots. In 2020 Lisa Page, a former FBI lawyer whom President Trump had attacked, found herself targeted by thousands of abusive tweets. An investigation found that "more than one in four of the replies to Page's tweet come from accounts likely to be trollbots."[19] Note the modifier "likely." Even sophisticated detection algorithms could not be sure who was human. Nor could investigators reliably determine the original source of a trolling campaign, or even what country it came from. So complete a detachment of information from accountability was without precedent.

Instead of privileging professionalism, digital media elevated amateurism and celebrity. The reality-based community is a professional network which rewards knowledge and expertise. By contrast, on social media, where attention is the coin of the realm, celebrity and virality are self-justifying. The original hope for digital media was that flat, unstructured networks would foster more participation by more voices and that better ideas would prevail. Sometimes that happened. Mostly, though, the medium turned out to favor professionals in the arts of manipulative outrage: the kinds of actors who were more skilled at capturing attention than at persuasion and who were more interested in dissemination than communication.

In January 2020 an obscure Twitter account with a history of spreading conspiracy theories posted a video deceptively edited to suggest that former vice president Joe Biden made racist remarks while campaigning for the presidency. Several writers for conservative outlets shared the doctored video on Twitter, where it quickly spread. Within about four hours, it had jumped to Facebook and multiple threads on the websites 4chan and Reddit. At that point, right-wing media began spreading it—and so did mainstream media, which embedded the video in stories debunking it (bad idea!). "Soon," reported Nick Corasaniti in his *New York Times* account of the incident, "any attempt to contain the spread of the disinformation in the video would prove futile."[20] Within only a day of the video's first surfacing on the fringe of the internet, a voter was asking Biden about it on the campaign trail. The system was spewing bilge instead of filtering it.

Disinfonomics

Finally, misinformation acquired a business model.

None of the technological changes I have mentioned would have mattered so much in the media environment of my childhood. People my age remember the three major TV networks (and what by today's standards was their paucity of news coverage), the two major newsmagazines (and their barely distinguishable editorial voices), and the one or two (but never more) major newspapers in every city, plus "rip and read" radio stations which bought their news from a handful of wire services. Leave aside whether you feel nostalgia for the media "Bigs" or are glad to be rid of them (and both feelings can be justified): there was a reason the gatekeepers were so few and influential. Information may want to be free, but knowledge wants to be expensive—very expensive. Just one investigative reporting project or academic study requires work by multiple full-time professionals and budgets into the tens of thousands and often much, much more. Whereas making stuff up is cheap.

Still, for many years reality-based institutions had a seemingly insurmountable advantage: distributing content was even more expensive than producing it. In pre-digital days, someone claiming that Hillary Clinton ran a pedophile ring out of a pizzeria might tell friends or print a brochure, but mostly the person would be ignored. Media owners (like Eugene Pulliam, the monopoly publisher of my hometown papers when I was a kid in Phoenix) could tilt news coverage, but a wholesale departure from reality would have destroyed their businesses and reputations.

To be sure, fake news existed, and entrepreneurs found ways to profit from it. Journalists of my generation affectionately remember the *Weekly World News*, which from 1979 to 2007 treated us to delectable headlines like "Clinton Hires Three-Breasted Intern," "Hillary Clinton Adopts Alien Baby," and "Bat Child Found in Cave." In 1992 politicos knew George H. W. Bush's re-election campaign was in trouble when *WWN*'s beloved "Space Alien" endorsed Bill Clinton for president. But to cover the Space Alien, that august publication had to employ writers and editors to make stuff up, artists to doctor photos, and sales teams to drum up ads for penile enhancement; then it had to pay for printing and buy rack space in supermarkets. The bat child was expensive to distribute and market, and the audience for him was limited and costly to reach. By contrast, the Associated Press could bundle reporting by news staffs everywhere and wholesale it to outlets around the world. Economies of scale favored real news.

Understandably, in the heyday of the Bigs, reality-based media became complacent about disinformation. There was not much demand for fake news and no business model for supplying it. Although the cost of disseminating information had fallen for centuries, no one foresaw that it would collapse to practically zero practically overnight. "By one estimate," writes Tom Wheeler, "the online delivery of a one-megabit file (1 million bits) costs one-tenth of one cent." In 2018 one Indonesian marketer told the *Daily Beast* he could publish articles—fake, real, whatever—on a network of more than

2,000 websites for $225. ("If you have an article for publishing, I can publish it. But for paid, sir.")[21] Nor did anyone foresee that information overload would suddenly make attention the world's most precious commodity—and that a globalized, mechanized bidding war for it would ensue. By 2017, Wheeler notes, online users were uploading the equivalent of 3 million Libraries of Congress every day. The old Bigs were caught unawares when digitization unbundled prepackaged media offerings like newspapers and TV, then decentralized distribution through social media and internet platforms, and then—perhaps most surprisingly of all—recentralized distribution, but now in the hands of new Bigs with undignified names like Google and Facebook and YouTube.

The new Bigs were more efficient at converting information into dollars than, say, a reputable statewide paper such as the *Arizona Republic* was in its heyday, and they could move content in quantities and at speeds which mocked traditional media. But with a crucial difference: they trafficked in information, not in knowledge, and in content rather than truth. They monetized eyeballs and clicks without pausing for reality checks, so that virality and profitability were a closed loop. The economic advantage of real news vaporized.

Many people, to be sure, will pay a premium for reality-based content (aka "news"). As I drafted this chapter, the *New York Times* announced that its subscription base had topped 5 million, the large majority of it digital—more readers than the *Times* could ever have reached in print alone. The problem was that most readers would not pay enough to cover the costs of producing news, or at least not as much news as the public had grown to expect. (As the digital-media pundit Frederic Filloux put it, "You can't sell news for what it costs to make.") The business model for reality-based journalism had been to use news to attract audiences and then sell those audiences to advertisers. When disintermediation demolished that model by moving advertising to Google and Facebook and Craigslist, news-gathering became a money-losing proposition. Reality-based news outlets began shrinking and shutting in droves. By 2018 newspaper circulation in the United States had fallen to its lowest level since 1940, the first year with available data. Newspaper advertising revenue had declined by 62 percent between 2008 and 2018, and newsroom employment had fallen by almost half.[22] In 2018 a report by the University of North Carolina's Hussman School of Journalism and Media found that more than 1,800 newspapers, a fifth of the national total, had vanished over the previous fourteen years, and many of the remnants were "ghost" papers, publishing little local news or original content.[23] Like the advancing Sahara, news deserts engulfed one community after another. The trend showed few signs of stabilizing. By the early 2020s, high-quality news was struggling to stay in business, while opinion, outrage, derivative boilerplate, and digital exhaust (personal data generated by internet users) enjoyed a thriving commercial market.

The Constitution of Wikipedia

And so reality fights an uphill battle in the digital age, disadvantaged by psychology, technology, system design, and economics, a potent combination. People argue about how the digital revolution compares with the upheavals caused by printing or the telegraph or broadcasting, but no one doubts it is a game-changer. Of course, the digital age brought inestimable good, but the crushing disappointment is that it unleashed so much sociopathy and slime. Retired four-star general Stanley McChrystal spoke for many, in a 2020 podcast interview with Sam Harris, when he said, "I really had a Pollyanna view that if you get enough sources in . . . the truth would win out, because it's the truth. That has not proven correct so far."

But is the current structure of digital media the only structure? Not necessarily. In the remainder of this chapter, I want to sketch glimmers of alternatives. Much of what has gone wrong is the result of antisocial system design. Better designs are possible. We know this, because such a design exists.

In March 2000 a couple of entrepreneurs named Jimmy Wales and Larry Sanger launched a radical new kind of encyclopedia, one which would harness digital technology to put knowledge of practically everything at practically everyone's fingertips. The visionary experiment flopped. The articles in Nupedia, as it was called, were written, edited, and peer-reviewed by experts and professionals, as with any conventional encyclopedia, except that the experts and professionals were asked to work for free. In its first year, Nupedia managed to publish only twenty-one articles.

While failing with Nupidia, however, Wales and Sanger came across so-called wiki software, which allowed anyone and everyone to edit online content in real time. Allowing anyone and everyone to write an encyclopedia seemed crazy; just imagine the junk people could post! Yet Wikipedia, as it was called, grew exponentially, boasting 200 articles in the first month, 18,000 in the first year, and 2 million before the end of 2007. By 2020 the English-language version alone had surpassed 6 million articles and 3.5 billion words; every minute, more than 100 edits were made.[24] And that was just in English; Wikipedia also boasted editions in more than 300 other languages. Moreover, its quality was generally high, rivaling that of the professionally published *Encyclopedia Britannica*, according to a 2005 review by the journal *Nature* of forty-two scientific articles. *Britannica* disputed the finding, but that Wikipedia was competitive showed it was working—and it was the eighth-most-visited website in the world. "It is the only not-for-profit site in the top ten, and one of only a handful in the top 100," wrote the journalist Richard Cooke in 2020. "It does not plaster itself with advertising, intrude on privacy, or provide a breeding ground for neo-Nazi trolling." Its contributors and entries could be quirky; its community was predominantly male; it contended with trolls and vandals; it struggled to make ends meet. Like anything ambitious, Wikipedia had its problems. But they were nothing like the failures and abuses which plagued other major social media. As Cooke wrote, "It is one of the few remaining places that retain the faintly utopian glow of the early World Wide Web. A free encyclopedia encompassing the whole of human knowledge, written almost entirely by unpaid volunteers: can you believe *that* was the one that worked?"

Clearly, Wikipedia did some things right. Some of those things had to do with its imaginative use of software. But its real distinction lay in the realm of social design. "Wikipedia succeeded even in the face of dire predictions that a knowledge source based on volunteers would be rife with errors and held hostage to those with an agenda," writes the philosopher Lee McIntyre.[25] "What actually happened, however, is that the many eyes looking at each entry soon sniffed out error and bias, resulting in a knowledge source that is astonishingly reliable, for what it is."

How?

First, Wikipedia built a community, not just a platform. "Wikipedia isn't a technological innovation at all; it's a social innovation," its co-founder and guiding spirit, Jimmy Wales, has written. "We discovered the basic idea of how to organize a community." He continued: "We're actually talking about very old-fashioned types of references. Good writing. Neutrality. Reliable sources. Verifiability. We're talking about people's behavior in the community. We're not talking about some kind of magic process. Quality matters, and a thoughtful community has emerged around that ideal."[26]

The community's values reflected a second defining characteristic: the community was reality-based. Unlike most social media, Wikipedia permitted only one page on each subject. There were no dueling, individualized, or fragmented realities. No algorithms served different pages to different people. You and I and everyone else see the same thing.

That is not to say that everyone agreed on the contents of every page. Far from it. Many entries were accompanied by discussion boards hosting vigorous, sometimes heated, debates. (One notorious edit war raged for years over the name of the city of Gdansk.) But participants argued about different views of the same thing. They subjected themselves to the disciplines of contestability. There is one reality-based community, and Wikipedia joined it.

As in other branches of the community, Wikipedians' conversations about their shared reality were decentralized. No one told them what entries to create or edit. The community, writes Andrew Lih, "usurps top-down authority, empowers individuals, and harnesses previously untapped labor of individuals previously isolated in separate social networks, but brought together by the internet."[27]

That sounds like the unstructured, anti-hierarchical utopia which the original World Wide Web promised but failed to deliver. Look more closely, however, and you immediately saw that being decentralized was not the same as being unstructured. Just the opposite. Wikipedia had hierarchies and gatekeepers, rules and norms, due process and accountability. For instance: although anyone could make an edit, or undo or redo an edit, the site had over a thousand so-called administrators who could block abusive users, delete and undelete articles, and lock pages targeted by vandalism. It also had what it called bureaucrats, a handful of super-administrators who could grant and revoke administrator privileges. It also had an arbitration committee, a kind of supreme court made up of trusted administrators. Administrators were vetted by the community, according to rules the community itself set, sometimes "requiring more than 1,000 edits and at least three months of experience just to get consideration," Lih writes. Experience and track record mattered, as elsewhere in the reality-based community. Anyone with an internet connection could contribute to an article or edit one, but well-established editors wielded much more influence than casual contributors.

Also, as in the rest of the reality-based community, Wikipedia inculcated a norm of objectivity: contributors should endeavor to set personal bias aside and write from a neutral point of view. But, again as in the rest of the reality-based community, Wikipedia did not rely on individuals to maintain superhuman dispassion. Rather, it built in multiple layers of accountability to other community members. Claims and facts had to be attributed to reputable sources, which anyone viewing a page could check. Someone who found inadequate sourcing could add a "{{citeneeded}}" tag. Every entry had an associated page displaying every edit and revision, allowing each modification to be traced to a particular user. Automated notifications allowed editors to monitor pages in real time for malicious or inauthentic behavior. Anonymous contributors were denied certain sensitive privileges, such as creating new pages. Abusers could be blocked or even ejected.

With all those handles for accountability, to whom was the community accountable? To itself, of course. Like the rest of the reality-based community, it debated itself: on discussion pages accompanying each entry; in an "articles for deletion" forum about whether to remove controversial or frivolous entries; in arguments between "inclusionists" and "deletionists" about which content did and did not belong.

Because literally no one was in charge, Wikipedia's curation reflected the obsessions and blind spots of its participants. Editors' passions, Richard Cooke writes, "can drive the site deep into incon-sequential territory—exhaustive detailing of dozens of different kinds of embroidery software, lists dedicated to bespectacled baseball play-ers, [and] a brief but moving biographical sketch of Khanzir, the only pig in Afghanistan." But here, again as elsewhere in the reality-based community, there was an element of self-correction. More traffic and editors flowed to pages of broader interest, where "{{citeneeded}}" tags and so-called stub entries directed attention to gaps. Marginalia was posted, but inattention kept it marginal. As with liberal science generally, the community was self-organizing: uncontrolled but not undirected.

All of that notwithstanding, Wikipedia's most vexing problem was peculiar to social media: vandalism and inauthentic behavior. Anyone could change any entry in ways obvious or subtle, in order to deceive, slander, self-promote, advertise, or just troll. "It takes a legion of dedicated users and administrators in the background of Wikipedia to keep things vandal-free," Andrew Lih writes.

Fortunately, that dedication came cheap—free, in fact—and or-dinary people could provide it. "The heroes of Wikipedia," writes Cooke, "are not giants in their fields but so-called WikiGnomes—editors who sweep up typos, arrange articles in neatly categorized piles, and scrub away vandalism. This work is often thankless, but it does not seem to be joyless. It is a common starting point for Wikipe-dians, and many are content to stay there."

In that respect, Wikipedia's workforce was distinctively ama-teur, in sharp contrast to the professionalism which marks so much of the rest of the reality-based community. But on closer examina-tion, the contrast was not so sharp. Wikipedia's social norms and incentives instilled a collective notion of integrity, defining right and wrong ways of doing things. Informally, specialization and exper-tise emerged because contributors gravitated to what they knew most about. Wikipedia, one might say, was a study in emergent profes-sionalism, replicating, informally, some of the vetting and standard-setting and training which traditional professions provide, but with less overhead.

Step back, and one sees that Wikipedia succeeded, like the rest of the reality-based community, by bringing multiple viewpoints to bear on a single, cumulating reality, then forcing them into critical conversation—into contestability—and toward mutual persuasion. Wikipedia's user guidelines say: "When discussion does not produce a conclusion, bringing wider attention to a dispute can lead to compromise. Consider getting a third opinion or starting a request for comment. Neutral editors aware of the dispute will help curb egregious edits while also building consensus about the dispute." That sounds just like liberal science.

In short, Wikipedia figured out how to bring the Constitution of Knowledge online. It made itself a microcosm of the reality-based community, and it embodied the community's commitments. *Fallibilism*: anyone can always be corrected and no entry in the matrix of knowledge is final. *Objectivity*: truth is public, not individual; it is what we persuade each other we know, not what you or I claim to know. *Disconfirmation*: we hunt for truth by correcting errors. *Accountability*: we answer to others and must justify our claims. *Pluralism*: we neutralize our biases by pitting them against each other. *Civility*: we try to keep conversations calm and impersonal. *Professionalism*: credentials, expertise, and track record count. *Institutionalism*: individuals come and go, but the community endures, organizing inquiry, promulgating standards, teaching values, archiving knowledge, connecting members, conferring honors, and more. (Wikipedia, a nonprofit organization, became an institution in its own right, and not just online; participants held meetups and gathered from around the world at an annual Wikimania conference, where a Wikimedian of the Year was named.) *No bullshitting*: we are here to be truthful, not to entertain or advertise or anything else. Accuracy is job one.

"Platforms" No More

The rub is that most social media *are* there to entertain, advertise, and everything else. Wikipedia is truth-driven, not ad-driven or revenue-driven. It is not commercial. It shows everyone the same reality, not a personalized feed. Its rules cannot be picked up and transplanted to the rest of the digital realm, because most of the digital realm is not in the knowledge business.

True. So return to the goal: for the most part, the digital realm does not need to be truth-seeking, only truth-friendly. Social media do not need to be like Wikipedia, but they can learn from Wikipedia. They are already doing so. Twitter, for example, debuted a new community feedback tool called Birdwatch—modeled on Wikipedia—allowing qualified users to identify and annotate tweets which they think are false or misleading, and also to rate the quality of other participants' annotations.[28] We do not need social media organizations to advance the frontiers of knowledge; we just need them to tilt toward truth instead of against it. That is a much smaller ask—though still hard, partly because of the digital world's cultural aversion to anything which smacks of publishing.

Until 2016 or so, the executives and technicians of the digital world treated epistemic valence as an afterthought, if they ever thought about it at all. The idea of telling people what to post or believe seemed repugnant. Let a thousand flowers bloom! Policing online speech is not our job! But 2016's perfect storm of disinformation, automation, and manipulation cast social media and the so-called platforms in a harsh new light.

A big social media organization is certainly not a newspaper, much less an academic journal. And one of the things it is, to be sure, is a platform, which is to say an open forum, for user-provided content. But Facebook, to take the most prominent example, is not just a platform. It is also a community, and communities implode if sociopathic behavior runs amok. It is a business, and businesses become unsustainable if they turn toxic to their customers or the society around them. And it is a publisher, packaging and distributing content to audiences whose attention it sells to advertisers, just as conventional publishers do.

The platform function implies little or no content regulation. But the other three functions *require* content regulation. If users swamp the network with material which scares other users, repels advertisers, poisons the brand, and systematically lies, the organization will have no choice but make some choices about what gets distributed and how prominently. It will need to promote some content over other content. It will need to make judgment calls. In some cases, it will need to exclude content or users altogether. In short, it will need to find an equivalent for the killer-app technology of old media: editing.

As I wrote this chapter, I noticed a headline in the *Washington Post*. "Facebook Takes Down Deceptive Trump Campaign Ads—after First Allowing Them." It seemed the president's campaign organization had run an ad urging Facebook users to "take the official 2020 Congressional District Census today," but a click led users not to the real government census but to a campaign survey which collected information and asked for money. Facebook initially allowed the ads, but when the speaker of the House complained, the company reversed course, saying, "There are policies in place to prevent confusion around the official U.S. census, and this is an example of those being enforced." Like it or not, and under whatever label, Facebook was exercising a version of what people in old media call editorial judgment. By 2020 Facebook was no mere "platform." It was using algorithms and humans and community flagging, and even complaints from House speakers, to screen over a billion posts a day and send problematic ones to thousands of content monitors, who made decisions based on Facebook's policies.

More: realizing that disinformation threatened the integrity of its product, Facebook set up a system routing prominent factual claims to outside fact-checkers. If a post was rated false, Facebook demoted it in users' news feeds, not censoring problematic content but reducing its prominence—and thereby, according to the company, slowing its spread through the network by 80 percent. If someone tried to share bad information, she would see a pop-up advising that the item had failed a fact-check and linking to better information. "None of these users are prevented from posting stories whose facts are in dispute," Regina Rini wrote in the *New York Times*, "but they are required to know that what they are sharing may be false or misleading."[29] If a user shared misleading information anyway, the next person would need to click past a warning ("Partly false information—checked by independent fact checkers") and an informational link ("See why") in order to view it.

Google, the search and advertising giant, adopted its own epistemic guardrails and speed bumps. It partnered with outside fact-checkers and used their results to label and promote verified news articles in its search results. It also included context about news publishers in search results, for example by displaying, alongside the results, information on topics covered by a publication and awards the publication had received. It blocked deceptive publishers' access to its AdSense program, cutting off their revenue stream. It barred some kinds of ads altogether—for instance, ads for shady medical treatments. It demoted certain kinds of misinformation in search results. And more. When I asked a Google spokeswoman about the company's anti-misinformation measures, the list she sent back ran to pages.

YouTube, Twitter, and other social media companies were busy developing their own guardrails, though less speedily than the Big Two. Pinterest allowed only posts from credentialed, reality-based public-health organizations to show up in searches related to vaccines.[30] Twitter pondered community ratings and real-time misinformation warnings.[31] Third-party developers, such as NewsGuard and the Duke University Reporters' Lab, began deploying automation to guide users to fact-checked information and reality-based sources.[32] There were all sorts of other efforts—by companies large and small, by universities and research organizations, by developers and innovators—to regrade digital media to slope toward truth.

Designing for Truth

From the vantage of 2020, the notion of a truth-friendly internet stretched the imagination. Wikipedia was celebrated precisely because its success was extraordinary. Although Facebook announced fistfuls of innovations and interventions and improvisations, not many experts felt optimistic about outrunning the tsunami of fraud and outrage. Facebook doubled its brigade of human content monitors, and might double it again and then again; but humans' capacity to filter content grows arithmetically, whereas robots' capacity for junky content and phony accounts grows exponentially. In a single six-month period in 2018, Facebook identified and eliminated a billion fraudulent accounts, which was good, but the sheer numbers suggested how easily a billion more could be created. And that was just on Facebook. What collection of stratagems and technologies could possibly keep up with disinfotech?

The real answer is that no one could know, and I certainly do not pretend to. Some general outlines are becoming discernible, however, and there is reason for hope and even optimism—if we understand the problem correctly.

It seems clear that there will be no magic bullet. Wikipedia began by getting some important things right. From the start, it committed itself to a single reality and to norms of neutrality and objectivity, and it understood itself as a community, not a "platform." In those respects, it was born as part of the reality-based community. The rest, though, was the product of trial and error and evolution and argument—just like liberal science itself.

In the rest of the digital media world, becoming truth-friendly will be even more organic and unpredictable. It will involve permutations of policy architecture, legal architecture, product architecture, and, especially, social architecture. Implementing those architectures will require human judgment, which is slow, and mechanization, which is fast, and so will require human-machine partnerships which by 2020 were already being invented and deployed at places like Facebook and Google.

On the policy front, companies and organizations of many kinds sifted questions like whether and how to place boundaries on user-uploaded content; how much anonymity is too much; how to define and weigh free-speech commitments; where to draw lines between outspokenness and harassment. On the legal front, a vigorous debate emerged over the future of Section 230, a U.S. statute shielding internet companies from civil liability for user-generated content—an exemption which was not available to offline publishers, and which either allowed free speech to flourish online or underwrote online harassment and fraud, depending on your point of view. (There was truth in both views.) Some countries, notably in Europe, adopted statutes requiring digital media to police their content and take down hate or fake news—an approach which would run afoul of the Constitution in the United States and which, in any case, chilled legitimate online conversations but seemed too rigid to stymie inventive trolls.

(In Germany, as *The Economist* reported in 2018, "Overwhelmed by the volume and wary of incurring . . . large fines, social media firms are erring on the side of censorship." Banned tweets included one by the very minister who had introduced the online hate-speech law.) Regardless, the legal debate, too, was only beginning.

In an interview with the podcaster Sam Harris in 2019, Jack Dorsey, Twitter's founder and CEO, said that the battle against misinformation and abusive online behavior would be won more by product design than by policy design. It was a powerful insight, borne out by experience both online and off. Wikipedia, for example, carefully designed its rules and policies, but it owed at least as much of its success to the way it was built, with incentives encouraging accountability, error-correction, persuasion, and the rest. Informed by that insight, Dorsey said that Twitter's early design decision to emphasize numbers of followers was a mistake, because it encouraged unbridled attention-getting behavior; and so, in 2019, he began talking about changes which help users follow conversations and topics, instead of personalities. Likewise, he regretted the "like" button, which encouraged performative, display-oriented content and emotional, unreflective sharing.[33] What might come of his ruminations was anyone's guess, but just thinking about building truth-friendliness and prosocial incentives into digital-media products opened new vistas of possibility.

For example, it was reckless to set up social media to propagate content everywhere instantaneously. Instantaneity inherently favored impulsiveness and outrage and shock value. Why not build in a waiting period before users' posts go live, or at least give users the option? Slowing things down—introducing friction, as Justin Kosslyn has put it—gives us time to recruit our slower-acting mental circuits, which are more rational and less emotional.[34] Why not, during the pause, route posts to algorithms which could tell me if a link I'm sharing has flunked fact-checking? Or let me appoint two or three friends as my personal panel of social editors, who could warn me if a bad joke is about to ruin my life? How about, along with the "like" button (or maybe instead of it), a "true" button which lets me rate posts' accuracy? The opportunity to rate posts for truthfulness—and the knowledge that my posts will be rated by others—might nudge me to care about accuracy, not just virality. Moreover, with the help of machine learning and outside fact-checks, the system could give users an epistemic credit score. A high trustworthiness score might earn me a gold star and more visibility. I would have reason to build a truthful reputation.[35]

The point of floating such notions is not to predict they would work. The point is to think about designing digital media with epistemic valence in mind. In November 2020, as Twitter sought to stem the tide of misinformation about the election and the COVID-19 pandemic, it introduced alerts warning users if they were about to share a post which had been rated false or misleading. "This is disputed," the alert said, in boldface type. "Help keep Twitter a place for reliable info. Find out more before sharing."[36] Users could still press the retweet button, but they would have to think first, and some of them might accept the suggestion to learn more. Would users make more informed choices? Or would alerts backfire by drawing more attention to bad information? Only trial and error could determine that. The important thing was that social media companies and developers and researchers were dreaming up and trying out truth-friendly innovations.

Internet 3.0

Still, as important as policy design and product design may be, the most transformational truth-friendly technologies will be social. Which is to say, *institutional.*

Web version 1.0 was ideologically allergic to institutional thinking. It celebrated being an ultrademocratic jumble of stuff. The online scramble was fun while it lasted, but with an efficiency which would have dazzled John D. Rockefeller, a handful of corporate behemoths rapidly consolidated search, advertising, social media. By 2020 Google controlled more than three-quarters of the search-advertising market, and it and Facebook, together, controlled more than half of all U.S. digital advertising. YouTube, Amazon, and several runners-up such as Microsoft and Twitter achieved almost comparable dominance in their domains. In the era of Web 2.0, the wild west had become a company town, to the astonishment and consternation of the World Wide Web's original libertarian constituency. "These tools which I thought were going to be the new gateway . . . to a new kind of collective human imagination ended up being the opposite," the media critic Douglas Rushkoff told the podcaster Sam Harris.[37] Many people still spoke of the digital media giants as platforms, as if they were passive providers of unstructured information spaces, but in reality they aggressively channeled and shaped information flows, although often without accountability or transparency or even understanding what they were doing.

Already under way, as I wrote this chapter, was the transition to Web 3.0, an era in which the platforms, or at least the important ones, began adopting institutional trappings. They were hard at work developing norms and incentives to guide themselves and their users toward pro-social, truth-friendly behavior. To be sure, that change entailed serious downsides, especially for people who had seen the internet as emancipatory. No one could feel entirely good about the power a few corporations were accumulating, or about the exploitive aspects of their business models. But institutionalization had its advantages, too. With Web 3.0, one could begin to see a change akin to the transition from the yellow press of the late nineteenth century to the more professionalized, truth-based journalism of the twentieth century—or medicine's transition from being the province of guesswork and hawkers to being a densely networked, truth-oriented profession. Digital media were starting to behave less like printers and more like publishers. They had realized that they could not thrive as enemies of truth, and that they could not even be neutral. Partly because they wanted to, but mostly because they had to, they began crafting epistemic standards and norms.

A striking example was Facebook's pathbreaking decision to establish an outside committee to decide which content to remove or demote. Realizing that it lacked both the know-how and the credibility to make millions of editorial decisions, Facebook announced in late 2018 that it would appoint a separate body of experts to make tricky calls about content. The oversight board, as it was called, would have its own bylaws, governance, and staff, and it would be supervised and financed by an independent trust. Its members would be subject to a code of conduct and could be removed by the trustees for violating it. The board would rule on take-down appeals from users and also on "significant and difficult" cases referred by Facebook itself. Its decisions would be binding on Facebook and would be published for all to read and debate, building a body of precedents. "The types of content that the board can review will grow over time, such as Groups and Pages, as described in the bylaws," Facebook said. "The oversight board is meant to be dynamic. It will need to remain responsive to shifts in how people use Facebook's services."[38]

A particularly interesting element was that the board could recommend policy changes to Facebook, so the oversight board and Facebook could check and balance each other dynamically, a concept familiar to James Madison. "Each of the entities will evolve, and how they relate to each other will evolve over time," Facebook's Brent Harris told me in an interview. And the board's independent structure was designed to allow other content-hosting companies to opt in. "We're hopeful we're building something people will look at and say, 'This is better than the way it's done today and we want to be a part of this,'" Harris said.

In the context of social media, Facebook's oversight board was a dramatic innovation. But as an example of setting up professional bodies to develop standards and bring order from chaos, it resembled the establishment of the Royal Society, the American Medical Association, the American Society of Newspaper Editors, and countless others. In other words, Facebook was doing what the reality-based community has been doing since Isaac Newton's day.

Another example of institutionalizing truth-friendliness online was less prominent but might turn out to be more important. It had to do with the organizing question of the Constitution of Knowledge: what is a fact, and who decides?

When I was trained as a journalist in the 1980s, the standard practice was to seek multiple points of view about every controversy in an effort to cover both sides (or all sides) of the story. For the most part, that practice promoted fairness and accuracy. Along the way, however, politicians and other public figures learned how easily they could manipulate journalistic two-sidedness to spread misinformation. They became adept at weaponizing the journalistic convention of balance. Trapped in an escalating conflict between two core values (fairness and factuality), some outlets decided they had a responsibility to "call the balls and strikes," as Bill Adair, a Duke University professor of journalism and public policy, has put it. What they did not want to do, though, was weigh in with their own opinions in news stories.

A solution surfaced in 2003, when a journalist named Brooks Jackson founded FactCheck.org. Reporters had been checking facts for a long time, but FactCheck.org was the first free-standing journalism organization dedicated to researching and refereeing public claims by politicians. In 2007 Adair launched a second major organization, PolitiFact. In the 2010s a raft of other fact-checking outlets were launched, until, by 2020, about 300 were operating in more than sixty countries and more than fifty languages. Their mission was to provide mainstream journalists and ordinary readers with the services of third-party arbiters. Instead of neutrally repeating a wrong or misleading claim, journalists could report that the claim had been independently rated as false, or they could consult fact-checks to decide whether to cover the claim at all.

But who is a fact-checker, and who a charlatan? What are the dos and don'ts? Who checks the checkers? In 2015, under the auspices of the nonprofit Poynter Institute, fact-checkers created their own professional society, the International Fact-Checking Network. It promulgated a code of ethics (emphasizing nonpartisan coverage, disclosure of funders and information sources, a show-your-work methodology, and the sine qua non of the Constitution of Knowledge, "a commitment to open and honest corrections"). It also conducted training, connected members, held conferences, and certified organizations which met its standards. (Not all who applied were approved: about a quarter of applicants for accreditation were rejected, according to a network official.)[39]

What began as a few teams performing a handful of spot-checks thus developed into a global network with an institutional hub. That hub, in turn, plugged into social media giants like Facebook, Google, and YouTube, which tuned their algorithms and search engines to favor fact-checked information. By linking the social networks to the fact-checking network, the digital media giants could start tilting their platforms toward truth.

Perhaps even more significant, once the fact-check organizations had formed a global network, they could identify and evaluate new claims faster than before and with less duplicative effort, and they could combine their fact-checks into a database of verified claims and known falsehoods. As their library of fact-checks grew, they began sorting and coding the items so that computers could read them and distribute them automatically. Say a politician repeats a claim that Hillary Clinton runs a child-sex ring out of a pizza parlor in Washington, D.C.; a computer scanning the news spots the claim, compares it with the database, and finds a previous rating of "false"; the computer reports the false claim to computers at social media outlets, and social media outlets demote or debunk it—all without human intervention and in less time than it took to read this sentence. That kind of seamless automation was impractical as of this writing, and even at its best could only supplement the judgments of humans, not supplant them; but anything like it could magnify the efficiency and speed of human fact-checkers by orders of magnitude.

As always, only trial and error will discover what works and what does not. (Some researchers dispute that fact-checking makes any difference.) The important point is that the commercial decisions and ideological preconceptions which made digital media so hostile to truth are being rethought. Error-correcting institutions and norms are taking shape online. Truth-friendly technologies and protocols are emerging. Above all, attitudes are changing.

Only a few years earlier, internet executives had made a point of renouncing any responsibility to truth. In a 2011 blog post headlined "The Tweets Must Flow," Biz Stone, a cofounder of Twitter, exemplified what in those days was the standard ideology: "We don't always agree with the things people choose to tweet, but we keep the information flowing irrespective of any view we may have about the content." By 2020 fewer people talked that way; the consequences of indifference to truth were too grim. During the COVID-19 pandemic of 2020, when misinformation and conspiracy theories spread faster than the virus itself, prominent digital-media companies took a host of measures to slow what some observers called the infodemic: everything from promoting verified videos on YouTube to removing fake reviews of health providers on Google Maps to elevating public-health agencies in search results.[40]

Making choices about truth and falsehood is sure to present social media companies with thickets of difficult choices. Many decisions will be controversial, and not a few will be no-win. But the pretense that platforms could take a neutral stance toward truth was always just that, a pretense. The real choice was to join the reality-based community or poison it. By 2020, for both better and worse—but on balance for better—the age of epistemic disregard was over. Many of the digital world's most formidable innovators and organizations had committed themselves to supporting truth rather than just delivering eyeballs to advertisers. Like Madison and Washington in the crisis of the 1780s, they had come to see the need for stronger, more capable institutions as an antidote to anarchy. They had applied for citizenship under the Constitution of Knowledge.

Unfortunately, other innovators and organizations, also formidable, were bent on stymieing them.

6

Troll Epistemology:
"Flood the Zone with Shit"

*Disinformation is an old enemy with
new weapons and powerful friends*

On September, 11, 2014, social media erupted with reports of a toxic leak from the Columbian Chemicals plant in Centerville, Louisiana. Residents living nearby received text alerts; local journalists received tweets; YouTube lit up with CNN footage. "A powerful explosion heard from miles away happened," someone called Jon Merritt tweeted. A person using the handle @AnnRussela shared an image of flames engulfing the plant. A Wikipedia page was even created for the disaster, complete with a link to a YouTube video.[1]

It was all fake: the texts, the tweets, the video footage. The plant's parent company, Birla Carbon, was puzzled. "There has been no release of such toxic gas, explosion, or any other incident in our facility," the company said in a statement. "We are not aware of the origin of this text message." Not long after, Duval Arthur, the homeland security director for St. Mary Parish, blamed the hoax on someone with a "sad, sick sense of humor."[2]

A troll, in other words. In yet other words: an epistemic sociopath.

What If You Could Do Anything?

In Book II of *The Republic*, Plato launches social philosophy's foundational inquiry by posing social philosophy's foundational question. Imagine discovering a ring which made you invisible so that you could behave with complete impunity. The person in possession of such a device "might with impunity take what he wished even from the marketplace, and enter houses and be with whom he pleased, and slay and loose from bonds whomsoever he would, and in all other things conduct himself among mankind as the equal of a god."[3] Why, Plato wonders, should a person facing no accountability or sanction ever behave justly or morally? Behind that moral question stood a political one: how, if at all, can a society be constructed to withstand the force of sociopathy?

"Sociopathy" is a modern word, and anachronistic in the context of ancient Greek philosophy, but useful all the same. A sociopath is someone who does not feel that social norms apply to her and who feels free to pursue naked self-interest whenever she can get away with it. She may conform to laws and constraints imposed from without, but only because doing so is to her benefit.

The American founders, like Plato, predate modern psychological jargon, but they possessed deep psychological insight, and they recognized that the problem of sociopathic behavior challenges every social order. Up to a point, rule-breaking and shamelessness can inspire breakthroughs in industry, politics, science, the arts, the military. But a little goes a long way. Too much leads to the downfall of a peaceful social order—especially a liberal social order, which depends on everyone's internalizing and following basically the same set of rules. America's founding generation feared sociopathic demagoguery as much as they did anarchy, and they understood that the two abet each other. In the *Federalist Papers*, Alexander Hamilton warned of the dangers posed by men with "talents for low intrigue and the little arts of popularity"—men who commence as demagogues and end as tyrants. Later, in a letter to President Washington, Hamilton warned that the "only path to a subversion of the republican system of the country" is by way of the ruthless demagogue who uses fear and flattery to "throw things into confusion [so] that he may 'ride the storm and direct the whirlwind.' "

Hamilton and his confrères were not worrying abstractly. One of the young republic's earliest challenges arose in the person of Aaron Burr, a man of exceptional talent, overweening ambition, and what today we might call narcissistic or sociopathic qualities. "He is a man of extreme and irregular ambition," Hamilton said of him, "selfish to a degree which excludes all social affections." Burr rose to the vice presidency in 1801 (only narrowly missing the presidency itself), killed Hamilton in a duel, and plotted to seize a swath of territory in the West over which he hoped to rule. Three decades later, with those memories still living, the young Abraham Lincoln used one of his first published speeches to warn of the havoc which might be wreaked by a "towering genius" whose ambition "thirsts and burns for distinction" and "scorns to tread in the footsteps of any predecessor, however illustrious." Lincoln's warning proved prescient. Ambitious sociopathy has brought down liberal (or relatively liberal) orders again and again, whether in the era of Lenin, Mussolini, and Hitler or in our own era of Vladimir Putin, Viktor Orbán, Rodrigo Duterte, Jair Bolsonaro, and Recep Tayyip Erdoğan.

And what of epistemic sociopathy? What if a person or regime has no scruples about truth and disregards it with impunity? That was a hallmark of illiberal countries and movements like Communism, to be sure. In the liberal democracies of the West, however, the Constitution of Knowledge seemed so sturdy for so long that systematic, regime-threatening lying seemed barely worth thinking about.

That changed in the twenty-first century. Digital technology and social media forged not one Platonic ring of impunity but an infinite number wielded by anonymous swarms. When the swarms connected with powerful state actors, first abroad and then in the person of the president of the United States, troll epistemology—a disaggregated, digitized, and often demented form of disinformation—rose to power.

Something New: Trolls and Shitlords

At around the same time as that nonexistent chemical plant explosion, a tempest called Gamergate swirled through the world of online video gaming. A swarm of harassers had ganged up on several women in the video-game industry, doxing them (that is, revealing personal details) and threatening them with rape and death. The swarm organized anonymously on platforms such as 4chan, Reddit, and Twitter; participants claimed to be a movement, though they had no leaders or manifesto. Someone I respected, a conservative feminist, told me at the time that Gamergate was a big deal and I should be concerned about it, but I could make no sense of it. It did not seem to be about anything. It just seemed . . . weird.

A self-appointed spokesman for Gamergaters was a young journalist named Milo Yiannopoulos. In 2014 he had joined the staff of *Breitbart News* and helped transform it into a pro-troll media franchise. Yiannopoulos was a natural provocateur with a fierce appetite for self-promotion and a willingness to say just about anything. In a 2016 interview with *Bloomberg Businessweek*, he described himself as "totally autistic or sociopathic. I guess I'm both."[4] A talented writer, Yiannopoulos became an advocate and theorist of trolling. In a 2016 *Breitbart* article called "Trolls Will Save the World," he described trolling as being outrageous on purpose, "to prank, to goad, to wind people up," thereby triggering self-righteous responses which only amplify the original provocation. He portrayed the practice as a form of social satire, sending up the "grievance brigade," as he called it. "I delight in offending people," he said in an interview with the U.K.'s Channel 4 News, "to make people think and perhaps to make people laugh." Were the trolls nihilistic vandals, eager to wreck reputations and lives, or merely merry pranksters out for lulz (internet slang for "laughs")? You could never be sure. "This is the essence of trolling," wrote Yiannopoulos: "keeping everyone else guessing as to whether you're really serious."

The trolls, however, knew what they were doing, and they were not just kidding around. In 2017 the *Huffington Post* unearthed a style manual for *The Daily Stormer*, a white supremacist website.[5] The guide advised using "naughty humor" to draw in curious readers, and then hammering them with a few repeated points "over and over and over and over again." The guide's author, Andrew Anglin, added, "The unindoctrinated should not be able to tell if we are joking or not. . . . This is obviously a ploy and I actually do want to gas kikes. But that's neither here nor there." He cited the propaganda tactics of Adolf Hitler. "Who cares whether they laugh at us or insult us, treating us as fools or criminals?" wrote Hitler, in *Mein Kampf.* "The point is that they talk about us and constantly think about us."

Trolls, despite their pose as online Jokers, seemed to grasp classic propaganda methods and had a knack for adapting them to the online world. Outrage and humor, they understood, were viral and addictive and could be weaponized to seize attention and occupy people's brains. In the 2015 documentary film *Welcome to Leith*, the white supremacist leader Craig Cobb told an interviewer: "I have a reputation online as speaking very, uh, meanly, I guess that's the word. Why? Because it shocks the limbic brain. To get people out of this lassitude of which they're mesmerized and hypnotized." They understood psychology. "Remember the main law: EMOTION IS THE HOOK, FACTS ARE THE SIDE DISH," propounded the trolls' style manual. They understood insurgent tactics and asymmetrical warfare. "We have the advantage of being an anonymous swarm with a singular goal," said the manual. "We don't have to play fair. We can say and spread whatever we want."[6]

The disrupters, many of them associated with the so-called alt-right (an internet-based backlash movement which had more to do with rage and nihilism than with any coherent ideology), ushered in a whole new argot: besides trolls and lulz, there were shitposters and shitlords and edgelords, cucks and cuckservatives and libtards and normies, ratioing and doxing and swarming and brigading. But what did they want, these seemingly nihilistic swarms and brigades? What was the purpose? Some spoke as if trolling was an end unto itself, aiming to anger and polarize for fun. A troll who went by the moniker Ironghazi told the *Daily Beast* that "the ultimate goal is making people mad online."[7] Studying the spread of hostile political rumors, several researchers (Michael Bang Petersen, Mathias Osmundsen, and Kevin Arceneaux) found that many trolls were motivated by a "need for chaos" and "a desire to tear down the system as such." Such trolls were status-obsessed yet socially marginalized, people likely to agree with statements like, "I think society should be burned to the ground." In other words, they were nihilists. Alarmingly, there seemed to be a lot of them. Almost a fourth of Americans either agreed with or were neutral about the statement, "I think society should be burned to the ground"—and 40 percent likewise did not reject the statement, "When I think about our political and social institutions, I cannot help thinking, 'Just let them all burn.'"[8]

Many other trolls, however, pursued more specific agendas. From the beginning, troll culture leaned to the right (much as cancel culture, as we will see in the next chapter, leaned to the left). Conservative activists had been using and refining the art of trolling since at least 1980, when the *Dartmouth Review*, with financial backing from conservative donors, shot to fame by baiting campus liberals and doxing gay students.[9] "One way to be effective as a conservative is to figure out what annoys and disturbs liberals the most, and then keep doing it," wrote Dinesh D'Souza, one of the *Review's* first editors, who went on to a career as a conservative provocateur. He added, "Yes, harpooning liberals is a lot of fun. I am especially fortunate because I get paid to do it."[10]

That second sentence hints at another motivation: profit. People like Alex Jones, who were nonentities in the reality-based world, discovered they could build commercial empires as conspiracy theorists. They could use their visibility to get on TV, hawk T-shirts, sell clicks to advertisers. Stefanie MacWilliams, who propagated the "Pizzagate" theory that Hillary Clinton was involved in a child prostitution ring hidden beneath a Washington, D.C., pizzeria, told the Toronto *Star*, "I really have no regrets, and it's honestly really grown our audience."[11] (This, after an armed man searching for child sex slaves entered the pizzeria, discharged his rifle, and put diners to flight.) In the runup to the 2016 U.S. election, a "growing group of Macedonian teenagers" discovered they could make thousands of dollars a month cooking up fake and inflammatory "news" for the partisan and gullible.[12]

The trolls' tactics hinted, though, at an even deeper agenda: an attack on knowledge itself. As the troll manual said, "The idea is to stack up so much doubt, emotional appeals, and circumstantial evidence ON TOP of facts that we create a landslide of anti-Hill[ary] sentiment that permeates through society." The idea they had hit upon was one with deep roots in the science of disinformation.

Firehose of Falsehood

Around 2014 internet researchers began to notice patterns. The doings of troll swarms were apparently not as random and opportunistic as they seemed. Researchers tracking anti-vaccination activists found an organized movement which was well funded and technically savvy. "Anti-vaccine activists established their narratives early on; in fact, the misinformation themes have remained largely unchanged since the early 1800s," wrote Renée DiResta, in a 2018 report.[13] The marketing techniques they used were almost as hoary: repetitive messaging, emotional appeals, endorsements by celebrities and influencers, and junk science. What was new was the adroit exploitation of online social networks. "Anti-vaccine activists have been at the forefront of leveraging all of the technological features social platforms provide," DiResta wrote.

That hoax about the chemical plant explosion in Louisiana? In fact, it was not the product of a "sad, sick sense of humor." It was a disinformation experiment by Russia's Internet Research Agency, the infamous state-sponsored troll farm in St. Petersburg, whose humans and bots and algorithms worked around the clock to design and refine viral fakery. In 2015 an online disinformation campaign convinced millions of people—including the governor of Texas—that a routine federal military exercise might be an Obama administration plan to round up political dissidents. That, too, turned out to be a Russian dry run for the much larger disinformation campaign of 2016.[14] Soon it became evident that countries around the world—big ones like Russia and Iran, small ones like Azerbaijan and Ecuador— were investing in what became known as state-sponsored trolling.[15] This was a realm far removed from lulz.

What trolls, unaffiliated and state-sponsored alike, had discovered was that because the internet was optimized for advertising, it was also ideally suited to disinformation campaigns on a previously impossible scale. "The entire toolbox of advertising technologies can be packaged together into coordinated campaigns that utilize both human and machine intelligence to optimize marketing," wrote the authors of a report for the New America Foundation in 2018. "All the tools of behavioral data collection available for the purpose of targeting communications into highly responsive audiences . . . are applied to the task of political disinformation."[16] Gradually, researchers developed a picture of what troll epistemology was really all about. In *Active Measures*, his history of disinformation wars, the historian Thomas Rid summed it up:

> At-scale disinformation campaigns are attacks against a liberal epistemic order, or a political system that places its trust in essential custodians of factual authority. These institutions—law enforcement and the criminal justice system, public administration, empirical science, investigative journalism, democratically controlled intelligence agencies—prize facts over feelings, evidence over emotion, observations over opinion. They embody an open epistemic order, which enables an open and liberal political order; one cannot exist without the other. . . . Active measures [a Russian term for disinformation] erode that order. But they do so slowly, subtly, like ice melting. This slowness makes disinformation that much more insidious, because when the authority of evidence is eroded, emotions fill the gap. . . . The stakes are enormous—for disinformation corrodes the foundation of liberal democracy, our ability to assess facts on their merits and to self-correct accordingly.[17]

The study of propaganda and disinformation has a long and distinguished history, which I will not attempt to rehearse here. The basics are well established. Propaganda is a campaign to influence public opinion without regard for truth, often (but not always) conducted by a state actor seeking some political outcome. It can exploit misinformation (false information), disinformation (deliberate falsehoods), and what has recently been called mal-information (information which is true but used misleadingly). Although the means vary widely, the end is this: *to organize or manipulate the social and media environment to demoralize, deplatform, isolate, or intimidate an adversary.*

State actors have traditionally understood propaganda and disinformation as psychological or informational warfare against an adversarial regime. Modern trolls view it the same way. By exacerbating conflict and mistrust in the target society, they can cause headaches for their adversary and potentially destabilize it. When the Russians mounted their information attack on the 2016 U.S. elections, they did not expect to elect Donald Trump, but they thought they could make the United States more polarized and less governable (and they were right). That was why, notoriously, they provoked both an anti-Islamic demonstration and a pro-Islamic counter-demonstration across the street from each other in front of an Islamic center in Houston.[18]

A good way to think about such attacks is as environmental. They attack not just individual people or facts but the whole information space. In a famous remark to the journalist Michael Lewis in 2018, Steve Bannon, the *Breitbart News* chairman who went on to become a senior strategist for candidate Trump and then President Trump, said this: "The Democrats don't matter. The real opposition is the media. And the way to deal with them is to flood the zone with shit."[19] *Flood the zone with shit*: although the formulation is crude, there could be no more concise and accurate summation of what modern information warfare is all about. All communities, and especially the reality-based community, rely on networks of trust to decide what is and is not true. People need to know whom they are talking to, whether that person is credible, which institutions confer credibility, and so on. Every aspect of trust and credibility is degraded when the zone is flooded with shit. In her classic 1996 essay, "Preposterism and Its Consequences," the epistemologist Susan Haack emphasized that the quality of the environment determines the quality of the intellectual work which gets done:

> The environment in which [inquiry] is conducted may be more or less hospitable to good intellectual work. A good environment will encourage genuine inquiry and discourage the sham and the fake; and the worst damage of sham and fake inquiry will be mitigated, and the contributions to knowledge that sham and fake reasoners sometimes make despite their dubious motivation will get sifted from the dross, if the environment enables mutual scrutiny among workers in

a field. . . . A bad environment will encourage sham and fake inquiry, and/or impede mutual scrutiny.[20]

Troll epistemology is by nature destructive and parasitic. It cannot create knowledge, build trust, or settle disagreements. It cannot develop new cancer therapies or discover new subatomic particles. It cannot even organize a coherent conversation. Only rarely can it directly attack and infest the core institutions of the reality-based community: the lab, the classroom, the college curriculum, the mainstream newsroom, the court of law.[21] What troll epistemology can do is degrade the information environment *around* the reality-based community. It can induce (in the words of the Harvard University researchers Yochai Benkler, Robert Faris, and Hal Roberts) "a condition that some propaganda seeks to induce, in which the target population simply loses the ability to tell truth from falsehood or where to go for help in distinguishing between the two."[22]

The concept of truth, the philosopher Hannah Arendt remarked, contains within itself an element of coercion.[23] If you believe something is true, you also believe you must believe it. The statement "The sky is blue, but I don't believe it" is grammatically correct but makes no sense. For a disinformation operative, the goal is to subvert truth's compulsion. That is difficult to do by changing people's minds, especially about identity-defining beliefs, as we saw in chapter 2. But making people confused and mistrustful is easier. Arendt "repeatedly called attention to a very particular kind of lying that she associated with the authoritarian governments of mid-twentieth-century Europe," writes the historian Sophia Rosenfeld. "This was a form of dissembling that was so brazen and comprehensive, so far from standard political fibbing and selective spin, that it left a population essentially impotent."[24] As Arendt famously wrote in *The Origins of Totalitarianism*, "The ideal subject of totalitarian rule is not the convinced Nazi or the convinced Communist, but people for whom the distinction between fact and fiction (i.e., the reality of experience) and the distinction between true and false (i.e., the standards of thought) no longer exist."

Russian propaganda became particularly adept at deploying what RAND Corporation researchers dubbed a "firehose of falsehoods."[25]

After Russian agents poisoned Sergei Skripal and his daughter in Britain in 2018, Russian media blamed Britain. And/or Ukraine. And/or it was an accident. And/or it was suicide. And/or it was a revenge killing by relatives. And/or Russia did not produce the nerve agent which was used. And/or an entirely different nerve agent was used. The claims' "contradictory character is not a flaw of the Kremlin's propaganda, but a feature," reported *The Economist*. "The purpose of the disinformation campaign is to drown Western intelligence in a cacophony of wild claims, rather than offer a coherent counter-narrative."[26] The *Washington Post*, publishing a flow chart of Russia's kaleidoscopic inventions, summarized what the Russian campaigns were up to: "They fling up swarms of falsehoods, concocted theories, and red herrings, intended not so much to persuade people as to bewilder them."[27]

A key to the success of any disinformation campaign is to trigger repetition and amplification in the target society's own media and political ecosystems. "A . . . large portion of the disinformation value-creation chain was outsourced to the victim society itself, to journalists, to activists, to freelance conspiracy theorists, and, to a lesser degree, to researchers," writes Thomas Rid. Somebody probably got a raise in St. Petersburg when an American senator (John Neely Kennedy, a Republican of Louisiana) parroted a Russian propaganda lie in a national news interview, saying "I don't know, nor do you, nor do any of us" whether Russian operatives had hacked and released Democratic emails. Likewise, Rep. Mark Meadows, a Republican defender of Trump, said, "I think what happens is when we start to look at the facts, everybody has their impression of what truth is."

I don't know, nor do you, nor do any of us. The firehose of falsehood aims not to persuade but to confuse: to induce uncertainty, disorientation, and attendant cynicism. A 2017 study found that 10 percent to 20 percent of Americans believed fake news stories which they were exposed to the year before; but for every gulled believer, two or three more people were unsure what to believe.[28] They were adrift from factuality and could no longer judge plausibility. As one woman, a retired teaching assistant, told the *New York Times*, "I guess I would have to say that I'm completely confused as to who is lying and who is telling the truth. I just feel helpless."[29] A man told the same paper, "There's no real news sources anymore. I don't trust anything."[30]

Epistemic helplessness—the inability to know where to turn for truth—was the desideratum of the firehose of falsehood. "The point of modern propaganda isn't only to misinform or push an agenda," the Russian dissident Gary Kasparov observed in a December 2016 tweet. "It is to exhaust your critical thinking, to annihilate truth." The goal was demoralization. In a chillingly candid interview in 1983, Yuri Bezmenov, a Russian intelligence defector who had specialized in propaganda and ideological subversion, explained: "A person who is demoralized is unable to assess true information. The facts tell nothing to him. Even if I shower him with information, with authentic proof, with documents, with pictures."[31]

(Dis)information Is Power

But why spend many millions of dollars and build national bureaucracies and international networks in order to demoralize people? As always with politics, the purpose was power. From a political point of view, demoralization is demobilization.

"It's to make people passive and not want to fight," the British journalist and disinformation expert Peter Pomerantsev told me. Working in and around Russian media in Moscow during the first decade of the century, he saw a new propaganda model take shape. Whereas Communism had tried to convince people it was forging a great socialist future, the newer model focused on sowing confusion and disseminating conspiracy theories. Pomerantsev thought it resembled an "unserious version of postmodernism." He noticed that as the Kremlin consolidated its control over media, it drove messages which were aimed not at motivating people to support the government but at demotivating them in order to make them feel helpless. "When you're surrounded by conspiracy theories, you feel you can't change anything, and there's nothing to guide you," he said. "The metanarrative is that there is no alternative to Putin."

What Pomerantsev called the "carnivalesque" qualities of Russian propaganda, and what trolls called lulz, were no mere lark. The sheer randomness and brazenness of the firehose of falsehood declared defiantly that no true north exists. The trolls could not be shamed or called out; they would merely shrug or laugh and move on to the next lie or conspiracy theory, then the one after that. "If there are no values and there are no institutions connected to those values, then it's OK to bomb people," Pomerantsev told me.

Or to steal. Putin and his cronies were not glowering ideologues in the mold of Lenin or Mao. They were rapacious thieves and kleptocrats. But who could be sure? "Putin is not corrupt," his propagandists would insist, "but his critics are corrupt . . . in fact, everyone is corrupt . . . *except* Putin!" Trolls hurled every charge, true or false or in between, back at the accuser. Donald Trump's famous retort to Hillary Clinton in a 2016 debate—"No puppet, no puppet, you're the puppet"—may have sounded infantile, but it was part of a strategy to ensure that every statement was mirrored by its opposite, that every truth was met not just with its denial but with inversion.

After all, any statement *might* be true. Conspiracism seized upon fallibilism's doctrine that any statement could in principle be wrong, and it inverted that, too, substituting the non sequitur that any statement could in principle be right. If a bunch of people profess a certain belief, mightn't they be on to something? How can you be sure they are wrong? "The new conspiracism—all accusation, no evidence—substitutes social validation for scientific validation," write Russell Muirhead and Nancy L. Rosenblum in their 2019 book, *A Lot of People Are Saying: The New Conspiracism and the Assault on Democracy*. "If *a lot of people are saying it*, to use Trump's signature phrase, then it is true enough." Reality and even sincerity were beside the point. "The new conspiracists do not necessarily believe what they say," write Muirhead and Rosenblum. "But they do not disbelieve it either." They just throw it out there. And then they throw something else out there. And something after that. Just when you think you might have a handle on reality, the next blizzard of conspiracies blows in.

In this way, troll epistemology could achieve something rather like censorship, only perhaps better, and certainly easier. Old-style censorship is expensive, inefficient, and leaky, especially in an open society like modern America. Suppose, instead of banning unwelcome ideas, you swamp and swarm them? In a landmark 2017 paper called "Is the First Amendment Obsolete?" the legal scholar Tim Wu argued that traditional censorship assumed that information and access to audiences were scarce and could be blockaded or bottlenecked. In the digital era, however, information (good and bad) is abundant; attention is what is scarce. So instead of blockading information, why not blockade attention? If you flood the zone with distractions and deceptions and just plain garbage, people's attention would be diverted and exhausted and overwhelmed. "Flooding can be just as effective as more traditional forms of censorship," Wu wrote. Traditional free-speech protections, such as America's First Amendment, could do nothing about it.[32]

To demoralization, disorientation, and de facto censorship, one might add a further virtue of disinformation, from the point of view of the authoritarian or kleptocrat. Recall, from chapter 2, conformity bias: we conform our beliefs to the beliefs of others in our social environment. By swarming social media platforms and using software to impersonate masses of people, trolls can spoof our consensus detectors to create the impression that some marginal belief held by practically no one is broadly shared. "Anyone, anywhere, with any kind of message, can manipulate a series of amoral and effective but dumb algorithms to create a perception of widespread popular belief, widespread popular consensus," Renée DiResta said in a 2020 podcast interview with *Lawfare*. Anti-vaxxers found they could spoof consensus to great effect. "Despite the fact that real-world numbers of anti-vaccine proponents are still a small minority, on social media they appear to hold the majority viewpoint," wrote DiResta.[33] By artificially inflating their following, they inflated their credibility, endangering decades of progress against scourges like measles.[34] In 2020, during the COVID-19 pandemic, three brothers used Facebook to gin up anti-quarantine protests—partly by creating the impression that the protests were an organic upswelling.[35] Russia used phony Facebook pages to create a false impression that Russia's client Saif Gaddafi had broad support among Libyans, the Stanford Internet Observatory reported.[36] Bots, echo chambers, and the manipulation of social media can make it impossible for even a diligent web-surfer to know where consensus opinion actually lies.

The point is not that the public is gullible and always falls for spoofing, trolling, and disinformation. The point is that by fouling and defrauding the information environment, troll epistemology could make it difficult to distinguish fact from fiction, to distinguish experts from imposters, to know the provenance of information, to assess what others do and do not believe, to know whom (or what) one is interacting with, and to orient yourself within the information environment. If you cannot be sure at any given time whether you are being manipulated or scammed, then the natural way to protect yourself is to assume that you are always being scammed, or to hunker down with online friends in your own private version of reality, or to take a demagogic politician's word for it.

Thus, when they succeed, trolls and their sponsors achieve something like the powers of Plato's invisibility ring, lying with impunity, mocking and marauding and harassing at will. When they succeed, they push us back toward a Hobbesian war of all against all, in which reality fragments and information warlords exert influence far out of proportion to their real-world power or political appeal. In a Hobbesian epistemic order, you can wage high-tech information warfare to make money, become famous, win followers, shield corruption, and gain power—dizzying heights of power, even control of the most powerful office on the planet.

"The Most Superior Troll"

We were warned. As we saw in chapter 1, in 2004 Trump had spoken admiringly of the disinformation tactics which flipped the narrative of Sen. John Kerry's heroism in the Vietnam War. We saw how, in 2013, he said it was "a great compliment!" to be named as a "most superior troll." He and his strategist Bannon and their followers knew what they were doing and were good at it.

Trump, fact-checkers found, uttered untruths and distortions at rates and volumes previously undreamt-of in American public life. In January 2020, the *Washington Post* fact-checking unit clocked him at twenty-two false statements *a day*. In December 2017, a tally by the *New York Times* estimated that Trump, in his first year, had uttered falsehoods at a rate sixty-two times higher than President

Obama.[37] The pace subsequently accelerated. In a single speech on March 2, 2019, he made 104 false and misleading statements, the *Post* found.[38] Over the course of three of his rallies, the *Post* rated between two-thirds and three-fourths of his statements as false, misleading, or unsupported by evidence.[39] When corrected, he would double down. The *Post* created a new "bottomless Pinocchio" category for falsehoods which were repeated more than twenty times.

Even accounting for whatever you believed to be the biases of the fact-checkers, there was no serious disputing that the volume and audacity of Trump's mendacity had broken through American politics' epistemic guardrails, such as they were. Like Russian disinformation, Trump's untruths were not just false but blatantly, ridiculously false, intended not to persuade but to convey that normal rules had been suspended and that the leader was the supreme authority. His very first act as president had been to assert that his inaugural crowd was larger than Obama's, in defiance of patently contradictory photographic evidence. ("He gave alternative facts," a member of his staff famously remarked, when asked about the press secretary's obvious falsehood.) He flagrantly contradicted himself, another way to flaunt his indifference to truth. One day he said his impeachment was hurting the stock market, then the very next day he bragged that the market was reaching new heights. He called government statistics showing unemployment declining under Obama "phony," but said the statistics showing unemployment declining in his own tenure were "very real." He denied saying what he had obviously just said. "The White House on Wednesday flatly denied that President Donald Trump had ever called the American criminal justice system 'a joke and a laughingstock,' just hours after Trump said precisely that during a televised Cabinet meeting," reported CNBC.com in 2017.[40] He repeated and amplified fabricated stories, such as the fictional murder of a U.S. border agent in 2018.[41] He smeared one of his critics with a completely made-up murder charge. On and on and on and on it went, a Putinesque carnival of lies. Nothing remotely like it had been seen in American civic life before.

The point, by now, must be obvious: Trump and his enablers and allies were engaged in a classic disinformation campaign, the sort of campaign which Yuri Bezmenov would have recognized immediately. Instead of using a traditional government propaganda agency, they coordinated their campaign on Twitter and other social media, where they elevated conspiracy theories and identified enemies. By lying not just occasionally but torrentially, they could confuse the public, flummox their antagonists, and turn the information space into a circus. By lying brazenly, gleefully, and self-contradictingly, they could assert their supremacy over truth and their imperviousness to accountability. By repeating and amplifying conspiracy theories, they could incite paranoia and undermine the claims of evidence and reason. By ignoring all factual corrections, reversing all accusations, and branding all reality-based media as "fake news," they could establish a false equivalence between trolling and truth. By attacking unwelcome academic research as "a Trump enemy statement" or "a political hit-job" or the like, they could diminish the credibility of science.[42] By weaponizing outrage, they could manipulate the public agenda and monopolize the national conversation. By creating a whirl of distortions and distractions, they could divert attention from their corruption and incompetence.

One could not but acknowledge Trump's virtuosity on a day like the one in August 2019 when the stock market fell, North Korea tested weapons, and protests erupted in Hong Kong. To change the subject, Trump created an uproar by encouraging Israel to refuse visas to two liberal members of Congress. Or the day in 2020 when U.S. deaths from the COVID-19 virus approached 100,000. A piece in the *Washington Post* described the White House's response: "In a flurry of tweets and retweets Saturday and Sunday, Trump mocked former Georgia gubernatorial candidate Stacey Abrams's weight, ridiculed the looks of House Speaker Nancy Pelosi (D-Calif.), and called former Democratic presidential rival Hillary Clinton a 'skank.'"[43] Meanwhile, less noisily, Trump had been busy replacing independent inspectors general in federal agencies with loyalists who were less likely to trouble him.[44] According to a memoir by John Bolton, a former national security adviser, in November 2018 Trump made a controversial public statement about Saudi Arabia to distract attention from his daughter's improper use of her personal email account.

"This will divert from Ivanka," Bolton reported Trump saying at the time. "If I read the statement in person, it will take over the Ivanka thing."[45]

No student of disinformation could have denied that Trump was, indeed, a "most superior troll." With skills he had honed for decades by manipulating journalists, deploying what he called "truthful hyperbole," and starring on reality TV, he was easily the most artful practitioner of disinformation since the 1930s. Anyone who did doubt his mastery ought to have been convinced when, after four years of softening up the public with one lie after another, Trump executed his coup de grâce, an astonishingly comprehensive, brazen, and effective campaign to convince the public that he had won the 2020 presidential election, or at least that the outcome was in doubt.

Fully seven months before the election, he commenced his propaganda war with a completely false but incessantly repeated attack on the validity of mail-in voting. He expected mail-in voters to lean Democratic, and so his goal was in that respect political; but his larger and more important purpose was to signal to his supporters in politics and conservative media that a major disinformation campaign was coming, and to organize and mobilize them to follow his lead. No one was surprised when, after the election, his now fully assembled propaganda machine unleashed a firehose-of-falsehood campaign on a scale never before attempted or even imagined in the United States. Using social media and mainstream media and the White House bully pulpit, and enlisting the voices of hundreds of Republican politicians, Trump and his allies disseminated made-up and sometimes mutually contradictory stories of conspiracies and malfeasance. Using litigation as a propaganda channel (an art Trump had perfected in his business career), they filed a blizzard of spurious lawsuits to overturn the election—knowing that despite losing every case in court, they could succeed at spreading doubt.

And succeed they did. Polls found that about a third of the American public, and about two-thirds of Republicans, believed that Trump was the rightful winner of the election.[46] Many others believed, incorrectly, that the outcome was unclear. Both results would becloud Joe Biden's presidency, perpetuate Trump's claims to be the real but robbed president, and—last but not least, from an information-warfare point of view—further divide already polarized Americans. As Thomas Rid writes in his history of information warfare, disinformation campaigns have taken many forms, but "the goals were the same: to exacerbate existing tensions and contradictions within the adversary's body politic, by leveraging facts, fakes, and ideally a disorienting mix of both." Dividing the country for political gain was what troll epistemology was up to; it was what the Russians were up to; and it was what Trump was up to—except that Trump was waging information warfare against the *American* body politic. Much as he was at war with his government's career bureaucracy and professional class (what he and his followers called, for sinister effect, the "deep state"), so he was at war with his country's epistemic constitution. By weakening it, by fouling the information environment, and by cultivating cynicism and confusion and division, he could dominate the news, demoralize his opponents, distract from his deficiencies, and, as he had said all those years before, "get away with it."

While Trump was president, he was often dismissed as a would-be authoritarian whose saving grace was his incompetence. That assessment might have been accurate in some respects, but it dangerously underestimated his skill and efficacy in the epistemic sphere. By the end of his term, he had succeeded in unmooring half or more of his party from its sense of truth and falsehood, even of right and wrong. In 2007 more than 70 percent of Republicans had said that for a president to be honest was "extremely important," according to a poll by the Associated Press and Yahoo—about the same proportion as among Democrats and independents. By the end of 2018, after only two years under Trump, a poll by the *Washington Post* found that only 49 percent of Republicans—not even a majority—rated honesty as extremely important.[47]

Putin himself might have envied Trump's achievement. As between the two of them, it was Trump whom historians would rate the greater innovator, for he had figured out how to adapt Russian-style disinformation tactics to American politics (no easy task). That lesson is not likely to be lost on other populists and demagogues, who can and will find new ways to refine and deploy the epistemic weapons which Trump pioneered. In that lamentable respect, we are all Russians now.

Conservative Media: "The Right and the Rest"

Troll epistemology sought to jam reality by causing confusion and chaos, but it did not stop there. It was able to do more: it split reality by creating its own world of alternative facts. It fomented what amounted to an epistemic secession. But Trump was only part of that story, and he appeared late in it.

The period after World War II was a time of unusual bipartisanship in the United States. Many Democrats were conservative and many Republicans were liberal, and collaborating and legislating across party lines was the norm. The same was true in the realm of knowledge; people disagreed on policy and politics, and indeed often on facts (were the Soviets ahead or behind in the arms race?), but they did not disagree much about the sources of epistemic authority.

Starting in the 1970s and accelerating in the Reagan years and beyond, the partisans began re-sorting themselves on ideological lines. Eventually, almost all conservatives became Republicans, and almost all liberals became Democrats. That made compromise and bipartisan governance harder, increased mistrust and hostility across party lines, and eventually turned the parties into contending tribes which not only disagreed with each other but feared and often hated each other. Meanwhile, the public lost confidence in many institutions, including the news media. Conservatives saw mainstream media as liberally biased, with some justification. First on talk radio, then on cable television, and eventually online, conservatives built a media counter-establishment. In some respects, that was a welcome development, diversifying the information supply and widening the ambit of received opinion.

There were signs, however, that the new conservative media establishment, or at least important portions of it, were promoting not only conservative viewpoints but also epistemic separatism, the idea that only conservatives could reliably grasp and report the truth. Rush Limbaugh, the doyen of conservative talk radio—so influential that he was an entire media counter-establishment unto himself—insisted that only he and like-minded sources could be trusted. He denounced what he called "the Four Corners of Deceit in our culture that . . . lie to students and the American people. The Four Corners of Deceit are government, academia, science, and the media."[48] In 2009, speaking of climate change but making a broadly applicable point, Limbaugh told his audience, "Science has been corrupted. We know the media has been corrupted for a long time. Academia has been corrupted. None of what they do is real. It's all lies!" He made his separatism explicit: "We really live, folks, in two worlds. . . . We live in two universes. One universe is a lie. One universe is an entire lie. Everything run, dominated, and controlled by the left here and around the world is a lie. The other universe is where *we* are, and that's where reality reigns supreme and we deal with it. And seldom do these two universes ever overlap."[49]

You recall from chapter 4 liberal science's empirical rule, which bars anyone from claiming authority over knowledge simply by dint of identity or tribe. By requiring that everyone be checkable by anyone, the empirical rule keeps millions of people and organizations talking to each other and working on the same reality-based project (albeit from many different angles of view), and it prevents social truth-seeking from degenerating into power struggles between warring tribes, the historical norm. By saying that checking only counts when done by *our* side, Limbaugh was repudiating the empirical rule. It was thus a flight from the Constitution of Knowledge altogether, and into the realm of cultism. Limbaugh was setting himself up as an information warlord, a commander of believers, and he amassed followers and imitators.

Others in the conservative media world were even more nakedly hostile to traditional journalism and its norms. "Screw journalism! The whole thing's a fraud anyway," said Matt Drudge, who ran an influential conservative website.[50] In a speech in 2017, *Breitbart News*'s Washington political editor, Matthew Boyle, said, "The goal eventually is the full destruction and elimination of the entire mainstream media." Mainstream media, he said, were not merely biased but crooked. "Journalistic integrity is dead. There is no such thing anymore. So everything is about weaponization of information."[51] Like certain academic postmodernists, conservative media had come to see all claims to objectivity as mere poses, cudgels in a political war.

"I've said it a lot," the Fox News commentator Sean Hannity said: "Journalism in America is dead."[52] And what might replace "journalism in America"? As it turned out, something rather different.

Politicians, preachers, and propagandists have strived to establish alternative realities since at least Plato's day, and they can succeed in closed communities like Jonestown and totalitarian states like North Korea. In as diverse and open a society as the United States, however, alternative realities are difficult to scale. Reality keeps intruding. Still, in the early twenty-first century, political polarization and media bubbles created new possibilities for separatism. In their 2019 book, *One Nation, Two Realities: Dueling Facts in American Democracy*, Morgan Marietta and David C. Barker posit a vicious spiral in which political polarization and epistemic separatism exacerbate each other. Factual disputatiousness, they write, "appears to skew the electorate, mobilizing ideologues but silencing moderates. The result is further retreat into like-minded bubbles, creating more distance and distrust, fostering greater polarization."

By 2014 researchers had noticed that the media sources trusted by conservatives and liberals were increasingly distinct. "When it comes to getting news about politics and government, liberals and conservatives inhabit different worlds," the Pew Research Center reported. "There is little overlap in the news sources they turn to and trust."[53] The researchers added an important caveat: "The study also suggests that in America today, it is virtually impossible to live in an ideological bubble. Most Americans rely on an array of outlets—with varying audience profiles—for political news. And many consistent conservatives and liberals hear dissenting political views in their everyday lives." Media bubbles, like filter bubbles, were not completely sealed. But they were growing more polarized, more isolated, and more radicalized—especially on the right.

The point is not that only conservatives lived in echo-chambers or believed fake news; plenty of progressives did, too. Nor is the point that conservative media were biased and other media were not. There was plenty of bias and bias-confirmation all over the ideological map. Rather, the point is that the conservative and non-conservative media universes were displaying different and asymmetric *systemic* behaviors. Research by Pew and others picked up one such asymmetry: although both liberals and conservatives tended to rely on bias-confirming sources, consistent liberals relied on and trusted a wider variety of sources. Liberals consumed CNN, MSNBC, NPR, the *New York Times*, and more; they said they trusted (more than distrusted) more than three-quarters of the news outlets on a list Pew offered. By contrast, consistent conservatives were "tightly clustered around one main news source," namely Fox News, and they distrusted most other sources. By 2020, Pew reported, about a fifth of partisans on both sides received political news from only partisan sources; among Republicans who occupied such news bubbles, fully 70 percent reported relying on Fox News—an astonishing level of concentration.[54] The sources which conservatives relied on, moreover, tended to be more extreme. "Prominent media on the left are well distributed across the center, center-left, and left," wrote a team of Harvard University researchers. "The center of attention and influence for conservative media is on the far right. The center-right is of minor importance and is the least represented portion of the media spectrum."[55] In other words, the media were bifurcating, and the conservative portion was spinning off to the right, precisely as Limbaugh had prescribed.

Conservatives were also seeing and digesting significantly more fake news. One study, by the political scientists Andrew Guess, Brendan Nyhan, and Jason Reifler in 2018, found that fewer than half of Americans visited a fake news website in the weeks before the 2016 election, but the visitors were not evenly distributed across the ideological spectrum: about six in ten visits to fake news sites came from the most conservative 20 percent of Americans. Trump supporters were more than twice as likely as Hillary Clinton supporters to visit untrustworthy websites; strikingly, fake news sites accounted for more than 10 percent of Trump supporters' overall news diet, versus only 1 percent of Clinton supporters' news diet.[56] Other research found that conservatives were more exposed to conspiracy theories and fake news, and were more likely to believe them. During the 2020 pandemic crisis, for example, polling by Yahoo News and YouGov found that 44 percent of Republicans, and half of people who relied primarily on Fox News, said it was true that "Bill Gates wants to use a mass vaccination campaign against COVID-19 to implant microchips in people that would be used to track people with a digital ID." Fewer than a quarter of Democrats and independents believed that bizarre claim.[57] Republicans were twice as likely as Democrats to believe that the COVID-19 virus was intentionally created in a lab.[58] And so on. "One consequence," wrote the political scientists Marc Hetherington and Jonathan Weiler, "is that conservative news media consumers are less likely to encounter news narratives that are widely shared by those who are not part of their political tribe. At the same time, when they do, those narratives may well seem that much more alien and unbelievable to them."[59]

What was going on? Were conservatives nuttier than liberals? More gullible? Although some liberals might have warmed to those explanations, a more likely cause was something else: mainstream media and right-wing media were increasingly in entirely different epistemic businesses. They were not ideological counterparts in the same knowledge-seeking enterprise. Mainstream media, whatever its ideological priors, was in the bias-*disconfirming* business. It remained grounded in conventional journalistic norms, such as checking information and correcting errors. Conservative media did some of that, but increasingly it was in the bias-*confirming* business. It was more interested in telling its audiences what they wanted to hear.

That is not to say that conservative media always lied or liberal media always told the truth. There were good reporters and fair-minded consumers on both sides. The difference, rather, seemed to be in the systemic incentives. Recall the analogy to a network of pumping and filtering stations. Fairly consistently, mainstream media were filtering fake news out and transmitting real news. But conservative media were often doing the reverse.

Think of it this way. Suppose you take a conspiracy theory and inject it into the mainstream media, and then watch what happens. If the mainstream media reported on it at all, they would typically debunk and then squelch it. After a news cycle or two, it would fade away. Conservative media might behave the same way toward a left-leaning conspiracy theory. But inject a right-leaning conspiracy theory, and the conservative system would tend to amplify it.

That was the finding of an exhaustive analysis of media networks and behavior published in 2018 by Yochai Benkler, Robert Faris, and

Hal Roberts, of Harvard's Berkman Klein Center for Internet and Society. "The consistent pattern that emerges from our data is that . . . there is no left-right division, but rather a division between the right and the rest of the media ecosystem," they wrote in *Network Propaganda: Manipulation, Disinformation, and Radicalization in American Politics.*[60] In 2016, they found, conspiracy theories and fake news were widely available to Clinton voters and to Trump voters, and both groups were comparably interested in hearing them. But the mainstream media ecosystem "was able to check disinformation and error on both sides, as mainstream and newer online media continuously checked each other's worst impulses and corrected error and overreaching." By contrast, "The insular right wing of the media ecosystem creates positive feedbacks for bias-confirming statements as a central feature of its normal operation." The mainstream media quickly squelched a fake story about Trump's having raped a thirteen-year-old, whereas conservative media disseminated and amplified a fake story about Clinton's involvement in a pedophile ring. Comparing those and other cases, the researchers said,

> underscores the fundamentally different dynamics in the right wing as compared to the rest of the American political media ecosystem. When observing right-wing conspiracy theories, we saw positive feedback loops between the core of that network—composed of Fox News, leading Republican pundits, and *Breitbart*—and the remainder of the online right-wing network. In those cases we saw repetition, amplification, and circling of the wagons to criticize other media outlets when these exposed the errors and failures of the story. By contrast, the mainstream media ecosystem exhibited intensive competition to hold each other to high journalistic standards, and a repeated pattern of rapid removal of content, correction, and in several cases disciplining of the reporters involved. Moreover, in none of these cases did we find more than a smattering of repetition and amplification of the claims once retracted.

To translate those findings into my vocabulary: when Trump came along, mainstream media were part of the reality-based community, but conservative media had one foot—sometimes both feet—out the door. Traditional and right-wing media outlets occupied diverging universes, not just in terms of what they believed, but in terms of how they believed.

Aspects of my argument will strike some readers as partisan. They may point out that I use Republican examples much more than Democratic ones; that I call out Trump more than, say, Hillary Clinton, and Fox News more than MSNBC. They may point out that there is nothing new about cynical political lying, and that all sides have engaged in it. (In 2012 Senator Harry Reid of Nevada, the Democratic Senate minority leader, leveled the made-up charge that Mitt Romney, the Republican presidential candidate, had paid no taxes for ten years. When he was criticized for the falsehood later, he replied, "Well, they can call it whatever they want. Romney didn't win, did he?") But the two information ecosystems' partisanship was not the epistemically important difference between them. In different circumstances, the partisan polarities might just as easily have been reversed. The important distinction is that the right and left had diverged epistemically and developed asymmetrically. As information systems, they were doing different kinds of things.

Epistemic Secession

Trump did not create the divergence, but he proved masterly at exploiting it. Like Limbaugh and Hannity and the rest, but even more brazenly, he savaged mainstream media, even encouraging physical attacks against journalists. He called the mainstream media "disgusting" and "a great danger to our country," even "the enemy of the American people," a sentiment with which almost two-thirds of Republicans agreed by August 2017.[61] He organized his political messaging around the conceit that, as Steve Bannon had said, "The real opposition is the media." He applied the label "fake news" to real news, and vice versa. "What you are seeing and what you are reading is not what's happening," he told his supporters. "Just stick with us, don't believe the crap you see from these people, the fake news." By contrast, he praised and amplified internet trolls: "The crap that you think of is unbelievable," he told them—intending "crap" as a professional compliment.

He encountered, then, a conservative media establishment which was already seceding from the Constitution of Knowledge, and a technological environment which already advantaged outrage and disinformation, and a public which was already polarized and vulnerable to disinformation. And he threw the full force of his personality, his following, the Republican Party, and the presidency of the United States into exploiting and heightening all of those trends. Together with his troll army and the conservative media counter-establishment, he was able to bring about something no ordinary troll, not even Vladimir Putin, could accomplish: an epistemic secession. Together, they created not just confusion and disorientation but a cultic alternative reality, anchored by the premise that Trump was never wrong but always the victim of conspiracies and lies.

Sometimes, in the alternative reality of the Trumpian echo chamber, day became night and night became day. Ukraine, not Russia, had interfered in the U.S. election in 2016. Biden, not Trump, had tried to sway Ukrainian prosecutors for political advantage. The special counsel's investigation was an attempted coup based on a hoax. The many documented ties between people in the Trump campaign's orbit and the Russians, as well as Trump's own public encouragement of illegal Russian intervention, were evidence of a frame-up by the Obama administration. Joseph Mifsud, a shadowy academic who had tried to worm his way into the Trump campaign, was not a likely Russian agent but an FBI plant. In the House impeachment hearings of early 2020, Trump's defenders used the firehose to question or deny almost everything (up to and including "that Joe Biden was a leading Democratic contender to face President Trump in 2020"), while airing conspiracy theories and innuendos.[62] Their strategy "seeks to create not just a counternarrative but a completely separate reality," wrote Ryan Broderick in *BuzzFeed News*. "Each round of GOP questioning is not meant to interrogate the witnesses . . . but instead to create moments that can be flipped into Fox News segments, shared as bite-size Facebook posts, or dropped into 4chan threads."[63] At long last, the inversion of reality reached its apogee with the claim that Trump was the landslide winner of the 2020 election and it was his opponent who was trying to overturn the results. Astonishingly, millions of Americans believed that on Inauguration Day Trump, not Joe Biden, would be sworn in.

Cults—religious, Marxist, Trumpist, and others—enmesh their adherents in infinite, impenetrable loops of self-reinforcing beliefs. They encourage and often require their members to isolate themselves from outside ideas and authorities. "Better to get your news directly from the president," Lamar Smith, a Republican congressman from Texas, said on the House floor, shortly after Trump came to office. "In fact," he added, "it might be the only way to get the unvarnished truth."[64] Inside the cultic bubble, every question has an answer, every implausibility an explanation, even if the answer is a change of subject or the explanation is that you cannot believe your own eyes and ears. "Everything you're seeing is deception," Rush Limbaugh told his listeners during the 2019 Ukraine scandal.[65] Indeed, disconfirming evidence is untrustworthy precisely *because* it disconfirms. When the Justice Department's inspector general found procedural errors but no political bias in the FBI's investigation of Russian efforts to influence the Trump campaign, Mike Lee, a Republican senator from Utah, asked him, "Is not the lack of evidence that you're talking about itself evidence of bias?"[66] Just so.

One finds oneself, here, in a world not just of dueling facts or even dueling realities, but of dueling epistemic regimes, one fallibilist and contestable, the other unfalsifiable and cultic. As we saw in chapter 2, mass alternative realities tend to be unstable and aggressive. Rejecting the tenets of the reality-based community, they feel excluded from it and threatened by it. Their frustration grows as reality-based institutions—mainstream journalists, the courts, scholars, government agencies—reject their claims, but being rejected only makes them surer that a conspiracy is afoot. As their anger and fear rise, they may finally resort to creed war, cold or hot. The rioters who stormed the U.S. Capitol to disrupt the counting of electoral votes on January 6, 2021, believed that right there in front of them, inside the building only yards away, Congress was in the process of reversing the people's will and stealing democracy. Given what they thought were the stakes, many of them saw little option but to take up arms in defense of truth. At the Capitol that day, the rebellion was against the Constitution of Knowledge no less than the Constitution of the United States, and what we saw—the use of force and intimidation to settle disputes about reality—was what we always see, sooner or later, where the Constitution of Knowledge loses its sway.

Blame Trump and his troll army and media enablers, to be sure; but remember that they could not have succeeded without their audiences' help. Disinformation and conspiracism spread in advanced, individualistic democracies like the United States not because their targets are sheeplike but because, to the contrary, so many people are active collaborators in their own deception. Feeling left behind by rapid social change or disrespected by the establishment, they seek explanations which scratch the itch for an emotionally cathartic story of good versus evil. Feeling that their voices and votes are disregarded and that mainstream paths to change are blocked, they search for a narrative which offers a heroic role in a millenarian drama. Encouraged by their connections on social media and sometimes in real life too, they eagerly join a club whose initiates purport to share privileged insight into hidden truths and future events. Conspiracy theories like QAnon and predictions that a military intervention would install Trump instead of Biden as president were delusional from any rational perspective, but emotionally they made perfect sense. "It's a fight between good and evil," one woman told the Associated Press in 2021, explaining why she spent hours every day scouring the internet for proof that the 2020 election was stolen from Trump. "She saw systems fail those most vulnerable," reported the A.P., "and her faith in the standard truth-bearers of American democracy—courts, Congress, the media—eroded. She felt she could trust nothing but believe anything. . . . 'Sometimes you feel like, gee, am I crazy?' she said. 'We know we're not insane, but our world has become very chaotic and we're just trying to sort it out.' "[67]

She felt she could trust nothing but believe anything: students of information warfare will recognize this as the state which disinformation campaigns seek to induce. By heightening political polarization, attacking established institutions, and fueling social mistrust, propagandists can make a portion of the public not only receptive to disinformation but eager to pitch in and help manufacture it. "A great deal if not all the time," writes the psychologist and law professor Dan Kahan, "misinformation is not something that happens to the mass public but rather something that its members are complicit in producing."[68] Far from blindly following what they are told, believers are convinced they are conducting their own rigorous investigations, that they will be the last to be fooled. Conspiracy theories like the ones about the 2020 election and the COVID-19 pandemic "are profoundly participatory disinformation campaigns," as the University of Washington's Kate Starbird told a *Lawfare* interviewer. "It is both top-down and bottom-up. At times elites and political operatives set the agenda, but the online crowd or the audiences help generate the narratives and piece together the evidence. So it's this two-way relationship."[69] Together, both leading and following each other, propagandists and their audiences dance away from reality.

Reality Pushes Back

The argument of this chapter is that disinformation is an old and well-known form of information warfare. Where strategic fundamentals are concerned, the modern disinformation campaigns waged by Donald Trump or Vladimir Putin or their allies and surrogates would seem familiar to propaganda operatives in the era of Lenin or Goebbels. What was new was the extraordinary toolset afforded by the digital revolution. Those new tools were seized upon by trolls and conspiracists, empowered by political polarization, captured and channeled by state actors, loosed into mainstream politics by sociopathic political figures, amplified by conservative media, and reinforced with the power of the U.S. presidency. Any one vector—digital technology, state support, polarization, sociopathic politicians, conservative cultism—would have made life easier for the aspiring information warrior. Together, they whipped up a perfect storm of chaos.

Cause for alarm, yes. Cause for fatalism—no. There are many reasons not to assume that troll epistemology will prevail over the Constitution of Knowledge, and many reasons to hope it will fail. The reality-based community has its share of vulnerabilities, one of which I take up in the next chapter. But troll epistemology has vulnerabilities of its own. It is, again, entirely parasitic and destructive; its inability to do anything constructive limits its sustainability and appeal. Its lies tend to collide unpleasantly with reality, as happened to the claim that Trump would be re-inaugurated on January 20, 2021. It relies on the information networks it targets to spread and amplify falsehoods, but those networks tend to wise up. It can coordinate its attacks but has little control over the demons it lets loose. It is not good at building durable institutions, because its norms are sociopathic. It is not good at maintaining its own situational awareness, because, as Thomas Rid notes, propagandists tend to become enmeshed in their own lies and half-truths.

Trolls use asymmetric information warfare—ambushes, swarms, anonymous raids, disruptive strikes—because they are weak, not strong. Their hope is to batter and undermine the reality-based community. They are dangerous, but their greatest threat lies not in their own capabilities but in their ability to exploit gaps in the Constitution of Knowledge's defenses: undermining its confidence, degrading its legitimacy, obscuring its principles, dividing its constituencies.

Even on those scores, troll epistemology's power is limited. Overestimating trolls is as mischievous as underestimating them. The business plan of trolling, like that of terrorism, is to cause fear out of proportion to the actual threat. Hyping disinformation risked making disruptive actors like Putin and Trump seem ten feet tall, which was exactly their goal. Most people, during the 2016 presidential campaign, did not go to fake news websites. Fewer than 10 percent shared fake news links on Facebook, according to a 2019 analysis by New York University's Social Media and Political Participation Lab and Princeton University. Republicans were four times more likely than Democrats to share fake news links—but still, fewer than a fifth of Republicans did so.[70] Brendan Nyhan and his colleagues found that the reach of fake news declined in the 2018 midterm election cycle, partly thanks to countermeasures by the media platforms.[71] During the pandemic in 2020, polls found that more Republicans (80 percent) trusted Trump for medical information than trusted the Centers for Disease Control. That seemed ominous. Yet it was still the case that the large majority of Republicans (74 percent) also trusted the CDC.[72] Conservative and mainstream media were drifting apart, not just ideologically but epistemically; but they were not disconnected altogether. In any case, disinformation seemed to have changed few people's minds about politics (because minds are so difficult to change); its influence was more in the nature of confirming what some people already preferred to believe, and confusing those who were unsure of what to believe, and, above all, normalizing political lying and the use of disinformation.

Overstating the fragility of the Constitution of Knowledge is likewise a mistake. The reality-based community would not have endured and expanded for four centuries unless it possessed formidable strengths: its institutional depth, its vast networks, its reserves of integrity. It can use those strengths to build resilience and resistance, and, after initially reeling from the shocks of the Trump era, it set about doing so.

The period before 2016, Thomas Rid remarked in an interview with *Lawfare* in April 2020, "was really the golden age of disinformation, because you could do it with ease and no one expected it to happen." But 2016 brought an awakening in the news media, the research community, the national security community, social media platforms, and elsewhere. As we saw in the previous chapter, social media companies hardened their networks by blocking coordinated inauthentic behavior, using humans and bots to moderate content, deploying fact-checks and warnings, and fixing vulnerabilities in their policies and products. Academic centers and nonprofit organizations sprang up around the world to track troll networks and alert governments and social media companies to threats. Schools began teaching media literacy, showing students how to distinguish fake news from the real thing. Journalism schools made sure that graduates learned how to detect fake sources and doctored images. Public education, though no silver bullet, seemed promising: research found that even simple interventions, like asking people to pause and think before sharing content, increased critical thinking. ("Even young children can learn to be more critical in their assessments of what's truthful," the *Wall Street Journal* reported.)[73]

Citizen resistance emerged, too. A 2020 study found that ordinary people could, and often did, use social media to correct misinformation—and that peer-based factual corrections were often effective, especially when citing trusted sources like the Centers for Disease Control.[74] Nonprofits organized networks of professional scientists to check online articles, and even a network of teen fact-checkers. In Europe, citizen activists, sometimes calling themselves "elves," developed networks to monitor and counter troll activity in real time, embedding themselves in chat rooms and Facebook groups where trolls incubated conspiracy theories and selected targets. "Some activists work in secret teams to challenge trolls directly on social platforms," reported Thomas Kent in *The American Interest*. "Others map entire networks of trolls and bots to help Facebook and Twitter shut them down."[75]

Journalists moved rapidly up the learning curve. They developed beats to cover, and uncover, disinformation campaigns. They became more sophisticated about adverting to conspiracy theories without always repeating them. They got smarter about inauthentic posts and deep fakes and algorithmic manipulation. Fortified by fact-checking, they became more willing to flag false information unambiguously: "Trump also repeated his false claim that . . ."—or "Giuliani also falsely claimed that . . ."—or "An ultra-Orthodox rabbi falsely described the measles outbreak as . . ." They made a point of contextualizing information whose sources might be inauthentic or suspicious, explaining at the top of stories—like ones about material found on a hard drive allegedly belonging to Joe Biden's son—where information came from and why it might be dicey.

Although there were, and could be, no comprehensive solutions to the disinformation threat, the adjustments being made by myriad actors offered the prospect of something like a stronger immune system—not invulnerable, but certainly less vulnerable. And the adjustments were coming quickly. "Not only do you have a much better network in place across the platforms and law enforcement and the research community who are looking out for this kind of stuff," said Ben Nimmo, the director of investigations at the internet research firm Graphika, in September 2020, "you also have a much more experienced press corps who are reporting on it, and they know the kinds of questions to [ask] and the kind of points to look for. And if you put all that together, it makes for a much healthier environment than we had four years ago, or even a year ago."[76]

Changes in practices among the reality-based community would make no difference if the public rejected the judgments of journalists or scientists or other reality-based professionals. But the public, too, showed signs of growing resilience. Despite, or because of, demagogic attacks on the mainstream media, public confidence that the news media try to report without bias rose 20 points between 2016 and 2017 in polling by the Newseum, and then rose five points more in 2019.[77] Large majorities (more than three-fourths in the Newseum's 2019 poll) agreed that "the spread of fake news and misinformation on the internet is a serious threat to our democracy." Although confidence in journalism remained well below the levels of the glory days, consumer behavior suggested a flight to quality. Audiences, especially younger ones, expressed declining trust in social media and shifted their consumption toward established news brands and paid subscriptions. "Young subscribers flock to old media," *Politico* headlined in 2017. During the COVID-19 crisis—not just the pandemic but the so-called infodemic—the traditional networks' nightly news programs, once written off as dinosaurs, enjoyed a resurgence. "Younger people have tuned in, too," reported the *New York Times*.[78] Trust in scientists, which had never collapsed as trust in journalists had done, also rose. By 2019 almost 90 percent of the public said they had a great deal or a fair amount of confidence in scientists to act in the public interest, and almost two-thirds said that the scientific method generally produces accurate conclusions, according to polling by the Pew Research Center.[79]

What one saw, then, was the reality-based community scrambling and struggling, innovating and improvising, to adapt to troll epistemology. With success? Yes. Falling short? Also yes. How well troll epistemology could thrive without a troll-in-chief in the White House was an open question. "The president's technique . . . is relentless and unforgiving: never admit any error, constantly repeat falsehoods, and have no shame about your tactics," the fact-checking group at the *Washington Post* wrote in 2020. "It will likely not be known for years if Trump has created a template for future presidents—whether he is an aberration or has changed the nature of the presidency."[80]

Part of the answer would be delivered at the ballot box, but much depends on the resilience of the reality-based community. And that depends on whether the reality-based community can meet a challenge from within: not chaos, but conformity.

7

Canceling: Despotism of the Few

Coercive conformity is corrupting
the reality-based community

On February 14, 1989, Ayatollah Ruhollah Khomeini, the supreme leader of Iran, called for the cancelation of the novelist Salman Rushdie.

When Rushdie published *The Satanic Verses* in 1988, at the age of forty-one, he was highly regarded in literary circles but not a public celebrity, and the book—a magical-realist novel about two Indian Muslims in contemporary Britain—did not initially make much of a splash. But in the weeks following its publication, Muslim protests swelled in Britain (Rushdie's home country) and abroad. After seeing a Pakistani protest on television, Khomeini issued an edict declaring the novel to be against Islam. He called on Muslims everywhere to murder Rushdie and anyone who had assisted in the book's publication. In the ensuing eruption, dozens of people were killed, including the book's Japanese translator, and many more were threatened. With Iran's multimillion-dollar bounty on his head, Rushdie was forced into hiding, under guard, for nine years. In that time, his marriage failed and his output declined. Echoes reverberated for years afterward. In 2018 Norwegian police filed charges in the shooting of William Nygaard, the publisher of the Norwegian edition, who was left for dead outside his home (but survived).

Beyond the killings and assaults and mass disruptions, the campaign had its desired effect. "Khomeini achieved something remarkable with his edict," wrote Daniel Pipes in his 1990 book on the crisis. "In Europe and North America (and many other regions too) he created an unprecedented climate of worry. Concerned for their personal safety, writers, publishers, booksellers, book-buyers, faculty, and students watched what they said."[1]

The phenomenon of thought vigilantism was ancient, but Khomeini showed that with the help of mass media it could be mobilized globally to reach anyone anywhere, literally overnight. A generation later, digital technology would make thought vigilantism even easier and faster. Like trolls and disinformation campaigners, cancelers, as they came to be called, discovered in social media an ideal technology for their purposes; but where trolls sought to confuse and disrupt, cancelers sought to chill and coerce.

Although James Madison did not anticipate the Rushdie affair and subsequent cancel campaigns, he did have relevant insights into a challenge they exemplified. What can be done when groups organize and agitate to get something they want at the expense of other groups or the larger society? In Rushdie's case, the group wanted Rushdie's head; other thought vigilantes were satisfied to get someone fired or ostracized. Often, of course, groups organized to pursue more benign claims, like subsidies for a favorite cause. Madison was aware of the general problem, which he knew had sunk democracies of the past. He called it the problem of factions—what today we often call special interests. "By a faction," he wrote in *Federalist* No. 10, "I understand a number of citizens, whether amounting to a majority or a minority of the whole, who are united and actuated by some common impulse of passion, or of interest, adverse to the rights of other citizens, or to the permanent and aggregate interests of the community."

The "mischiefs of faction," Madison understood, put democracies in a bind, because democracies cannot prevent citizens from forming interest groups. The alternative was to control the *effects* of factions by limiting the harm they could do and even making constructive use of them. But no prior democracy, Madison knew, had sustainably met that challenge; in time, some faction would rob or oppress the rest of the population.

Characteristically, Madison came up with a counterintuitive solution. There must be a lot of factions, and they must differ from each other. Small, homogeneous republics, like the ones Rousseau called for, were prone to factional capture. Instead, a large, pluralistic republic would ensure plenty of factional diversity, and diversity would ensure that no one faction could prevail. "Extend the sphere," he wrote, "and you take in a greater variety of parties and interests; you make it less probable that a majority of the whole will have a common motive to invade the rights of other citizens; or if such a common motive exists, it will be more difficult for all who feel it to discover their own strength, and to act in unison with each other."

The United States has grown in population nearly a hundred-fold since Madison wrote *Federalist* No. 10, and its diversity has grown apace. One might have thought the country would long since have fallen apart. Yet, in the bigger scheme of things, it is more democratic and more stable and more protective of minority rights than ever. The second great liberal social system, the market economy, likewise has grown in scope and inclusion by many orders of magnitude. And, as we saw in chapter 3, the reality-based community of science and journalism and other truth-seeking, fact-based professionals has extended its sphere spectacularly, and its global reach and geographic diversity continue to increase exponentially. Experience has borne out Madison's counterintuitive claim: liberalism and diversity are allies. They thrive together and need each other. Extending the sphere brings headaches, but ultimately it makes us stronger.

But diversity has opponents, and many of them are inside the reality-based community. They champion diversity but neglect—or outright oppose—the most important kind.

"The Chief Danger of the Time"

In 1859 a London-born polymath named John Stuart Mill published his gemlike essay *On Liberty*, which soon became the starting place for modern conversations about freedom of speech. Educated by his stern father, Mill worked as a colonial administrator in the British East India Company and served briefly in the House of Commons, but he never had a professorial appointment or even attended university (which he and his father deemed a waste of time). That did not prevent him from becoming the nineteenth century's most influential English philosopher, cited more than any other today; and *On Liberty* is his most cited book, as potent as it is concise. If you studied it in high school or college, you probably read the second chapter, "Of the Liberty of Thought and Discussion." There Mill lays out three interlocking arguments for tolerating, even welcoming, ideas and opinions which we believe to be wrong, even indefensible. First, however certain we may feel, we may nonetheless be wrong in our own beliefs, and the opinion we reject might be true (classic fallibilism). Second, it is rarely the case, particularly in morals and politics, that one opinion is entirely true and the other entirely false. "There is a commoner case than either of these; when the conflicting doctrines, instead of being one true and the other false, share the truth between them." Thus only "the steady habit of correcting and completing his own opinion by collating it with those of others" can allow us to piece together the whole picture. Third, even in cases where one view is firmly established as the correct one, contending with alternatives prevents intellectual torpor and dogmatism: "However unwillingly a person who has a strong opinion may admit the possibility that his opinion may be false, he ought to be moved by the consideration that however true it may be, if it is not fully, frequently, and fearlessly discussed, it will be held as a dead dogma, not a living truth."

Together, Mill's arguments nod in the direction later taken by Charles Sanders Peirce and Karl Popper: knowledge is a social phenomenon. It is a product of human interactions, not just individual reason. It requires comparing viewpoints. Wherever there is only one person or opinion, fact and faith become undistinguishable. "In an imperfect state of the human mind," wrote Mill, "the interests of truth require a diversity of opinions."

What happens if a community becomes hostile to a diversity of opinions? That question brings us to the chapter of *On Liberty* which you are less likely to have read in college. In the comparatively over-looked third chapter, "Of Individuality, as One of the Elements of Well-being," Mill argued that innovation, creativity, and intellectual breakthroughs depend on individuality, unconventionality, and genius. Genius is inherently scarce, and it "can only breathe freely in an atmosphere of freedom." Somewhat surprisingly to Americans today, Mill held that the most dire threat to freedom comes not from state repression but from social conformity, which leads to a shortage of diversity—diversity of inclination and interest and talent, but especially, he implied, diversity of opinion. "Precisely because the tyranny of opinion is such as to make eccentricity a reproach, it is desirable, in order to break through that tyranny, that people should be eccentric." His stark conclusion: "That so few now dare to be eccentric marks the chief danger of the time."

The chief danger! That is a strong claim, and one which, today, seems itself a bit eccentric. In the twentieth century, state repression was far and away the most serious threat to free thought and expression, and contemporary liberal societies like the United States have certainly not lacked for individuality, at least not since the cultural and sexual and intellectual and social emancipations of the 1960s. Or so I thought. Only in the new century did it dawn on me that Mill was on to something, for reasons rooted in epistemology and confirmed by psychology.

Objectivity Comes from Diversity

Today's philosophers of science have largely come around to Mill's view. Without pluralism and viewpoint diversity, transcending our biases is impossible, even in principle. Perfect objectivity will always elude us, but we come much closer if we follow the empirical rule by checking our views against others' different views, which of course is possible only where people disagree. "A homogeneous community will be hard-pressed to realize which of its assumptions are warranted by evidence and which are not," wrote the historian of science Naomi Oreskes in her 2019 book, *Why Trust Science?* "After all, it is hard to identify prejudices that you share. A community with diverse values is more likely to identify and challenge prejudicial beliefs embedded in, or masquerading as, scientific theory."[2] Shared assumptions—like psychiatry's insistence in the mid-twentieth-century that homosexuality was a mental disorder—become invisible or unchallengeable or both. "From all this it follows," wrote the philosopher Helen E. Longino in her landmark 1990 book, *Science as Social Knowledge*, "that the greater the number of different points of view included in a given community, the more likely it is that [the community's] scientific practice will be objective."[3]

Objectivity improves, then, as a function of viewpoint multiplicity and diversity, and diminishes as a function of viewpoint monopoly and homogeneity. In chapter 3 I stressed how the globalization of the reality-based network brings more minds to bear on problems, but just as important, maybe more so, is that it brings *different* minds to bear, many from places and perspectives which never before had the opportunity to contribute. A nice example comes from biology. Homosexual behavior is common in the natural world, which seems peculiar to evolutionary biologists. After all, sterile sex would seem to be a waste of precious reproductive energy. Or . . . maybe not. When a group of researchers with mixed sexual orientations came along to ponder the problem, it occurred to them to question the background assumption and invert the hypothesis. Perhaps what is costly, in evolutionary terms, is the cognitive equipment and anatomical differentiation required for opposite-sex relations. In that case, homosexuality might be costless, from evolution's point of view; what would need explaining is the *rarity* of homosexuality. Reporting on that theory, *The Economist* commented, "It raises the question of which other facets of scientific knowledge might be being obscured because the backgrounds of practitioners in those fields do not lead them to ask unconventional questions." Paging Mr. Mill!

Spirals of Silence and Zombie Science

Psychology and sociology affirm what epistemology predicts: if a community falls prey to intellectual conformity, it descends down a kind of epistemic rabbit hole, a "spiral of silence."

That evocative term comes from a 1974 article by the German sociologist Elisabeth Noelle-Neumann. Individuals, she posited, fear social isolation. They have a "quasi-statistical" organ which monitors their social environment and continually assesses the distribution and intensity of opinions around them. As we saw in chapter 2, conformity bias is strong; we harmonize our beliefs and even our perceptions with those of the people around us, often without being aware of doing so. Also, as we saw in chapter 6, our opinion-sensing "organs" can be spoofed. Autocrats can use state media and censorship to make people believe that the leader enjoys broad support and that hardly anyone dissents. Online propagandists can use algorithmic amplification and fake personas to make a small group like anti-vaxxers seem like a big, respectable school of thought. In a manipulated or repressive social environment, people who follow the cues around them will misread the distribution of opinion. The person who believes herself to be in the minority will assume that her views are losing ground. The more isolated she feels, the less inclined she will be to express her view, and the more pressure she will feel to conform. You see how the spiral forms: "The more individuals perceive these tendencies and adapt their views accordingly, the more the one faction appears to dominate and the other to be on the downgrade," wrote Noelle-Neumann. "Thus the tendency of the one to speak up and the other to be silent starts off a spiraling process which increasingly establishes one opinion as the prevailing one."[4]

The spiral of silence has some odd characteristics. In principle, a view which may initially not represent a consensus at all, which indeed is in the distinct minority, can make itself first seem dominant and then actually become dominant as holdouts fall silent, succumb to doubt, or convert to what they think is the prevalent view. Spoofed consensus can become real consensus, or at least close enough to be indistinguishable. Moreover, as we know from totalitarian states, once the spiral forms, even obvious facts can fail for a long time to interrupt it. As diversity dries up, the community spins ever further into its own looking-glass world.

All the while, the members of the community can be engaging in what seems to them to be rigorous criticism and debate. In their 2019 book, *The Misinformation Age: How False Beliefs Spread*, Cailin O'Connor and James Owen Weatherall explain the perverse dynamics. Imagine a scientific community which bifurcates into two hostile camps. Imagine also that the camps lose trust in each other and stop communicating. They attend separate conferences, publish in separate journals, teach in separate schools. The individual members of both camps remain conscientious, hard-working scientists. Nonetheless, something has gone wrong. "Now, instead of steadily trending toward consensus, either right or wrong, scientists regularly split into polarized groups holding different beliefs, with each side trusting the evidence of only those who already agree with them." The polarization is stable: "No amount of evidence from the scientists who have adopted the correct belief will be enough to convince those who adopted the wrong belief," write O'Connor and Weatherall. "Worse, once they find an action they all agree on, they will keep performing that action regardless of any new evidence. They will do this even if all the scientists come to believe something else is actually better, because no one is willing to buck the consensus."

Even strong evidence can fail to burst an epistemic bubble, partly because of information cascades, in which (write O'Connor and Weatherall) "incorrect statements of belief can snowball as people's judgments are influenced by others in their social environment." I believe that you are giving me good empirical information, but you are actually recycling what I told other people who then told you. Without realizing it, we are talking to ourselves. As in a stock bubble, none of us is consciously following the crowd. We are each making rational decisions based on what appears to be solid evidence—unaware that we are trapped in a closed loop.

The result can be to reverse the epistemic valence of critical persuasion so that it points away from reality, even in the face of countervailing evidence. "Conformity nips the spread of good new ideas in the bud," write O'Connor and Weatherall. "Of course, conformity can also nip the spread of bad ideas in the bud, but we find that, on average, the greater their tendencies to conform, the more often a *group of scientists* will take the worse action. . . . Pressures from their social realm swamp any pressures from the world."[5]

I italicized "group of scientists" to emphasize that O'Connor and Weatherall are not describing religious cults or political parties; they are describing scientific communities which have been, in effect, zombified. Individuals' personal commitment to the Constitution of Knowledge can help prevent zombification, but it is no guarantee. Wherever a viewpoint monoculture takes hold, a bubble can form. People inside the bubble will perceive themselves to be engaging in vigorous contestation and criticism—unaware that what they are actually doing is confirming and re-confirming their shared biases.

There is nothing new about any of this. A chillingly accurate description of spirals of silence was written in 1840 about the United States of America. "I know of no country where, in general, there reigns less independence of mind and true freedom of discussion than in America," wrote Alexis de Tocqueville, in the second volume of his masterpiece, *Democracy in America*. He explained:

> In America, the majority draws a formidable circle around thought. Within these limits, the writer is free; but woe to him if he dares to go beyond them. It isn't that he has to fear an auto-da-fé, but he is exposed to all types of distasteful things and to everyday persecutions. A political career is closed to him; he has offended the only power that has the ability to open it to him. Everything is denied him, even glory. Before publishing his opinions, he believed he had some partisans; it seems to him that he has them no longer, now that he has revealed himself to all; for those who censure him speak openly, and those who think as he does, without having his courage, keep quiet and distance themselves. He gives in; finally, under the daily effort, he yields and returns to silence, as though he felt remorse for having told the truth.[6]

Purism vs. Pluralism

The First Amendment gives no protection against spirals of silence. Neither does mere lip service to intellectual pluralism and viewpoint diversity. The only prophylactic is the real thing, actual intellectual pluralism and viewpoint diversity. Go out and actively seek a variety of viewpoints. Find outlooks which make you uncomfortable. Find thinkers who may seem strange, unorthodox, unsafe. If everyone around you agrees with you (or seems to), you are doing it wrong. And viewpoint diversity means *viewpoint* diversity; other kinds of diversity, while important, are not substitutes. A demographically diverse roomful of people with identical views is a bubble.

I am not suggesting that every Jew go and talk to a neo-Nazi, or that historians reconsider whether the Holocaust happened, or that psychiatry revisit the claim that homosexuals are mentally ill. The Constitution of Knowledge owes its efficiency to producing a body of knowledge, an archive of settled claims which do not need constant relitigating. The reality-based community is conservative, in the sense that it conserves what it has learned and reopens closed accounts reluctantly. When new evidence turns up or experts develop new arguments, then reexamining an established claim may be in order, but the vast majority of claims against settled knowledge do not deserve research budgets or investigative-reporting teams and are rightly ignored. Viewpoint diversity does not imply that anything goes. Plausibility, credentials, consistency with known facts: all of those screens matter. Inevitably, people disagree about which propositions are settled knowledge and which are (or should be) in serious dispute, but consensus forms over time, and the community respects that consensus.

What I am saying, rather, is that to use intimidation or social coercion to *suppress* intellectual diversity violates the Constitution of Knowledge, whatever the ostensible justification. Mill was right: conformity casts a pall over inquiry, often a deeper pall than that of official censorship. I am suggesting that when we encounter an unwelcome and even repugnant new idea, the right question to ask is "What can I learn from this?" rather than "How can I get rid of this?"

Well, that sounds fun. Like *Star Trek*—seek out new life and new civilizations! Boldly go where no one has gone before! Unfortunately, as we saw in chapter 2, most people would rather have dental surgery than confront strange new ideas. Over the millennia, people have gone to endless trouble to find reasons to suppress, punish, and banish dissent. In *Kindly Inquisitors*, I argued that today's challenges to free thought and liberal science fall into three buckets. One is *fundamentalist*, grounded in certitude: your ideas are so definitely and obviously wrong that you must be evil, stupid, or ignorant to believe them, and no one should have to encounter them. A second is *egalitarian*, grounded in fairness: your ideas are oppressive in and of themselves, and expressing them disadvantages some perspective or group; or, as some argue, the very idea of objective truth silences or marginalizes oppressed groups—and any number of other variants. A third is *humanitarian*, grounded in harm: your ideas hurt me or my group in a way which is violent or akin to violence, and so expressing or tolerating them violates my human rights. Variations on those themes go back for centuries and can be found on the political left and right and everywhere in between.

I said much more about those arguments in *Kindly Inquisitors*. Here, suffice to say that all of them militate against viewpoint diversity. Instead of being pluralist, they are purist. Instead of seeking to pit biases against other biases and prejudices against other prejudices, they seek to eliminate bias and prejudice from the get-go—an Augean task which first polices culpable words, then culpable ideas when different words are recruited, and finally culpable minds when bad ideas keep popping back up. Purists, I wrote in 1995, "are doomed to hunt and hunt and hunt, scour and scour and scour."[7] That remained the case twenty-five years later, but by then an especially troublesome wrinkle had emerged.

Diversity Is Dangerous . . .

In 2020 journalists and other employees of the *New York Times* launched a protest, both internally and on social media, against their own newspaper. The op-ed page had published a controversial article by a U.S. senator named Tom Cotton; the editorial page editor, James

Bennet, was forced to resign. The drama was complicated, but one aspect stood out. As the paper's own account reported, "Times employees began tweeting a screenshot of Mr. Cotton's essay, most with some version of the sentence: 'Running this puts Black @nytimes staff in danger.'"[8] There are communities—Bible studies, support groups, fan clubs—whose members can legitimately seek safety from unwelcome viewpoints, but journalism is not one of them; entering hostile emotional and intellectual territory is in the job description. By 2020, however, what had come to be called "emotional safetyism" had spread through the reality-based community.

It was a new(ish) variant of the general humanitarian argument that "words that wound" are a form of violence, not metaphorically but actually. Long-standing First Amendment doctrine had allowed narrow restrictions on true threats and incitement to imminent lawless action, but the "words that wound" doctrine went much further: speech deemed hurtful or oppressive is literally violence or oppression—an act, not an idea. As a law professor once said, "To me, racial epithets are not speech. They are bullets."[9] A civil rights lawyer (who, one would think, might understand the difference between hearing conservative arguments and actually being shot) justified student activists' blockading and deplatforming of a conservative speaker this way: "It doesn't make sense for you to be pursuing a degree somewhere and for someone to put a bullet in your head."[10] Obviously, violence and oppression are human rights violations. It necessarily follows that speech deemed violent or oppressive not only can be suppressed, it *must* be suppressed.

At around the same time that the "words that wound" doctrine began getting traction in academic circles, it received an assist from an unexpected quarter. Starting around 1980, the federal Equal Employment Opportunity Commission promulgated regulations forbidding employers to let workplaces become pervasively hostile environments for members of minorities who were protected by employment discrimination law. The original idea was that a worker who had to endure, say, targeted racial bullying on a daily basis was a victim of discrimination. That seemed plausible, but the idea proved hard to contain. By the mid-1990s, the doctrine was being used to sue an employer who printed a Bible verse on paychecks (which a court found to be religious harassment of non-Christians). A university forced a graduate student to remove a photo of his bikini-clad wife from his desk, because someone filed a harassment complaint. A library worker was forced to remove a *New Yorker* cartoon from his work area after coworkers said it harassed them. The town of Murfreesboro, Tennessee, removed a painting from a public exhibit in City Hall after a city employee filed a hostile-environment complaint about it.[11] Those incidents and others like them should have been seen as flashing red lights, but weren't.

The "words that wound" doctrine and the hostile-environment doctrine flowed together, and eventually—perhaps inevitably, in an increasingly therapeutic and medicalized society—they merged with a third stream. Words and ideas can have emotional impact. They can be hurtful. Emotional injury and physical injury are both injuries, and thus are two forms of the same thing, and so any speech or idea which upsets someone is "assaultive," and if the victim is a minority, the assault is a hate crime. Surely, if we are entitled to be safe from physical violence in the public streets, we are also entitled to be safe from emotional violence in the public discourse. It is not enough, then, to react *after* someone feels offended or upset; we must proactively scrub the environment of unsafe ideas, lest we encounter them unexpectedly or, even worse, unavoidably. (The employee who said she was harassed by the art in Murfreesboro claimed the right not to have the painting "thrust in my face on my way into a meeting with my superiors.")

The Constitution of Knowledge acknowledges that ideas and words can be subjectively hurtful. To help us cope and mitigate the harm, it pushes us to interact civilly, depersonalize our disagreements, listen attentively, substantiate our claims, and wage our controversies through mediated channels like edited journals. It also recognizes that certain kinds of speech—true threats and targeted personal harassment, for example—are off limits. (U.S. First Amendment jurisprudence defines and delimits those exceptional cases.)[12] And it understands that going out of one's way to be empathetic and spare individuals from unnecessary indignities is ordinary decency. In general, it does a good job of encouraging civility—certainly better than any authoritarian system can manage.

But it also recognizes that criticism, by its very nature, can be painful and humiliating. Even in the hard sciences, as we have seen, debates can become angry, personal, and emotionally wounding. In response, the Constitution of Knowledge offers tough love. It requires us to accept a certain amount of emotional bruising. It asks us to be thick-skinned. It reminds us that speech alone has no magical powers to harm, and that we can reframe it and choose how we interpret it, which is not true of bullets. (If someone calls me a "fucking faggot," I interpret her as telling me that she needs counseling, not that I am a fucking faggot.) What the Constitution of Knowledge does *not* allow is treating criticism, offense, or emotional impact as equivalent to physical violence, or protection from emotionally hurtful expression as a right. If subjectively hurtful expressions are violence, then criticism is violence, and then science is a human rights violation.

Emotional safetyism rejected all those strictures as so much oppression, at least where minorities are concerned, and it soon proved even less containable than its precursors. It boiled down to the idea that any claim of endangerment ends the conversation.[13] Not everyone demanded emotional safety everywhere, all the time; but no one could say where, precisely, the right to safety began or ended. "There should be places where you feel uncomfortable, because that's how people grow as students and as future leaders," one college student acknowledged. (So far, so good.) "But I do not feel that college campuses need to be places where students feel unsafe. I'm not 'uncomfortable.' I feel threatened."[14] What was the difference between feeling uncomfortable and feeling threatened? No one could say.

Psychologists suspected that the emphasis on feeling safe grew from a parenting culture which increasingly "prepared the road for the child, not the child for the road," as Greg Lukianoff and Jonathan Haidt argued in their 2018 book, *The Coddling of the American Mind*. Be that as it might, by the late 2010s the vocabulary of emotional safetyism had become ubiquitous. People who objected to ideas they deemed hurtful found themselves armed with a powerful rhetorical weapon and limitless potential targets.

. . . and "Safety" Isn't Safe

In *Kindly Inquisitors*, I had a lot to say about the "words that wound" doctrine. I argued that words are not bullets, that stopping words does not stop bullets, and that confusing words with bullets is a tragic error. I will not repeat that discussion here, but I will update it by mentioning some of the reasons why emotional safetyism is inherently—not merely incidentally—incompatible with free speech, intellectual diversity, the pursuit of knowledge, and social peace.

Emotional safetyism is silencing. If an idea makes you feel unsafe, you can hardly be expected to have a conversation about it: that would be dangerous. If you are told by someone else that your idea makes her feel unsafe, you are in no position to argue the point: she is the expert on how she feels. Worse, defending yourself against a charge of violating emotional safety is itself unsafe, because it denies the danger. "She began the session by instructing the white people in the room not to defend ourselves if something was said in the session that made us feel defensive," said a woman who underwent corporate racial-sensitivity training. "It made me much more cautious. . . . I was worried as I interacted with my POC [person of color] co-workers. Oh, am I going to say something wrong? . . . And faced with the choice of do I stick my neck out and go for this interaction . . . or do I just put my head back down and sit back down at my computer, it was often easier to do the latter."[15] The only "safe" thing to do when someone plays the safety card is to end the conversation.

Emotional safetyism makes you neurotic. If you constantly scour the environment for danger, you will see danger. Haidt and Lukianoff write: "What is new today is the premise that students are fragile. Students think they are in danger and therefore need more protection. Even those who are not fragile themselves often believe that others are in danger and therefore need protection. . . . Stated simply: many university students are learning to think in distorted ways, and this increases their likelihood of becoming fragile, anxious, and easily hurt."[16] In the lexicon of emotional safetyism, a promiscuously used word is "traumatized." At Harvard, students who demanded a law professor's removal from his position as faculty dean of a residential house said that his service on the defense team of the disgraced movie executive Harvey Weinstein was "not only upsetting, but deeply trauma-inducing."[17] If interacting with a defense lawyer was trauma-inducing, one wondered what might *not* be trauma-inducing.

Emotional safetyism causes conflict. "If you . . . encourage students to find more things offensive (leading them to experience more negative impacts)," Haidt and Lukianoff note, "and you *also* tell them that whoever says or does the things they find offensive are 'aggressors' who have committed acts of bigotry against them, then you are probably fostering feelings of victimization, anger, and hopelessness in your students. They will come to see the world—and even their university—as a hostile place where things never seem to get better. If someone wanted to create an environment of perpetual anger and intergroup conflict, this would be an effective way to do it."[18]

Emotional safetyism rewards overreacting. In an environment where feeling unsafe, or claiming to feel unsafe, gives you power, it pays to feel *very* unsafe. The reality-based community rewards reasoned claims which can be defended when challenged; the safety-based community rewards emotional demonstrations which put challengers on the defensive. "Students were just screaming that we were trying to 'kill them,' " said a Williams College professor who sought to adopt the Chicago principles, a free-speech statement.[19] In a confrontation between Nicholas Christakis (a Yale professor) and a group of angry students, this exchange occurred:

> *Christakis:* So I have a vision of us, as people, as human beings, that actually privileges our common humanity, that is interested not in what is different among us, but what is the same. . . . I believe, even though I am not like you in the sense of my superficial appearance, that I can sit down and talk to you and understand your predicament, that I can listen to you. If that's not true, if you deny that, then what is the reason that you ask to be heard, by me or anyone else?
> *Student:* Because we're dying![20]

Emotional safetyism ignores consequences. Censorship and suppression do not make harmful ideas or thoughts go away. More often, they do the opposite. The only clear winner in the controversy over Senator Cotton's allegedly unsafe article in the *New York Times* was Cotton himself, who (the *Washington Post* reported) was "only emboldened," was "enjoying the fallout," and raised $200,000 from the controversy.[21] Again and again, history shows that censorship draws attention to the views it seeks to suppress. Adolf Hitler played the Weimar Republic's censorship laws like a violin, putting up posters with captions like "Crooks can speak anywhere in Germany, but Hitler is banned." (Later, when he came to power, he used the Weimar censorship laws to justify his own much harsher censorship regime.)[22] Appeals to safety allow for no consideration of their real-world effects. When *Reason* magazine's Robby Soave asked a graduate student whether deplatforming a speaker might backfire by creating a martyr and discrediting student protesters, the student granted the point but said it was not his concern. "I'm worried about people feeling safe and comfortable on campus," he said.[23]

Emotional safetyism is a censorship machine. There is no idea, person, or behavior it cannot reach. When the *Crimson*, Harvard's student newspaper, asked the U.S. Immigration and Customs Enforcement agency to comment for a news story about an anti-ICE protest at the school, the student government condemned the request for causing "feelings of unsafety." (Admirably, the student journalists stood firm: "Fundamental journalistic values obligate the *Crimson* to allow all subjects of a story a chance to comment.")[24] Truman State University in Missouri rejected an animal-rights study group, citing the "emotional risk" it might cause among students.[25] Marchers carrying rainbow flags with a star of David (representing Jewish Pride) were kicked out of a lesbian pride march in Chicago because the flags "made people feel unsafe," according to a march organizer.[26] What do a comment from federal officials, an animal-rights group, and Jewish Pride flags have in common? Precisely nothing, except that someone claimed they were unsafe.

Emotional safetyism is politicized. People always believe their political opponents are dangerous. No wonder that Brown University students objected to a speaker whose "fiscal conservatism and free market ideology" caused "real, tangible state violence against marginalized communities" and thus amounted to "hateful rhetoric which actively makes others less safe."[27] And that Harvard students filed a civil rights complaint asserting that allowing Supreme Court Associate Justice Brett Kavanaugh to teach there would create a hostile environment. The complaint, they said, would give them "a right to our feeling of being safe."[28] And that students at Emory University protested chalkings on campus which said "Trump 2016." "I'm supposed to feel comfortable and safe," one student said. "I don't deserve to feel afraid at my school."[29] Threatened with protests, New York City's Lesbian, Gay, Bisexual and Transgender Community Center canceled a panel featuring conservatives who planned to encourage sexual minorities to "walk away" from the Democratic Party. "Permitting this event to proceed would make many of our community members feel unsafe," the center said.[30] Because emotional safetyism has no limiting principle, it can politicize literally everything and reach into every cranny of social life. Though it ran amok in left-wing precincts, it was a handy political weapon; conservatives, you could be sure, would in due course adopt it.

Emotional safetyism catastrophizes everyday interactions. An uproar at Yale was set off by a professor's email about students' Halloween costumes. Two members of Bowdoin College's student government faced impeachment proceedings because they attended a party where some guests wore tiny sombreros. In condemning the transgressors, the student government said it stood by "all students who were injured" because the incident had "create[d] an environment where students of color, particularly Latino, and especially Mexican . . . feel unsafe."[31] The concept of microaggressions turned life's everyday misunderstandings and faux pas into rights violations and traumas, reinterpreting ordinary interactions as assaults and encompassing—well, anything, including such statements as "Where are you from?" and "I believe the most qualified person should get the job."[32]

Emotional safetyism trivializes physical violence. If words are just as violent as bullets, then bullets are only as violent as words. We lose the vocabulary to distinguish between having an unpleasant verbal encounter and having your head broken. "It's violence to misgender or to alter a name of a trans person," said a questioner at a Democratic presidential debate in 2019, when the moderator accidentally mispronounced her name.[33] Senator Cotton's controversial *New York Times* article "wasn't just an opinion, it felt violent," one union activist at the paper said.[34] *Felt* violent? Millions of Americans, including countless minorities, know what violence feels like, and it does not feel like an op-ed piece in the *New York Times*.

Emotional safetyism excuses real violence. If words are violence, then using physical violence to silence a speaker is justifiable self-defense. "A scheduled February appearance [at the University of California at Berkeley] by right-wing provocateur Milo Yiannopoulos prompted masked agitators to throw Molotov cocktails, smash windows, hurl rocks at police, and ultimately cause $100,000 worth of damage," wrote the columnist Bari Weiss, in 2017. "The student newspaper ran an op-ed justifying the rioting under the headline 'Violence helped ensure safety of students.' Read that twice."[35] Yes, do. The author of the op-ed article wrote, "A peaceful protest was not going to cancel that event. . . . Only the destruction of glass and shooting of fireworks did that."[36] The author failed to mention that "people who were there said that protesters attacked them, beat them, pepper-sprayed them," and that at least four people who had shown up to attend the event were injured, two with concussions, broken or bruised ribs, cuts, and burns and welts from pepper spray.[37] Still, given the author's premise, his logic was sound. Physical violence had prevented emotional violence.

Emotional safetyism patronizes minorities. It assumes that we want to be "safe" from words or ideas; that we will wilt in the heat of an argument; that we need protection from "assaultive" words and should run to the authorities to get it. Homosexuals were stereotyped as weak ("pansy," "limp-wrist," "sissy," "fairy"), African Americans as childish, women as delicate. Gay people and other minorities fought for legal equality by joining arguments and winning them, and we fought for cultural equality by defeating the stereotype of weakness. The last thing we need is to resuscitate it. Thanks, but keep your emotional "protection."

Emotional safetyism distracts from the real problem. "We are not safe when these violent words are among us," the legal scholar Mari Matsuda wrote in 1993, as the equivalence of words and violence was gaining traction.[38] One imagined gangs of racist words swinging chains and smashing heads in back alleys. But false and harmful words are not the problem; false and harmful *ideas* are the problem, and suppressing them does not defeat them: demonstrating that they are false and replacing them with better ideas defeats them. Homosexuals did not win our battles for equality by censoring claims that we seduced children or were mentally ill or subverted the country's security; we won them by holding the false claims up to the light of evidence and argument. We won by correcting, not by coercing. Thank goodness we lacked the power to stifle our opponents; we needed to hear them in order to identify them, confront them, rebut them, and discredit them. Fighting ignorance and hate by chasing "words that wound" and trying to expunge "unsafe" talk is like fighting global warming by breaking all the thermometers. Hatred comes from fear and ignorance, and confronting reality, not hiding from it, is the answer.[39]

Emotional safetyism undermines pluralism. Diversity is inherently uncomfortable and sometimes emotionally unsafe. The genius of the Constitution of Knowledge is that it forces us—in a systematic, organized, and usually civilized way—to confront unfamiliar and unwelcome ideas, to contend with them, to compare them with our own. Physical safety is assuredly a civil right; but a right to feel safe from words or ideas is a right to criminalize giving offense. It creates a positive obligation to cleanse the world of emotional danger—and so of intellectual diversity.

In her 2001 convocation address, Ruth Simmons, the president of Brown University (and the first Black president of an Ivy League university), said this: "I won't ask you to embrace someone who offends your humanity through the exercise of free speech. But I would ask you to understand that the price of your own freedom is permitting the expression of such opinions. . . . I believe that learning at its best is the antithesis of comfort. The process of discovery need not make us feel good and secure." Just so. The process of social learning—creating knowledge—is good and heathy and important, but it cannot promise to be reassuring or affirming or safe.

Simmons's point, to be clear, was not that anyone should be gratuitously offensive. "We will not stop hoping that men and women will rise above gratuitously specious utterances," she said, "but even if they do not, we must fight with all the force within us to preserve their right to be heard even as we work hard to expose the error of their logic." The Constitution of Knowledge is far better than any alternative system at encouraging and institutionalizing civility, but it makes no guarantee. Civility, impersonality, and considerateness are best practices, not enforceable entitlements. As Salman Rushdie said, "What is freedom of expression? Without the freedom to offend, it ceases to exist."

The Rise of Cancel Culture

Emotional safetyism could not have achieved the cultural momentum that it did without an assist from the new technologies and tactics I described in the last two chapters. Later, the whole bundle would become known as canceling, but they were on the rise years before they won a nickname.

I began paying attention to canceling in 2014. Brandon Eich, a new chief executive of the internet company Mozilla, was fired after an outcry against him on social media. Eich had been appointed to lead the company on March 24, but activists, egged on by an online dating company which sensed a publicity bonanza, campaigned against him because in 2008, six years earlier, he had donated $1,000 to a ballot initiative overturning gay marriage in California. At the time of his donation, most Americans, including many liberals and Democrats (and presidential hopeful Barack Obama), opposed same-sex marriage. From the perspective of 2014, however, that was no excuse. Only eleven days after being appointed, Eich was dumped. Mozilla issued the customarily worded apology. "We're sorry. We must do better."

Legally speaking, activists had every right to criticize Eich, and Mozilla had every right to choose a chief executive who was not a magnet for controversy. Yet something seemed troubling—troubling enough so that I and dozens of other advocates of same-sex marriage wrote a public letter expressing our dismay. There was no evidence, we pointed out, that Eich "believed in or practiced any form of discrimination against Mozilla's LGBT employees. That would be a very different case. He was pressured to leave because of personal political actions he took at a time when a majority of the American public shared his view. . . . So the issue is clearly presented: is opposition to same-sex marriage by itself, expressed in a political campaign, beyond the pale of tolerable discourse in a free society?" If so, would every CEO be forced to agree with activists or risk losing her job?

We suspected, in 2014, that the Eich incident augured worse to come, but we did not foresee that social media could unleash a tsunami. That was evident after the 2013 incident involving the woman who tweeted a bad joke and, over the course of an airplane flight, became the subject of an international shaming campaign. She was an ordinary person, not a prominent CEO, but now ordinary people were in the crosshairs. When the journalist Jon Ronson interviewed people who had been targets of shaming campaigns, he found "everyday people pilloried brutally, most often for posting some poorly considered joke on social media. . . . The people I met were mostly unemployed, fired for their transgressions, and they seemed broken somehow—deeply confused and traumatized."[40]

It could happen to anyone, over anything. In 2020 a data analyst lost his job after tweeting an accurate summary of academic research about protest and voting behavior. Twitter users called him a racist, and employees and clients of his company complained that his tweet had threatened (of course) their safety. "Come get your boy," one accuser tweeted to the man's employer. The analyst apologized the next day: "I regret starting this conversation and will be more careful moving forward." To no avail. He was fired and kicked off a progressive listserv.[41]

In 2019 a former employee of a small coffee-roasting company in Portland, Oregon, discovered that Nancy Rommelmann, a writer and the wife of the company's owner, had co-anchored a podcast criticizing aspects of the #MeToo movement. The ex-employee emailed company employees and the media charging that Rommelmann's "vile, dangerous, and extremely misguided" views made the company potentially (what else?) unsafe. A group of the company's employees and alumni took the cue, sending Portland's news media a protest letter saying, "This cannot be tolerated." Hammers fell fast. "The staff quit and we couldn't hire people to replace them," Rommelmann told me. "They accused me of being dangerous to their physical safety." A vendor refused to service the company's machines because his wife was angry. The wholesale business collapsed. Two out of the company's four cafés closed. "My husband is devastated," Rommelmann told me in an interview. "He's trying desperately to sell the business." Eventually, the couple pulled up stakes and moved to New York City for a fresh start.[42]

As high-tech intimidation gained currency, it spread from one venue to the next. My own field, journalism, was not spared, as incidents at the *New York Times* and elsewhere revealed. In 2020, the curator of the San Francisco Museum of Modern Art told a staff meeting that to avoid collecting the work of white men would amount to "reverse discrimination." Soon afterward, according to an account in *Artnet News*, "a group of former employees who have been advocating for change at the museum created a petition calling for his resignation, which had been signed by 180 people as of publication time." In a social media post, the petitioners said, "His response included *violent language* [my italics] claiming 'reverse racism.' Gary must be removed from his job, effective immediately." The curator apologized for his "offensive term," promised to contribute to "true diversity"—and resigned, saying he could "no longer effectively work at SFMOMA."[43]

And, of course, academics were frequent targets, often of other academics. In 2018, during a visit to Rhodes College, in Memphis, Tennessee, I met a young philosopher named Rebecca Tuvel. The year before, she had published an article (peer reviewed—a serious piece of work) in *Hypatia*, a feminist philosophy journal, defending so-called transracialism: "Since we should accept transgender individuals' decisions to change sexes, we should also accept transracial individuals' decisions to change races." For a month the article went mostly unnoticed. But then a sociology graduate student found it and posted a denunciation on Facebook. "I refuse to allow this garbage to gain traction," wrote the grad student, although her next sentence acknowledged that she had not, in fact, read Tuvel's article. Another Facebook poster demanded that Tuvel "and her white supporters" pay reparations. By the end of the day, a Facebook commenter had escalated to the inevitable question: "Can we get this person fired?" Other social media activists chimed in, attacking the article as "wack shit" and "epistemic violence" and its author as transphobic, racist, crazy, stupid, and a Becky (a term of sexist abuse which also happened to be a diminutive of Tuvel's first name). The "words that wound" doctrine was invoked right on cue: Tuvel's article, one professor claimed, "enacts violence and perpetuates harm."[44] Hundreds of academics signed an open letter demanding, among other things, that *Hypatia* retract the article. As the journalist Jesse Singal and the philosopher Justin Weinberg documented at the time, the letter grossly mischaracterized Tuvel's article, suggesting that the letter's authors either had not read the piece or had chosen to distort it.[45] In an anguished public response, Tuvel responded:

> So much wrath on electronic media has been expressed in the form of ad hominem attacks. I have received hate mail. I have been denounced a horrible person by people who have never met me. I have been warned that this is a project I should not have started and can only have questionable motivations for writing. Many people are now strongly urging me and the journal to retract the article and issue an apology. They have cautioned me that not doing so would be devastating for me personally, professionally, and morally.
>
> So little of what has been said, however, is based upon people actually reading what I wrote. . . . I have never been under the illusion that this article is immune from critique. But the last place one expects to find such calls for censorship rather than discussion is amongst philosophers.[46]

Some academics privately told Tuvel they wished they could support her but could not stick their necks out; some were so fearful that they claimed privately to be on her side but signed the public condemnation anyway.

Nothing in Tuvel's years of training had prepared her for the onslaught; nothing could have. Her first instinct was to leave academia. She did not leave, but, she told me, "I developed a newfound respect for how brutal it is to be the receiving end of a social media pile-on. The psychological impact was far more significant than I ever would have anticipated. I was made to feel I did something absolutely horrific. I wanted to disappear. The shame cut deep."

Khomeini Showed the Way

I could list more examples of high-tech thought vigilantism, but if you were reading the newspapers you saw more than enough. Each was unique in its details, but they had a distinct family resemblance. Their ideology might have flowed mostly from the political left, but their tactics had a forebear in the granddaddy of cancelations.

Khomeini's 1989 campaign to cancel Rushdie and *The Satanic Verses* aimed, of course, at the most literal kind of cancelation, physical assassination. Its modern descendants used a more sophisticated (and legal) approach, that of character assassination. Launching a campaign against a graduate student who defended studying racial differences in intelligence, a professor tweeted that his intent was to "ruin his [the student's] reputation permanently and deservedly."[47] The goal is to turn the target into a pariah, shunned by employers and professional connections and polite society. Jonathan Kaiman, a journalist who was targeted in a successful pressure campaign, lost his job, his book contract, and his standing in the professional organization he had led. He found himself unemployable as a journalist and, when I spoke to him, was hoping to go to law school. "It really is absolutely cataclysmic," he told me. "Some people rebound, but very few. Most people wind up just flat on their backs." Long after the vigilantes move on, their targets may find themselves shunned or blacklisted. Often their life trajectories are altered permanently, as Rushdie's was. When he was approached at a social function by an aspiring writer who told him *The Satanic Verses* had changed her life, he replied, "Well, that's good, because it ruined mine."[48]

Notice a detail of the Tuvel case discussed above: the campaigners did not feel any need to read the work they were campaigning against. The same was true in the Rushdie affair. Virtually none of his denouncers had read *The Satanic Verses*. Few even bothered to read extracts. Many of them, like the graduate student who launched the campaign against Tuvel, acknowledged or even bragged about not reading what they were supposedly protesting. "I do not have to wade through a filthy drain to know what filth is," a member of India's parliament said.[49]

Just so. Canceling is not fundamentally about the ideas or even the people it targets; it is about virtue signaling and bonding with your group: making a public show of defending sacred values against some perceived threat or impurity. "There is something dark and vaguely cultish about this particular brand of politics," a young queer activist named Yarrow Eady wrote in a perceptive article in McGill University's student newspaper in 2014. "Groupthink becomes the modus operandi. When I was part of groups like this, everyone was on exactly the same page about a suspiciously large range of issues. Internal disagreement was rare. The insular community served as an incubator of extreme, irrational views."[50]

As with online outrage, so also with canceling: the ostensible target, whether a person like Rushdie or Tuvel or a piece of work like *The Satanic Verses* or Tuvel's article, is not the campaign's real subject at all, but rather a convenient object for a show of group solidarity. If Rushdie had not come along, some other target might have served just as well. In the summer of 2020, almost 600 "members of the linguistic community," as they called themselves, sent a letter to the Linguistic Society of America demanding that Steven Pinker, a prominent Harvard linguist, be removed from "both our list of distinguished academic fellows and our list of media experts." They could not cite any examples of professional misconduct or assert plausibly that Pinker was not distinguished or expert. Instead, they had combed through Pinker's writings and Twitter feed and come up with a handful of complaints which were trivial if not absurd (Pinker had used the phrase "urban crime," had cited a Black scholar on the decline of overt racism, had described a public shooter as "mild-mannered," and so on). The indictment's arbitrariness—one might comfortably say silliness—was part of its point: "No one engaged in public life could be confident of avoiding speech that might be deemed problematic by the standards used in the Pinker letter," wrote Conor Friedersdorf in *The Atlantic*.[51]

Pinker was a tenured professor with a national following, too big to take down—but that, too, was part of the point. In an important respect, the ostensible target—Steven Pinker—was not the campaign's real target, or at least not its main target. The real target was the onlooking audience of much less powerful people who understood that they might be next, and that if Pinker could be targeted, certainly they could be. "This letter wasn't really about Pinker at all," wrote a graduate student named Shaun Cammack. "In fact, it has a very specific function—to dissuade lesser-known academics and students from questioning the ideological consensus. . . . There are 575 people opposing Pinker for his views, and in the small world of academia that signals an extraordinarily high cost to dissent."[52] Pinker would be fine, but the smaller fry would get the intended message, which was to steer a wide berth around disapproved ideas or thinkers.

The targeted person's first instinct will be to apologize, whether out of shame or just to get her normal life back. But because the campaign's objective is not to persuade her but to make an example of her, apologizing rarely helps. In fact, it backfires, proving to the shamers that their outrage was justified and that their tactics are working.[53] Rushdie's expression of "profound regret" brought this response from Khomeini: "Even if Salman Rushdie repents and becomes the most pious man of all time, it is incumbent on every Muslim to employ everything he has got, his life and wealth, to send him to hell."

Because canceling is performative—a show one puts on for one's social group—rather than argumentative, it has no interest in evaluating an idea. Normally, it has no real interest in ideas at all. For that reason, there is literally no telling what might trigger a campaign. No one could have predicted that Khomeini would alight on Salman Rushdie's obscure novel and turn it into a global crisis. Or that Tuvel's article or Rommelmann's podcast would trigger firestorms. In 2020, literally overnight, a family-owned Middle Eastern food business in Minneapolis found itself facing boycotts, doxing, death threats, and more after someone found racist tweets by the owner's daughter— from eight years earlier, when she was a troubled fourteen-year-old. "In a matter of hours, a family that I had known as warm, open-minded, and dedicated to using food to bridge the differences among Jews, Arabs, and all people became infamous as the most racist Muslims in the Midwest," wrote one observer.[54] Think of the unfortunate data analyst who tweeted out an accurate description of reputable scientific work. No one could have predicted the uproar and his subsequent firing, and that, really, was the point.

Once a campaign is triggered, it is open ended; the originators can commence it but not control it. Khomeini decreed that the campaign against *The Satanic Verses* should begin by murdering Rushdie, but he let the mob decide where it might end. Legalistically, Iran argued that the decree became irrevocable when Khomeini died; but even if Khomeini had lived to change his mind there was no guarantee that his inflamed vigilantes would stand down. The same is true with a modern cancel campaign: once a pile-on begins, how long it may last and how far it may go is anyone's guess. The pillory, which for centuries was a staple of official punishment in the United States and many other places, was eventually banned partly because courts could not control the amount of abuse which passing villagers meted out; some victims were jeered, others pelted with excrement, and others killed. Canceling, likewise, can turn out to be anything from a nuisance for the victim to a career-ending catastrophe, without rhyme or reason or predictability, depending on the ebb and flow of mob justice.

Secondary boycotts (a prominent feature of McCarthyism in the 1950s) are among cancel culture's most characteristic hallmarks: would-be defenders, friends, and employers of the main target are implicitly warned that they could share the same fate. So might anyone who criticizes the cancelers. Khomeini condemned not only Rushdie and his book but "all the editors and publishers aware of its contents." Among the many killed were two Muslims living in Belgium who had expressed reservations about Khomeini's edict. No wonder, then, that even sympathetic colleagues and friends are reluctant to support a target of canceling; they are frightened, and rightly so. Just as important, potential employers and associates also join the boycott. "I'm operating on the assumption that the corporate world is closed to me," Jonathan Kaiman, the canceled ex-journalist, said. "One thing I realized very quickly when I was being canceled is that your relationships aren't contingent on what individuals think of you; they're contingent on what individuals think *other* individuals think of you. The punishment is that stigma, and it's a stigma that might never fade."

Notice, too, that cancel campaigns reduce a human individual to a single point in time, a single incident, often yanked out of context or deliberately distorted. Whereas critical culture weighs the totality of a person's character and career in evaluating her credibility, cancel culture does the opposite. Any scholar or public figure who has been mobbed over a single tweet or a misleadingly quoted line of text knows that reducing an entire career to one complaint is the most frustrating and unfair aspect of canceling—and that protesting "Read it in context!" or "Look at what else I've written!" does no good at all. Nor did it do Rushdie any good to point to his distinguished career as a novelist who had assumed many voices and expressed many ideas. His record counted for nothing against the supposed transgression he had allegedly committed in a couple of passages in a book which his cancelers had not even bothered to read.

Cancel campaigns are not interested in fair criticism or persuasion. They want to isolate, intimidate, and demoralize. If a campaign can drive its targets from polite society, then it can spoof people's consensus detectors and seed a spiral of silence. Some people will fall for the spoof and accept the apparent judgment of the crowd. Others will remain inwardly skeptical but, as Tocqueville said, "yield and return to silence."

Am I Canceling You Right Now?

But wait. Might not the indictment of "cancelation" itself be a kind of canceling? Didn't I just insist that words are not bullets? But here I am, condemning as "cancelers" people who are merely engaging in criticism. Sure, death threats and harassment should be off limits. What happened to Rushdie was totally unacceptable. But someone who makes controversial statements should expect to be criticized. If a lot of people are appalled by something, shouldn't they speak up against it? Isn't that the whole point of free speech? Even demands for someone's firing are expressions of opinion; why shouldn't Brandon Eich's critics say he is unfit to lead Mozilla, if that is what they think?

Therefore (continues the argument) the whole idea of cancelation is at best meaningless, at worst just another way to shut down debate. "Government inhibition of speech is wrong, full stop," wrote Elizabeth Picciuto, when the public conversation about canceling reached a boiling point in 2020. "Threatened and actual violence in retaliation for speech are wrong, full stop. Firings, deplatformings, and social stigma for self-expression are not always wrong. They are wrong on a case-by-case basis."[55] Hannah Giorgis, another writer, put the point concisely: "Critical tweets are not censorship."[56]

Giorgis and Picciuto had a point. To address it, we must be a bit more specific about what canceling—or coercive conformity, as I think of it—is and is not. Both criticism and coercive conformity take the form of people arguing about something, but they belong to very different worlds. Criticism expresses arguments or evidence with the goal of influencing opinion through rational persuasion. It belongs to the realm of truth-seeking. Canceling belongs to the realm of propaganda warfare: like other forms of information warfare, it seeks to organize and manipulate a social or media environment to demoralize, deplatform, isolate, or intimidate an adversary. Like disinformation and trolling, its interest is not in discovering knowledge but in shaping the information battlefield.

In practice, the line between criticizing someone and canceling her can be fuzzy and subjective, and we will sometimes have to argue about where to draw it. Reasonable people could dispute whether the firing of the *Times* op-ed editor showed intolerance or reasonable editorial judgment. Shouting "canceling!" profligately makes you part of the problem and turns "Who's shaming whom?" into a finger-pointing contest. ("Remember," the journalist Jesse Singal quipped, "the way to fight the shaming of online shamers is to shame the shamers' shamers!")

One could grant that point and still recognize that, in principle, criticizing and canceling are different kinds of things, pointing to very different values. Criticism seeks to engage in conversations and identify error; canceling seeks to stigmatize conversations and punish the errant. Criticism cares whether statements are true; canceling cares about their social effects. Criticism exploits viewpoint diversity; canceling imposes viewpoint conformity. Criticism is a substitute for social punishment (we kill our hypotheses rather than each other); canceling is a form of social punishment (we kill your hypothesis by killing you socially). Criticism reflects the values of the Constitution of Knowledge, seeking to inquire and learn. Canceling reflects the values of propaganda, seeking to manipulate the information environment.

How to tell the difference? When are you being canceled, as opposed to criticized? Here are some good diagnostic indicators:

- **Punitiveness:** Does what is being said to or about you have the goal or foreseeable effect of jeopardizing your livelihood or isolating you socially? Are people denouncing you to your employer, your professional groups, your social connections? Are you being blacklisted from jobs and social opportunities? The Constitution of Knowledge punishes the idea, not the person; cancel culture punishes the person, not the idea.

- **Deplatforming:** Are campaigners attempting to prevent you from publishing your work, giving speeches, attending meetings? Are they claiming that allowing you to be heard is violence or makes them unsafe? The Constitution of Knowledge relies on diversity of expression; cancel culture prevents it.

- **Grandstanding:** Is the tone of the discourse ad hominem, ritualistic, posturing, accusatory, outraged? Are people flattening distinctions, demonizing you, slinging inflammatory labels, and engaging in moral one-upsmanship? Are people ignoring what you actually said and talking about you but not to you? The Constitution of Knowledge rewards careful, rational argumentation; cancel culture rewards demagoguery.

- **Reductionism:** Are you being condemned on the basis of one or two things you may have said or done, taken in isolation and shorn of context? Are people collapsing the totality of your character and career down to a single mistake or offense, without regard for your other contributions and accomplishments? The Constitution of Knowledge builds reputational credibility over decades; cancel culture demolishes it overnight.

- **Orchestration:** Does criticism appear to be organized and targeted? Are the organizers recruiting others to pile on? Are you being swarmed and brigaded? Are people hunting through your work and scouring social media to find ammunition to use against you? The Constitution of Knowledge relies on independent observers; cancel culture relies on mob action.

- **Secondary boycotts:** Is there an explicit or implicit threat that anyone who supports you will get the same treatment that you are receiving? Are people putting pressure on employers and professional colleagues to fire you or stop associating with you? Do people who defend you, or criticize the campaign against you, have to fear adverse consequences? The Constitution of Knowledge relies on independent judgment; cancel culture relies on bullying.

- **Inaccuracy:** Are the things being said about you incorrect? Do the people saying them seem not even to care about veracity? Do they feel at liberty to distort your words, ignore corrections, and make false accusations? The Constitution of Knowledge puts accuracy ahead of politics; cancel culture puts politics ahead of accuracy.

The more of those information-warfare tactics you are encountering, the surer you can be that you are being canceled, not criticized. Most of the time, in real life, the difference will not be hard to see.

"You're Going to Get Your Ass in Trouble"

As with disinformation and trolling, so also with cancel campaigns: underestimating their strength is a mistake, but so is overestimating their strength. Like terrorism, they work by inspiring disproportionate fear. Campaigns can fail, especially if their targets—individual and institutional—have backbones. Rebecca Tuvel, for instance, was not fired or punished. Her department and her university's administration stood behind her. *Hypatia* refused to retract her paper. Prominent academics came forward to condemn the attacks on her, and she received, she reckoned, a thousand supportive emails. In due course, she received tenure and became chair of her department. Perhaps most significant: after weathering her crisis, she found new strength. "I was always an ardent defender of academic freedom and free speech," she told me. "I'm even more so in the wake of all of this, because I appreciate just how grave the threat to those values is nowadays."

I asked her to elaborate. Call-out campaigns are "nauseatingly predictable," she said, "especially if you're white and publishing something controversial related to race, or cisgender and publishing on trans issues. I know professors who will not touch certain topics with a ten-foot pole in the classroom for fear of getting a report filed against them. Self-censorship is everywhere. It's a serious problem that makes me concerned for the future of academia."

As I spoke with academics and university students, I lost count of the number who echoed Tuvel's worry. In journalism and law and certain other sectors of the reality-based community, coercive conformity had made inroads, but in universities it was reconfiguring the whole intellectual landscape, for students and professors alike. As a professor told me, "There is no bigger filter bubble than any selective university in the United States. It is definitely the case that at these institutions, which are supposed to be founded on the idea of a marketplace of ideas, there are all kinds of expressions you can't say now. Anything that relates to race or gender, you had best keep your mouth shut if you have a point of view that deviates from the predominant woke one. You're going to get your ass in trouble."

Surveying professors is challenging from a statistical point of view, because samples tend to be small and representativeness is hard to ensure. Still, available evidence suggested that "you're going to get your ass in trouble" was a very common sentiment. When Aaron Kindsvatter, a University of Vermont professor who teaches graduate students to become psychotherapists and counselors, surveyed professors in his field, fewer than a third said they would feel secure disagreeing in the classroom with prevalent views on race, sexuality, gender, social class, or religion. Two-thirds or more said they were at least "a little" concerned that having an open class conversation on such topics could result in their being reported to authorities, receiving bad course evaluations, suffering damage to their reputations and careers, and being shunned by colleagues; around a fourth said they were "extremely" or "very" concerned. Yet almost 90 percent of the professors agreed that exposure to adverse views, even if sometimes offensive, benefits students.[57] In other words, many professors were frightened to teach in the way they thought best for their students. They felt pressured to shortchange their students and themselves. "I used to say things in class just to be provocative—because I think the university is not a place where one should feel intellectually comfortable," one professor told me. "I never do that anymore because I don't want to deal with a dozen complaints to the dean."

Where students were concerned, the evidence of widespread chilling was beyond dispute. In 2018 a Gallup poll found that 61 percent of students said their campus climate prevented some people from

saying things they believed because others might find them offensive—an increase of seven percentage points over 2016, only two
years before.[58] A 2019 poll by the Knight Foundation found more
than two-thirds of students saying their campus climate precluded
students from expressing their true opinions because their classmates
might find them offensive.[59] Other surveys returned similar results.[60]

Actually, self-censoring was almost as prevalent off-campus.
Among Americans generally, according to a 2020 poll by the libertarian Cato Institute, 62 percent said that the political climate prevented
them from saying things they believed because others might find
them offensive—an increase of four percentage points over 2017.[61]
That was disturbing, to say the least. But there was this difference:
the whole point of higher education is to practice and teach critical
inquiry by testing and contesting ideas and opinions, and the university's charge is to create an environment where contestation can
happen freely and openly, *especially* about controversial issues. The
chilling of the intellectual climate on campuses and in classrooms
represented not just an unfortunate social development but a cata-
strophic failure of universities to defend and fulfill their mission. It
was a breach of their promise to their students and to the Constitution of Knowledge.

Students felt the chill and were unhappy about it. "Students across
the political spectrum want more opportunities to engage with those
who think differently," a study by three professors at the University
of North Carolina at Chapel Hill reported in 2020.[62] In that survey, a
plurality of *liberal* students at the school said there were too few conservative speakers. A progressive student at a leading East Coast liberal arts college told me, "I have not had as many conversations from
different ends of the spectrum as I'd like to." (She consoled herself
that she had been exposed to a variety of left-wing views.) A student
at a California college bemoaned "the inability for many individuals
to have necessary conversations with one another," adding that there
were so many politically correct tripwires that "many students choose
to forgo conversation altogether in order to avoid causing harm or offense." A student at a major research university told me, "On today's
college campus, the risks of engaging in debate of controversial topics
vastly outweigh the benefits. It's fascinating to see how, in order to

avoid social repercussions, many students are censoring themselves and just repeating the belief of the group in order to not stand out. Why would you counter a point when you know you are going to be judged, shamed, and maybe ridiculed for holding it?" Universities, and especially elite universities, were becoming sinkholes of socially enforced conformity: Mill's nightmare.

There was no mystery about the main source of the chilling. And it was not, chiefly, "tenured radicals" on the faculty. Aggressively politicized professors and administrators sometimes did shame or persecute conservatives (and liberals), but they were the exception, not the rule. In the Chapel Hill survey, most students (liberals and conservatives alike) said that professors were generally open-minded and encouraging of participation across the political spectrum. Students at Chapel Hill reported worrying more about censure from fellow students than from faculty. When the 2019 poll by Heterodox Academy asked students why they were reluctant to express their opinions, more than 60 percent cited the worry that other students would criticize their views as offensive, versus fewer than half who cited criticism from professors or fear of receiving a lower grade.[63] Students I interviewed said the same thing: they perceived most professors, including most left-wing professors, as bending over backward to encourage debate. "The professors are pretty open to hearing these [conservative] ideas and are even willing to throw opposing ideas at students to spark those conversations," a student at a liberal arts college told me. "It's really outside the classroom where you have the peer pressure against those ideas and voices."

What students were chiefly afraid of was social exclusion and moral rejection. Students were frightened, mainly, by each other. They feared social death—a fate which frightens humans, very often, more than physical death.

"It's the Unasked Questions"

In academia, the chilling of expression among students and faculty was one sign that the Constitution of Knowledge was in trouble. The distortion of scholarship was another.

In 2015 a group of five social psychologists and a sociologist

raised an alarm. In an article titled "Political Diversity Will Improve Social Psychological Science," José Duarte, Jarret Crawford,
Charlotta Stern, Jonathan Haidt, Lee Jussim, and Philip Tetlock announced some striking findings. Already left-leaning in the late twentieth century, social psychologists had become overwhelmingly so in
the twenty-first. "The field is shifting leftward," they said; "the ratio
of liberals to conservatives is now greater than 10:1, and there are
hardly any conservatives in the pipeline."[64] Other surveys found even
more lopsided ratios. In 2016 a survey of members of the Society for
Experimental Social Psychology found that, among 326 respondents,
the number identifying as right of center was . . . eight.[65] The lack of
ideological diversity, the six authors said in 2015, was creating blind
spots and generating flawed research. "If left unchecked, an academic
field can become a cohesive moral community, creating a shared reality that subsequently blinds its members to morally or ideologically
undesirable hypotheses and unanswered but important scientific
questions," they wrote. For example, they continued, researchers
into unethical behavior were defining it according to progressive notions of feminism and environmentalism. (Not automatically taking
a female colleague's side in her sexual harassment complaint was
"unethical," for instance, as was a worker's placing the well-being of
her company ahead of unspecified harms to the environment.) Other
researchers made false assumptions about conservatives or assumed
that prejudice was the exclusive domain of the right. "Political discrimination is a reality in social psychology," the authors said. The
cost was borne by disadvantaged conservative scholars, to be sure,
but also by social psychology itself. "More political diversity would
help the system discover more truth," they concluded bluntly.

By the latter part of that decade, the evidence was incontrovert-
ible. Viewpoint diversity was an endangered species in many academic fields, especially the social sciences and humanities. According
to periodic surveys by the Higher Education Research Institute (at
the University of California at Los Angeles), the share of professors identifying as conservative—after a long decline—had fallen to
under 12 percent by 2017, and moderates (who had accounted for
40 percent in 1990) had declined to 28 percent. The slack had been
picked up by professors identifying as liberal (48 percent) and far left

(12 percent). That still left a fair salting of conservatives and moderates in academia as a whole, but in some disciplines non-liberals were almost entirely absent. A study of voter registration patterns among more than 8,000 professors in fifty-two schools found about five Democrats for every Republican in chemistry, economics, and math—but seventeen Democrats for every Republican in psychology, history, and philosophy, and upward of forty Democrats for each Republican in sociology, English, and anthropology, among others. (In anthropology, among fifty-six respondents, the number of Republicans was zero.)[66] A study of faculty voter registration in five fields (economics, history, journalism, law, and psychology) found a ratio of twelve Democrats to each Republican; in more than 40 percent of academic departments, Republican registrants were as scarce as registrants of minor parties, if not scarcer. Conservatives in the social sciences were much more underrepresented than were, say, Blacks or women.[67] Although data on university administrators were harder to come by, administrators appeared to be even more lopsidedly left-leaning than faculty.[68]

The problem was not that progressivism was a wrongheaded ideology; no one doubted that it contributes valuably to scholarship. Nor, even, was the problem that leftists were particularly prone to excluding the other side. It was true that conservative scholars experienced discrimination; progressive scholars often openly acknowledged discriminating. "In decisions ranging from paper reviews to hiring, many social and personality psychologists said that they would discriminate against openly conservative colleagues," wrote Yoel Inbar and Joris Lammers in a 2012 study. "The more liberal respondents were, the more they said they would discriminate."[69] When they looked more closely, though, researchers found that academic ideologues of both sides were about equally likely to discriminate against the other, if given the opportunity. One study of academic philosophers found that a significant minority of scholars on both the left and the right openly acknowledged willingness to discriminate against the opposite ideology.[70] Another study, of faculty members at four California State University campuses, found that "both liberals and conservatives expressed a similar explicit willingness to discriminate against each other," with anywhere from about a fifth to almost half of academics saying they would prefer to hire someone who shared their politics (depending on the discipline).[71]

As left-leaning academics grew in preponderance, however, they increasingly were in a position to discriminate in ways which conservative academics could not—thereby accelerating the disappearance of conservatives. "The problem is not progressivism," wrote Jon A. Shields and Joshua M. Dunn Sr. "It is the absence of conservatives from many important domains of inquiry."[72] Academia had long leaned to the left, as William F. Buckley had famously complained in his 1951 polemic, *God and Man at Yale.* In 1969, before the modern culture wars commandeered campuses, only a minority of professors, 27 percent, were right of center.[73] If, however, a fourth of your colleagues were conservative, you could expect to encounter at least some conservatives as you conducted research, submitted to journals, and underwent peer review and performance evaluations. You would need to contend with their views. By the 2010s, however, the diversity drought had reached the point where an academic might go through her entire professional life, from training to tenure and beyond, in a conservative-free bubble. Writing in *Quillette* in 2019, the cultural and political historian Christopher Dummitt recounted that in his graduate training he assumed that gender was a social construct because there seemed to be no other view on the matter.

> I never engaged—at least not seriously—with anyone who suggested otherwise. And no one, at any point of my graduate studies, or in peer review, ever did suggest otherwise—except in conversations, usually outside of academia. And so I was never forced to confront alternative, biologically oriented explanations that were at least as plausible as the hypothesis that I'd dressed up with the air of certainty. . . . The only real criticisms I received were admonitions to strengthen the paradigm.[74]

No wonder results were often distorted. Researchers found bias-related flaws in, among other disciplines, psychology, sociology, gender studies, and philosophy. Looking at the social sciences broadly, Cory J. Clark and Bo M. Winegard found evidence of a pervasive, often unquestioned ideology they called equalitarianism, which attributed all group inequalities to prejudice and discrimination.[75] Undoubtedly, prejudice and discrimination harm groups and deserve to be called out. But, wrote Clark and Winegard, "when the majority of scientists in a discipline share the same sacred values, then the checks and balances of peer review and peer skepticism that science relies upon can fail. Peer review, critical engagement, skepticism, and the other virtues of science . . . become tyrants that promote and protect the sacred values of the scientific community."[76]

More insidious than the distortions which were apparent were the hypotheses never entertained, the research never undertaken: losses to knowledge which were literally inestimable. "It's the unasked questions," one professor told me. "There are certain topics you hesitate to go near out of fear you'll be ostracized, you'll be cut off from the herd."

The decline of diversity did not infect all fields, all students, all professors (though it probably infected most universities to some significant degree). Academia still produced excellent research—by volume, surely more than ever. But zombification had proceeded far enough, and long enough, to have corrupted whole departments and disciplines, and to have distorted and politicized whole fields of research. "It is unfortunately true that a good deal of social science today is unreliable, due to its infection by political ideology," wrote the epistemologist Lee McIntyre. "Even in universities, in some fields there is no clear line between 'research' and political advocacy."[77] Ominously, there were signs that the collapse of diversity was propagating itself across generations. Research by the political scientists Kenneth B. McIntyre and Stacy G. Ulbig found that the more time left-of-center and minority students spent on a university campus, the more their support for viewpoint diversity declined. The effect was not particularly large, but, the authors commented, "the mere fact that students become less rather than more supportive of the free exchange of ideas the longer they spend on the university campus does not bode well for the future of liberal education in America."[78]

Tyranny of the Few

But here arises a puzzle. Most students do not want to drive conservatives from campus and most professors do not want to discriminate against conservatives. Most students do not want to go to college to hear only one point of view and most professors do not want to politicize their classes. Most scholars have not abandoned the tenets of intellectual pluralism and do not want their research to be distorted or chilled.

For all the talk of leftist hegemony on American university campuses, 22 percent of students were self-reported conservatives in 2019, and a fifth were Republicans, according to the Heterodox Academy poll. Another fifth were self-described moderates. The share identifying as liberal was 42 percent, a plurality but not a majority; the "very liberal" share was only an eighth. On elite campuses, especially the liberal arts colleges, the ultra-liberal share was probably higher. Even so, anecdotal and survey evidence suggested that the hard-core intolerant represented a distinct minority, even of liberals. At Chapel Hill, fewer than a quarter of self-identified liberal students said that the school would be better off without conservative students, or that they would not have a conservative student as a friend. In the 2018 Gallup survey, 10 percent of students said that violence was acceptable at least sometimes as a way to keep controversial speakers from being heard, and 37 percent said the same of shouting speakers down—figures which were far too high, but which still represented numbers well short of majorities.[79] Surveying the scene at Chapel Hill, the researchers there concluded, "Although we document ways in which political hostility emerges disproportionately from the political left at UNC, this hostility often comes from a *minority* of campus liberals."[80]

Here again, my interviews were consistent with the surveys. "I don't know many people, not many students, even, who are in the camp of wanting to shout down people or deny speakers," David C. Barker, a political scientist at American University, told me. "I think that the very intolerant mindset from the left reflects a small minority of students, and certainly of faculty." Many people on campus, students and faculty alike, had mixed feelings about free speech, supporting it more in the abstract than when asked about hard cases like (alleged) racism or hate speech—an ambivalence which is an eternal characteristic of public attitudes about free speech, on campus and off. The hard-core intolerant, though, were a much smaller group. "Truly illiberal tendencies are limited to about 20 percent of college students," wrote *The Economist* in 2017.[81]

How could a minority silence and chill so many, to the point of torpedoing universities' entire mission? An answer comes from an improbable quarter: political economics. A field known as "public choice" concerns itself with the ways in which narrow pressure groups can out-organize and dominate much larger majorities. Consider American rice farmers. From 1995 to 2019, U.S. rice subsidies cost almost $17 billion.[82] The benefits were concentrated on a small set of farms; two-thirds of the money went to the biggest 10 percent of the farms, each of which received an average of almost $1.3 million. You could be sure they were organized, resourced, and determined to defend their subsidy, and woe unto the legislator who would try to zero it out. Meanwhile, the cost was spread over the whole U.S. population. Rescinding the entire amount would have saved each of about 140 million taxpayers about $120 over the period, or less than five dollars a year: too little to notice, much less to organize against. If a group opposing rice subsidies did manage to organize, the rice lobby would pull out all the stops to defeat it. But usually, as the economist Mancur Olson showed, the asymmetry between concentrated benefits and diffused costs is such that the majority interest does not organize at all. Over time, pressure groups accumulate, capturing resources which might have flowed elsewhere. If the process is not checked, entire economies and societies can calcify and rot.[83]

The same public-choice arithmetic applies in the epistemic economy. Once organized, intellectual pressure groups capture resources and influence. They impose taboos, guard sacred beliefs, dominate hiring and tenure decisions, and build administrative empires, all of which accumulate over time, distorting and calcifying the intellectual economy. As the groups become more entrenched and better resourced, they can make challenging them very painful. Understandably, most people do not bother. "You just don't want to be the next one," a professor (at a relatively conservative college) told me.

"It's so much easier to avoid. The anecdotes are enough to frighten a lot of people. You can wind up eating your faculty lunches alone. Just sort of cut off. Before we express a view, we put out our antennae. You figure out is it safe in this room or this environment to express my views, and if you don't think it is, you shut up."

Over time, as taboos and dogmas pile up on one side of the argument, spirals of silence form. Another professor said, "There's a small group of very vocal, very active students who are attempting to restructure societal systems and will engage in a kind of retribution. Oftentimes the way they do that is what they report in, say, course evaluations. They will write things that are very liable to be investigated. It's a little difficult to tell where my paranoia begins and their intention to get revenge comes into play. It's just getting so difficult to talk about anything, whether it's related to politics or not, that I feel I am constantly tiptoeing through a minefield." His metaphor reminded me of members of Congress who complain about the difficulty of legislating while trying to pick their way through minefields of interest groups.

The point is not that any particular group of activists or their cause is good or bad or right or wrong. All pressure groups, whether they are rice growers or minority-rights advocates, believe they are on the side of the angels, and they may be right. No one doubts that progressive perspectives have enriched academia and contributed valuably to knowledge. The problem arises when *other* groups and *other* ideas are absent or silent or fail to organize. To say it the Millian way: the problem arises where lack of contestation hardens even true opinions into dogmas. To say it the Madisonian way: the problem arises where the republic of science becomes too small, intellectually speaking— when its sphere contracts instead of extending.

Importantly, there has been significant support, including from the left, for extending the sphere. Some of the sharpest critiques of ideological monocultures in academia came from within academia. "I have been raising a fuss about these issues since 2011," Jonathan Haidt, a prominent voice for expanding intellectual diversity, wrote in 2016:

In that time I also moved from the left to the center, politically. I am no longer a progressive. So you might expect that I've been ostracized, but I have not. Nothing bad has happened to me. Some of my colleagues believe that the political imbalance is not a problem. But the majority response has been, roughly: "This is really interesting. We really, truly value diversity, and we agree with you and your co-authors that diversity of viewpoints is the kind that confers the most benefits on groups. But gosh, how are we going to get more?"[84]

Similarly, most Americans, including most left-leaning Americans, do not want to see debate chilled and speech policed. A poll in 2018 found 80 percent of Americans, including 74 percent aged twenty-four to twenty-nine, agreeing that "political correctness is a problem in our country." A solid majority of traditional liberals thought political correctness was a problem; the only group which did not think it was a problem was progressive activists, who made up only 8 percent of the population.[85]

Both inside the reality-based community and in the public at large, the Constitution of Knowledge still had large numbers of supporters. The question was how to mobilize them to push back.

8

Unmute Yourself: Pushing Back

Defending the Constitution of Knowledge
requires confidence and counter-mobilization

On a January day in 1838, a young lawyer—only twenty-eight but ambitious and talented beyond his years and humble origins—took the stage at the Young Men's Lyceum in Springfield, Illinois, for what history would remember as his first great speech. The topic, "The perpetuation of our political institutions," was no mere abstraction to Abraham Lincoln, or to his audience. James Madison, the last titan of the founding generation, had gone to his grave almost two years before; the last signer of the Declaration of Independence, Charles Carroll, had died in 1832. The revolutionaries who had built the republic "were a forest of giant oaks," said Lincoln. "They are gone." He and his generation were on their own, inheritors of a precarious experiment.

Could they sustain it? Lincoln was worried. Democracy's enemies, he warned, were not without but within. "If destruction be our lot, we must ourselves be its author and finisher," he said. "There is even now something of ill omen amongst us." Around the country, mobs had taken justice into their own hands, lynching Blacks who were suspected of fomenting insurrections and whites who were accused of gambling. "The innocent . . . alike with the guilty fall victim to the ravages of mob law." Without the wise and restraining influence of the Founders, how could the country preserve the Constitution, which requires ordinary people to exercise wisdom and restraint?

Two things were needed, Lincoln said. First, every American should respect and revere the law. "Let reverence for the law be breathed by every American mother to the lisping babe that prattles on her lap." (Lincoln's style had yet to achieve the biblical cadence and Euclidian concision of his maturity.) Reverence for the law must "become the political religion of the nation." Even unjust laws should be obeyed until they can be changed.

Yet the people must defend the law with their heads as well as their hearts. They must trace out and master the Constitution's logic—lest, as J. S. Mill would put it a generation later, the principles underlying the Constitution become dead dogmas rather than living truths. "Reason—cold, calculating, unimpassioned reason—must furnish all the materials for our future support and defense," said Lincoln.

Almost by definition, a religion—even a political religion, in Lincoln's phrase—is something we do not subject to cold, calculating, unimpassioned reason. By calling for Americans to regard the Constitution with both religious devotion and analytical rigor, Lincoln's demands seemed contradictory, and the breakdown he feared came to pass, during his own presidency. Yet since then, Americans have filled his assignment surprisingly well. They revere the Constitution, yet they debate it constantly and sometimes criticize it unsparingly. As Lincoln hoped, by using their hearts and their heads, Americans have kept their experiment alive long past the age when most democracies die.

And how has the Constitution of Knowledge fared? It too, faces challenges not only from enemies on the outside but from corruption and complacency within. It, too, demands both reverence and reason. Members of the reality-based community must pursue truth passionately while remaining coolly mindful of its elusiveness. They must search for knowledge boldly while accepting that on most days all they will find are mistakes. They must believe that knowledge is knowable and facts are factual while also remembering that even the most obvious certainties might be wrong. They must commit themselves wholeheartedly to the Constitution of Knowledge while acknowledging its limits and the limits of those who uphold it.

Again, the answer must be: the Constitution of Knowledge has fared surprisingly well. The reality-based community manages to revere and follow the Constitution of Knowledge without viewing it mystically or uncritically. The growth and success of the reality-based community speak for themselves. To feel awestruck, one need only think about the global mobilization of brainpower against COVID-19. As I said in chapter 1, the Constitution of Knowledge has faced constant challenge, and its advocates need to wake up every morning and justify its very existence from scratch—today, tomorrow, and forever. Yet here it is, bigger and more capable than ever.

Still, the Constitution of Knowledge does not just take care of itself. It needs a strong and positive defense. More particularly, it requires strengthening all three legs of a triadic defense, each reinforcing the other two. Members of the reality-based community need to reinforce our institutions, our solidarity, and ourselves.

It's the Institutions, Stupid!

If there is one message this book seeks to impart, that is it. Individuals talking to each other, no matter how big the network, are just people gabbing. Even truth-seeking individuals who cherish rigor and accuracy are likely to go unheard amid the din. The reality-based network's institutional nodes—its filtering and pumping stations—are what give the system its positive epistemic valence. The techno-utopians of the information revolution assumed that knowledge would spontaneously emerge from unmediated interactions across a sprawling peer-to-peer network, with predictably disappointing results. Without the places where professionals like experts and editors and peer reviewers organize conversations and compare propositions and assess competence and provide accountability—everywhere from scientific journals to Wikipedia pages—there is no marketplace of ideas; there are only cults warring and splintering and individuals running around making noise.

That is why the corruption of reality-based institutions is so dangerous: when, for example, a U.S. president alters the weather forecast, makes false murder accusations, and attacks news media and law enforcement and intelligence agencies and every other reality-based institution; when universities let research integrity take a backseat to social justice, students' comfort, pressure groups' demands, administrators' agendas, or anything else. Defenders of the Constitution of Knowledge therefore need to think about institutional fortitude, not just intestinal fortitude.

Individuals' courage and integrity matter profoundly, of course; but courage and integrity do not come out of nowhere. Institutions, as Yuval Levin has noted, *form* the individuals who pass through them.[1] They store and transmit values. When law enforcement put away Michael Cohen, Donald Trump's lawyer-consigliere, it sent a message about lawbreaking. When the National Oceanic and Atmospheric Administration's inspector general investigated political interference with the weather report as potentially a "major breach of scientific integrity," it sent a message about corrupting science. When CNN fired three prominent journalists for faulty reporting, it sent a message about journalistic standards.[2] When, on a single day in 2018, more than 300 newspapers ran synchronized editorials against the president's claim that the news media were the enemy of the American people, they sent a message about journalism's independence. When seventy-five universities (at this writing) adopted versions of the so-called Chicago principles—guaranteeing "the broadest possible latitude to speak, write, listen, challenge, and learn"—they sent a message about academic freedom. When Purdue University added a module on the First Amendment to its orientation program, ensuring that, by 2020, every graduate knew free speech fundamentals, it was sending a message about constitutional rights and responsibilities. Institutions define and instill integrity. They defend us, which is why it is so important that we defend them.

Diversifying the Academy

In academic institutions, unfortunately, the commitment to viewpoint diversity and free inquiry has faltered, and the public has noticed. In 2019 almost 40 percent of Americans told the Pew Research Center that colleges have a negative effect on the country, a dramatic increase from 26 percent seven years before. The change was driven by a collapse of confidence among Republicans and Republican-leaning independents: in the space of only four years (2015 to 2019), the share saying that colleges have a negative effect on the country grew by a whopping 20 percentage points, to almost 60 percent.[3]

Well publicized incidents of campus intolerance and one-sidedness have convinced a lot of people that universities are in the indoctrination business. In academia, as we saw in the previous chapter, conservative voices are few and getting fewer, to the point of almost disappearing in some disciplines. If anything, according to the political scientists Morgan Marietta and David C. Barker, conservatives underestimate the leftward tilt of university faculty: "Their [conservatives'] rejection of university knowledge might be even greater if citizens accurately perceived the true degree of ideological imbalance on campus."[4] Not only does academic one-sidedness distort research and chill debate, as we have seen; it also sabotages public confidence in the whole reality-based project—a gift to all the enemies of academia. Inevitably, the ideological skew also attracts interest from politicians, especially conservative ones. By 2019 seventeen states had passed laws professing to protect speech rights at public universities, and more were sure to join. If you think state legislators are reliable stewards of academic freedom and integrity, I have a bridge to sell you.

For academia, time is running out to take viewpoint diversity seriously—meaning just as seriously as other kinds of diversity. That might entail making positive efforts to recruit and hire and promote conservatives and others who challenge campus orthodoxies in their teaching and research; at a minimum, it entails identifying and eliminating discrimination and other obstacles to conservative faculty and students. It entails welcoming conservative speakers, making them safe, and defending them from mobs and deplatformers; consistently disciplining bad actors who bully or harass people who have controversial views; repudiating the use of ideological litmus tests (like commitments to a progressive interpretation of diversity) when hiring and promoting scholars and staff; disowning emotional safety as a community value (while ensuring physical safety); ceasing to treat everyday interpersonal conflicts as triggers for administrative action, and instead encouraging students and faculty to work out their disagreements face-to-face; ridding campuses of speech codes and "bias incident reporting systems" which chill candid conversations; using an objective "reasonable person" standard instead of a subjective, feelings-based standard when evaluating claims of speech-related harm or harassment; banning any investigations of students and faculty members for First Amendment–protected speech, absent a showing of probable cause that professional standards were violated.

"Principles of academic freedom must be institutionalized," the scholars Thomas Simpson and Eric Kaufmann write. Statements of principle are well and good, but "inadequate to effect real change," they argue. "For a set of principles to be effective, there need to be procedures which ensure that individuals and committees actively comply."[5] They call for the establishment of campus academic freedom champions, staffed to investigate reports of political discrimination, compile data about viewpoint diversity, and make recommendations for improvement. The idea of establishing one more campus bureaucracy to keep tabs on all the other campus bureaucracies has its downsides, and there is no guarantee that an academic freedom bureaucracy would not itself be captured and politicized. Still, the broader point seems correct: universities need to make defending pluralism a top institutional priority, not an afterthought. If they do not, politicians—the world's worst judges of scientific integrity—will try to do it for them.

In 1915 the University of Utah summarily fired four professors who had allowed a graduation speaker to criticize the Church of Jesus Christ of Latter-day Saints; seventeen other faculty members resigned in protest. In response to the crisis, the fledgling American Association of University Professors issued a "Declaration of Principles on Academic Freedom and Academic Tenure," urging concrete steps to institutionalize academic freedom, such as tenure protections and "suitable judicial bodies, composed of members of the academic profession, which may be called into action before university teachers are dismissed or disciplined." Universities around the country and even the world responded by building the norms and safeguards of intellectual inquiry and classroom discourse which underpin the modern academy. A century later, the academic world needs to make another such watershed commitment, this time to viewpoint diversity and intellectual pluralism.

Countering Canceling

In much the same way that activist students and professors can make life miserable for anyone who crosses them on campus, off-campus cancelers have figured out how to bully and intimidate almost at will by targeting people's employers and professional associates with denunciations, boycotts, and demands for firings. Because employers are not in business to defend speech rights, employment is the soft underbelly of the culture of free speech. Why should a business ever fall on its sword to protect a controversial employee when there are always plenty of noncontroversial candidates for the job?

Employment law could change that calculus. U.S. federal and state laws already protect workers from discrimination based on race, gender, sexual orientation, religion, disability, and more. For decades, a handful of states have also barred employment discrimination based on political activities, such as canvassing for candidates.[6] Amid the blaze of cancelations targeting employers, it makes sense to extend such provisions to constitutionally protected speech.

There are precedents. In 2015, when Utah added sexual orientation to its employment-discrimination protections, it forbade employers to fire, demote, or blacklist anyone "for lawful expression or expressive activity outside of the workplace regarding the person's religious, political, or personal convictions . . . unless the expression or expressive activity is in direct conflict with the essential business-related interests of the employer."[7] In 2020 a congressional bill protecting gay and trans people from discrimination, called the Fairness for All Act, included a similar provision.[8] Stronger, clearer protections for workers who exercise their free speech rights would at least partially balance employers' lopsided incentives to throw controversial employees to the dogs.

Still, antidiscrimination protections are cumbersome to enforce; employers who want to fire somebody can usually find reasons other than the real one, and not all employees have the stomach or resources for litigation. More important than legal pressure, therefore, is the development of countervailing social pressure on employers not to reflexively kowtow to cancelers. Publicly praising companies which defend their employees' speech rights, and criticizing them when they fail, would help restore balance. Something like that worked when Trader Joe's, a grocery chain, came under fire for branding which some activists deemed racially insensitive. After initially wavering, the company stood its ground after it "heard from many customers reaffirming that these name variations are largely viewed in exactly the way they are intended."[9]

Most important of all is for employers and companies to internalize resistance to cancelations, especially by preparing for attacks. In order to defend their values when a crisis hits, organizations need to identify and declare their values ahead of time; otherwise, they panic and cave in. They can prepare by (for example) setting up internal procedures preventing a rush to judgment against targeted employees; by pre-committing to evaluate the totality of an employee's work history and character rather than acting on the basis of a single controversial action or allegation; by offering recourse and support to employees who are targeted on social media (or by bullies inside the company); by promulgating guidelines for human resources and communications executives to follow when cancel campaigns boil up; and, above all, by expressing a commitment to their employees' off-workplace speech rights. By hardening their defenses, organizations make themselves more resilient if hit by cancelers—and therefore less tempting as targets.

Media and Government

At this writing—perhaps surprisingly—the organizations working hardest to build institutional barriers to propaganda and intimidation are the ones most often criticized for doing too little: social media companies. Figuring out how to moderate oceans of content non-arbitrarily is a herculean job, but major companies—Facebook, Google, Twitter—are spending millions, hiring thousands, and innovating to do better. By comparison, academia, which is the sector one might hope would fight hardest against propaganda and bullying, is doing the least.

Mainstream media organizations are in between. Reality-based journalists can be proud of doing their jobs with determination and professionalism during the Trump administration despite relentless vilification by the president and his many allies. At the same time, though, their commitment to reporting as objectively as they can—a hard-won norm which emerged from more than a century of partisanship and yellow journalism—has come under challenge as never before. Mainstream media outlets find themselves under growing pressure from activists and interest groups within their own ranks to bend coverage toward social justice (as defined by the political left, usually) and to deplatform, or at least disfavor, contrary views. Some journalists, especially younger ones, ridicule the idea of objectivity as a "view from nowhere" and call for replacing it with "moral clarity," by which they seem to mean their own political values.[10] As progressive moralism filters through newsrooms, conservative, center-right, and even moderate journalists report self-censoring to stay out of trouble with editors and colleagues.

Bringing cancel culture and ideological uniformity into newsrooms can only distort coverage, enlarge blind spots, and further alienate the public. "Any degree of what feels like cancel culture in a newsroom is a terrifying thing," Tom Rosenstiel, the executive director of the American Press Institute, told me. "A newsroom where there isn't argument over stories is a dysfunctional newsroom."

The best way to ensure healthy arguments is to ensure viewpoint diversity. Surveys find, to no one's surprise, that mainstream newsrooms lean to the left, although not as uniformly or extremely as in, say, academic humanities departments.[11] "We have to recruit more ideologically diverse newsrooms or the product will suffer from unconscious bias which the journalists who produce it won't even recognize—and that's, I think, where we are," Rosenstiel said. "That was occurring even before Trump, and then this became a wicked problem, where these newsrooms, because there are so few conservatives, are even less hospitable to conservatives." To break the cycle, media organizations need to recruit for ideological diversity, in addition to the more standard diversity categories. Newsrooms need to become "more woke in both directions," Rosenstiel said: "they need people who are of color and different generations to say, 'The way you're thinking is white and middle aged,' *and* people who are conservatives to say, 'The way you're thinking is very liberal.' If you're going to be serious about this, you have to consider ideological diversity."

Reality-based government agencies and professionals—from the CIA and the FBI to medical regulators and even the National Weather Service—also faced a war on objectivity. "There is intense, unrelenting pressure from Trump and his White House to bend the norms of objectivity and independence that have always been a hallmark of the American government," Peter Strzok, a former FBI agent, told *Lawfare's* Benjamin Wittes in a 2020 interview.[12] Under the circumstances, what seems remarkable is how many government professionals have stood their ground. As I wrote this chapter, news broke that a former head of the Department of Homeland Security's intelligence division had blown the whistle on efforts by political appointees to tone down assessments of Russian election interference.[13] "Heroic" is the only adequate word for an official who comes forward to accuse his superiors of turning a blind eye to the country's enemies. Others in the government, such as Anthony Fauci, the director of the National Institute of Allergy and Infectious Diseases, fought tooth and nail to resist White House efforts to shade the truth about the COVID-19 pandemic. Justice Department prosecutors withdrew from cases rather than signing misleading briefs and politicizing their legal work. State Department and military officials sacrificed their careers to tell the truth to Congress.

Still, even brave individuals can withstand the onslaught of unreality for only so long. They need legal and institutional backup. New laws need to be passed, and old ones given teeth: laws to forbid the president to fire inspectors-general except for cause; to thin the ranks of political appointees in scientific, law-enforcement, and intelligence agencies; to insulate prosecutors from political pressure; to require that the reports of inspectors-general and special counsels be shared with the public and Congress; to provide stronger protections for whistle-blowers; and to repair many other holes which Trump and his cronies tore in the fabric of reality-based government.[14]

It Takes a Group to Stop a Group

In 2020 a group of about 350 faculty and staff members of Princeton University signed an open letter demanding that the university create a faculty committee to "oversee the investigation and discipline of racist behaviors, incidents, research, and publication on the part of the faculty." Exactly what qualified as racism was to be determined by the committee itself. The call for what amounted to an anti-racist Committee of Public Safety was antithetical to every tenet of the Constitution of Knowledge: it was authoritarian, anti-empirical, and arbitrary, and that was just the letter A. That so outlandish an idea attracted significant support, much less hundreds of endorsements, smacked as much of fear as ideology; sure enough, when *The Atlantic*'s Conor Friedersdorf interviewed signers, he found that "multiple signatories are vehemently opposed to the demand beneath which they put their names."[15]

Around the same time, I heard from a worried professor at another university that faculty in his department were circulating a proposal to embed anti-racism (as defined, again, by the activists themselves) in every aspect of the curriculum. The proposal included "the development of anti-racist curriculum within each course," integrating "anti-racist policy activism" into the internship program, holding "a ceremony that ritualizes our program's commitment to anti-racism," and "insert[ing] the Black Lives Matter symbol into our website and onto the cover of our student handbook." Rituals and ceremonies? Iconic symbols? Short of sacrificing a goat in the dean's office, a clearer demand to convert a curriculum into a cult would be hard to imagine. Yet the professor who contacted me feared opposing the proposal. "A single professor or even a small group of professors who are determined to push back against these ideas or preserve the integrity of the university is just not effective," he told me. "I feel there is absolutely nothing I can do as a single tenured professor to stop this. It's like trying to hold back the ocean with a broom."

His voice, and the sub rosa voices of Princeton faculty who endorsed a letter they disagreed with, were the voices of demoralization. They were voices of individuals who feel isolated, outnumbered, fearful, and therefore helpless.

In his book *Free Speech and Liberal Education*, the political scientist and free-speech champion Donald Downs stresses the importance of counter-mobilization: "The actions of a few students can set the public tone of an institution if counter-voices and counter-actions remain dormant."[16] At the Cato Institute, a libertarian think tank in Washington, he elaborated:

> It's really a minority of students that are pushing this. . . . They're not being countered. They're getting some support from the campus bureaucracy and social media . . . and it's making people afraid to fill the public space with counter-views in favor of free speech. So the minority viewpoint is prevailing. . . . So it's really incumbent on people who want to support free speech principles to speak up, and to organize and mobilize.[17]

Just so. Organized minorities beat disorganized majorities every time. When pressure groups meet with organized opposition, they retreat. When they do not, they advance.

Because of the lopsided arithmetic of public choice, counter-mobilizing is a challenge: each individual will be tempted to hang back and hope that someone else will do the risky and difficult work of organizing, which often means that no one does it. Still, America's civic culture can counter-organize against canceling and coercion, and is already doing so.

In 1999 Alan Charles Kors and Harvey Silverglate—a professor and a lawyer conjoined by their passion for free speech and their worries about campus intolerance—organized the Foundation for Individual Rights in Education. FIRE launched with a successful public campaign defending the speech rights of Tufts University's Christian Fellowship, which had been denied recognition as a campus group because of its viewpoint. That effort proved to be a template for many other public campaigns on behalf of muzzled or persecuted students and faculty. A few years later, the group added litigation to its armory, suing public universities which violate First Amendment rights. Some universities defend their violations to the bitter end, but others turn to FIRE for guidance. By backing speech rights with publicity campaigns, legal action, expert advice, and moral support, FIRE mobilizes free speech constituencies on campus and evens the odds when conflicts arise. According to FIRE, the proportion of university speech policies which clearly and substantially violated First Amendment principles (thus earning the group's "red light" rating) fell to around 20 percent in 2020: still too high, but far better than almost 80 percent which earned red-light designations in 2009. Just as important, FIRE's support gives students like Sam Foer, whom we met in chapter 1, support and confidence to find their own voices.

In 2015 a conversation between three academics about the lack of viewpoint diversity in their disciplines turned into a blog, then a membership organization—and then Heterodox Academy, which in 2020 boasted more than 4,000 members, nearly all of them university professors. Jonathan Haidt, one of the founders, had publicly fretted since 2011 that ideological uniformity was skewing his discipline, social psychology; he and his cofounders—the sociologist Chris Martin and the law professor Nicholas Rosenkranz—believed that remedies should come from within the academy, sailing under the colors of science, not politics. By 2020 the group boasted a substantial following, including more left-leaning academics than right-leaning ones.[18] "Our commitment to heterodoxy within the academy has taken shape as a response to the rise of orthodoxy within scholarly culture—when people fear shame, ostracism, or any other form of social or professional retaliation for questioning or challenging a commonly held idea," the organization declared in its mission statement. Importantly, Heterodox Academy speaks the language of science, appealing to academics' professional integrity as truth-seekers, something they care about.

At the University of California at Berkeley, after efforts to disrupt a speech by the alt-right provocateur Milo Yiannopoulos turned violent in 2017, an undergraduate named Manu Meel, along with several friends, founded BridgeUSA, originally as a free speech group, then broadening to support empathetic dialogue on and off campuses. "Those kids who feel fervently but are being silenced or are being forced to change their minds—our job is to figure out how to empower them," Meel told me. As of this writing, the group boasts thirty-five college chapters, and counting. Another effort to make the world safe for viewpoint diversity is Braver Angels, a national grassroots depolarizing movement which sponsors open, participatory debates both among students and the general public. Anyone can show up to speak on either side of an issue or even both; the only rule is to use strict parliamentary procedure (to encourage civility) and sincerely say what you really believe (no bullshitting, no grandstanding). Online, Braver Angels debates attract hundreds and might scale to thousands. On colleges campuses, students love the format, which creates a safe space for honest disagreement and feels to many students like a jailbreak from groupthink. On one occasion, student activists who showed up intending to disrupt a debate wound up participating instead. Yet another promising initiative, this one for middle schools and high schools, is debate-centered instruction. Instead of just memorizing facts or writing reports, students work in teams to build and argue a case, a format they find engaging and empowering. By learning to advocate views they may not share, they develop epistemic resilience, the capacity to encounter adverse ideas without melting down.[19]

"The students are activating and they're clearly hungry for these conversations," Deb Mashek, the executive director of Heterodox Academy, told me. "They're creating groups, events, formats. Students are creating opportunities for not just dialogue but actually learning from people with different perspectives." FIRE's Nico Perrino reported the same trend. "We've seen a huge uptick in interest in campus free speech issues," he said, "including the founding of new organizations devoted to those issues, or existing organizations who made it a bigger part of their work." He substantiated his claim with a list too long to reprint here. As I worked on this chapter, I learned of Princeton alumni organizing a new group to defend free speech there, and also a coalition of professors organizing a new group to defend academic freedom nationally.

The larger culture is fighting back, too. A few weeks before I wrote this chapter, 157 prominent writers and intellectuals, many of them left-leaning, signed a public letter in *Harper's* magazine condemning the spread of cancel culture. "The free exchange of information and ideas, the lifeblood of a liberal society, is daily becoming more constricted," the letter said, citing "an intolerance of opposing views, a vogue for public shaming and ostracism, and the tendency to dissolve complex policy issues in a blinding moral certainty."[20] Around the same time, a center-left writer and academic named Yascha Mounk founded Persuasion.community, a gathering place and online journal for pluralists who feel ready to fight back. "Too often," the group declared, "the advocates of free speech and free institutions have been passive, even fatalistic. It is high time for those who believe in these enduring ideals to stand up for our convictions."

Even the victims of canceling are finding each other and organizing. I first connected with Jonathan Kaiman, whose canceling cost him his job, his book contract, and his career as a journalist, when I learned that he and his girlfriend, Charlotte Arneson, were creating what they called the UnCancel Project, a support network for people whose lives are upended by shaming campaigns. When Kaiman's case was publicized, his inbox filled with inquiries from others whose own canceling episodes had left them unemployed, depressed, sometimes suicidal. He and Arneson planned to create support networks, provide referrals for services like legal advice and counseling, gather data and research on canceling, and raise public awareness of the human costs. "The driving force is letting people know they're not alone," Arneson said. "We're often the first people someone has talked to about this. Just let them know they're not alone and have someone to talk to."

As the gay community realized decades ago, the first step toward liberation is finding others and joining forces. Quite rapidly, the realization is sinking in that the three top priorities for pushing back against coercive conformity are, in order of importance: organize, organize, and organize.

We Have Met the Snowflakes and They Are Us

Still, in the end, although institutions and organizing are essential, it comes down to individuals.

As different as their methods and politics may be, disinformation and coercive conformity are both forms of information warfare. Cancelers and trolls share the goal of dominating the information space by demoralizing their human targets: confusing them, isolating them, drowning them out, deplatforming them, shaming them, or overwhelming them so that they give up on pushing back. Demoralization is demobilization. At bottom, individuals must decide whether to submit, and so the most important thing to say to individuals is this: don't be a snowflake.

In the culture wars, the term "snowflake" originally caught on among conservatives to mock students who profess to be traumatized by microaggressions and Halloween costumes. The term is not particularly accurate, though. Some student activists are coddled and fragile, no doubt, but many express their moral values with passion and sometimes bravery. In 2017, after students at Middlebury College were criticized for disrupting a speech by a conservative scholar, some of them wrote that the protesters "did not believe that registering respectful disagreement was enough. They took the great risk of standing up for their principles, at the expense of their reputations, to insist that some views are not worthy of a platform at one of the most elite colleges in the country."[21] One could doubt that protesting a conservative speaker at a very progressive college entailed any great reputational risk, but the students were right about one thing: even if their behavior was misguided, they had shown the courage of their convictions, which is the most potent weapon in any debate.

If it applies to anyone, "snowflake" more aptly describes people who profess to support intellectual freedom and diversity but fail to speak up for it—especially tenured professors, whose jobs are among the world's safest, yet who often dive under the furniture when academic freedom is challenged. Some lack courage, but others lack the confidence and conviction to speak out. Friends of the Constitution of Knowledge have been on the defensive for so long, especially in academia, that they are unsure how to respond, and they doubt that anything they say could or even should make a difference. "Classical liberals just have not produced the emotive narratives and reasoned arguments to resist 'social justice,'" one professor told me. "Most academics won't join a pile-on, but most won't oppose one. Not because they're scared, but because most don't feel strongly about academic freedom or wish to be associated with those who do." Remember, spirals of silence instill self-doubt, not just self-censorship.

On college campuses, when I give talks about free speech and pluralism, there is a question I hear again and again. Often it comes from a first-year or second-year student, and often from a straight white male, but sometimes I hear it from faculty members or minority students, like a gay freshman who was ostracized by the campus LGBT group for his comparatively moderate (though still center-left) views. The questioner will recount being disqualified from conversations because of his privilege. Or race. Or gender. Or sexual orientation. Or cultural insensitivity. Or conservatism. Or non-leftism. Or something. For whatever reason, he is told he cannot participate. If he does participate, students are quick to judge, to condemn, to isolate. "Students with differing opinions are often placed in morality hell before a conversation can be had," one student, a Hispanic sophomore at a leading university, told me. "In my experience, discussions far too often cease to be a deliberate analysis of ideas and instead turn into a five-versus-one barrage. Unfortunately, it ends in an attack on the person and not the idea: 'You are a bad person for having this belief.' This has been my experience on numerous occasions."

Although there are many variations on the theme, my student questioner—I'll call him Theaetetus, in tribute to that wondering young man of ancient Athens—asks something which amounts to this: "When people disqualify me or deplore me or attack me personally or gang up on me, how can I respond? What should I say?"

When I first encountered that question, my instinct was to suggest snappy comebacks. "Tell them you won't be bullied. That good arguments are identity-blind. That every individual brings a unique perspective. That they just might learn something from differing views." I suggested all kinds of zingers, but I could never find the perfect one. My suggestions seemed more like theoretical postulates than something a teenager might say in a conversation.

So I tried passing the buck back. "I can't tell you what to say," I told Theaetetus. "I know how to talk to my generation, but you'll have to figure out how to talk to your generation." That, needless to say, was even less satisfying.

At last, I came around to this: "Really, what you say when someone disqualifies you isn't all that important. What really matters is *that* you say. What matters is that you not shut up. They can disqualify you, disapprove of you, denigrate you, turn their backs, drown you out. But they cannot silence you, unless you let them. Just by speaking out, you are breaking a spiral of silence and refusing to be manipulated.

"Remember, you are never as alone as silencers want you to believe. If your point of view commands good evidence or strong arguments, you can be sure that other people share it or can be brought around. Spoofed consensus is an illusion which can collapse overnight when people start speaking out. That was why the Soviet Union worked so feverishly to repress dissidents like Sakharov and Amalrik and Sharansky; and why it fell nonetheless."

Whenever I can, I tell the story of Franklin Kameny, the pioneering gay rights activist who changed the world by not shutting up. You can read that story in the afterword to *Kindly Inquisitors*, or in Eric Cervini's fine biography.[22] Despite the vindictiveness of the U.S. civil service (which fired Kameny from his government job in 1958, revoked his security clearance, and ignored his protests), the indifference of the U.S. Supreme Court (which declined to hear his lawsuit against the government), the contempt of the U.S. Congress (whose members called him "disgusting," among other choice adjectives), the condemnation of the American psychiatric establishment (which declared him mentally ill), the harassment by J. Edgar Hoover's FBI (which investigated and hassled him), the hostility of the law (which made him a criminal), and the antagonism of mainstream American society (which viewed him and other homosexuals as predatory and obscene)—despite all of that, he would not be silenced. "Gay is good!" he said to anyone who would listen, which at first was nobody. He founded a pioneering gay rights organization, he helped other blacklisted homosexuals fight for their rights, he organized protests, he ran for Congress, he confronted psychiatrists. And he, not the forces arrayed so massively against him, prevailed. He lived long enough to accept the government's apology and receive one of its highest honors.[23]

"Demoralization," I tell Theaetetus, "denies your agency. It makes you feel helpless. Don't let them do that. You are not helpless."

Andrew Zeller was a twenty-three-year-old graduate student when I met him at Purdue University, where he was the president of the graduate student government. He had become involved in student government to keep an eye on student-activity funds, but then he heard Greg Lukianoff, the president of FIRE, give a lecture about campus speech restrictions. "It was super, super interesting to me," he told me. "I had had no idea of the level of abuses." He also learned that Purdue's own policies were hazardous to free speech, having received FIRE's "yellow-light" rating. "We're going to take this on," he decided. "We're going to be a green-light institution," earning FIRE's top rating.

The story I expected to hear was about an uphill battle against fanatical campus activists and foot-dragging administrators. Actually, Zeller said, "it wasn't terribly difficult to get people to say we want to be the best there is on free speech." Arguing that "this is for the benefit of all the causes which anyone in the audience might support, regardless of where their particular political allegiances might be," Zeller won a joint resolution of the graduate and undergraduate student councils. Before long, Purdue was a green-light school, and it also became the first public university to sign on to the Chicago statement on free expression. "That was awesome, more success than we could have hoped to have," Zeller said. He was just as surprised when the student government's board leapt at the idea of sponsoring a campus lecture series—beginning with talks on free speech, my own among them. Meanwhile, according to Steve Schultz, Purdue's general counsel, faculty members said that if the university was going to embrace the Chicago statement, students needed to understand their First Amendment rights and responsibilities, which led to Purdue's inclusion of seventy-five minutes about free speech in its freshman orientation. So the whole thing snowballed after one student broke the ice. "Nothing was as hard as we expected it to be," Zeller recalled.

In 2016 a group of radical students at Reed College took to disrupting a required humanities course for freshmen. "It's the heart of the academic experience at Reed," wrote Chris Bodenner in *The Atlantic*. Or it was, until Reedies Against Racism (RAR), declared that the course "perpetuates white supremacy" and showed up to

protest every lecture. "I am intimidated by these students," one professor wrote. "I am scared to teach courses on race, gender, or sexuality, or even texts that bring these issues up in any way—and I am
a gay mixed-race woman."[24] But after a year of disruptions, other
students began speaking up. When activists arrived in class to shout
and wave signs, an African American student in the front row stood
up and said, "This is a classroom! This is not the place! Right now
we are trying to learn!" The hall broke into applause and cheers. "I
don't want to hear it," a protester yelled back. A second voice rang
out: "This is as much his space as it is your space!"[25] In that room,
at that moment, the spiral of silence was broken. "This school year,"
reported Bodenner, "students are ditching anonymity and standing
up to RAR in public—and almost all of them are freshmen of color."
The spoof was exposed; the protesters' power was shattered. "Support for RAR seems to be collapsing," wrote Bodenner. "RAR's list
of demands keeps growing, but its energy is now focused on Wells
Fargo."

Sometimes, of course, change is harder than it was for Andrew
Zeller at Purdue. No guarantees. "Remember, though," I tell Theaetetus, "pushing back against coercion and bullying always works
better than remaining silent, and it always rebalances the odds meaningfully; the only question is how much. But if you are a snowflake
and the other side is not, then the result is pre-ordained."

Free Speech Is the Only Safe Space for Minorities

Well, that was a good pep talk, but Theaetetus still hesitates. His
would-be disqualifiers and silencers hit back with what seems like a
powerful argument. Free speech and intellectual diversity may sound
good on paper, they say, but in the real world it defames, oppresses,
and injures minorities and the marginalized.

"Of all the arguments against robust free inquiry and intellectual
diversity, this one has been the most effective at instilling guilt and
self-doubt among people like you and me," I tell Theaetetus. "And
among all the arguments, it is the one which truly breaks my heart."

There are many variations on the theme that minorities need
protection from hateful and harmful ideas. One version holds that

free speech and objectivity are oppressive. As students at the Claremont Colleges put it in a 2017 manifesto (demanding that the colleges "take action" against conservative journalists on the student newspaper), "free speech, a right many freedom movements have fought for, has recently become a tool appropriated by hegemonic institutions. It has . . . given those who seek to perpetuate systems of domination a platform to project their bigotry. . . . The idea that the truth is an entity for which we must search, in matters that endanger our abilities to exist in open spaces, is an attempt to silence oppressed peoples."[26] A variant is that free expression in the real world is a zero-sum game. "Granting speech opportunities to some often denies speech opportunities to others," a law professor wrote in 2018.[27] The most straightforward claim—the oldest and simplest argument against free expression—is that toleration allows people to say bad and wrong things: "For too long, a flawed notion of 'free speech' has allowed individuals in positions of power to spread racist pseudoscience in academic institutions, dehumanizing and subjugating people of color and gender minorities," a Middlebury student wrote in 2017.[28] Or, as a university administrator wrote, "Free speech protections . . . should not mean that someone's humanity, or their right to participate in political speech as political agents, can be freely attacked, demeaned or questioned."[29] And so on, and on.

In the real world, however, the claim that censorship or enforced orthodoxy protects minorities and the marginalized has been comprehensively disproved, again and again and again. "Censorship has always been on the side of authoritarianism, conformity, ignorance, and the status quo," write Erwin Chemerinsky and Howard Gillman in their book *Free Speech on Campus*, "and advocates for free speech have always been on the side of making societies more democratic, more diverse, more tolerant, more educated, and more open to progress."[30] They and former American Civil Liberties Union president Nadine Strossen, in her powerful book *Hate: Why We Should Resist It with Free Speech, Not Censorship*, list the horrors and oppressions which have befallen minorities in the name of making society safe from dangerous ideas. "Laws censoring 'hate speech' have predictably been enforced against those who lack political power," writes Strossen.[31]

In America, under the Alien and Sedition Acts, authorities censored and imprisoned sympathizers of the opposition party (including members of Congress) and shut down opposition newspapers; under the Comstock laws, they censored works by Aristophanes, Balzac, Oscar Wilde, and James Joyce (among others); under the World War I anti-sedition laws, they convicted more than a thousand peace activists, including the Socialist presidential candidate Eugene V. Debs, who ran for president in 1920 from a prison cell.[32] In more recent times, when the University of Michigan adopted one of the first college speech codes in 1988, the code was seized upon to charge Blacks with racist speech at least twenty times.[33] When the United Kingdom passed a hate-speech law, the first person to be convicted was a Black man who cursed a white police officer.[34] When Canadian courts agreed with feminists that pornography could be legally restricted, authorities in Toronto promptly charged Canada's oldest gay bookstore with obscenity and seized copies of the lesbian magazine *Bad Attitude*.[35] All around the world, authorities quite uncoincidentally find that "hateful" and "unsafe" speech is speech which is critical of them—not least in the United States, where, in 1954, the U.S. Postal Service used obscenity laws to censor *ONE*, a gay magazine whose cover article ("You Can't Print It!") just happened to criticize the censorship policies of the U.S. Postal Service.

Everywhere you look in the world, countries and cultures which have embraced the Constitution of Knowledge are where social equality and minority rights have advanced the most. That is no coincidence: as I argue in *Kindly Inquisitors* and in chapter 4 of this book, criticism and contestation advance moral knowledge, not just scientific knowledge. The advance of equality for sexual minorities in America is a sterling example. The biggest breakthrough for gay equality was not the Stonewall riot of 1969; it was the Supreme Court's ruling in 1958, more than a decade earlier, that the government's censorship of *ONE* was illegal. That decision gave Frank Kameny and other homosexuals the weapon they needed: their voice.

Frederick Douglass, who was born a slave, knew what he was talking about when he said in 1860, after an angry mob broke up an abolitionist meeting in Boston: "Slavery cannot tolerate free speech. Five years of its exercise would banish the auction block and break every chain in the South." (He added, significantly: "To suppress free speech is a double wrong. It violates the rights of the hearer as well as those of the speaker.") The late Representative John Lewis, whose head was bashed in by white supremacists, knew what *he* was talking about when he said, "Without freedom of speech and the right to dissent, the civil rights movement would have been a bird without wings." (Among Lewis's many arrests and jailings was one for carrying a sign which said, "One man, one vote." Unsafe!) Hosea Williams, another great civil rights leader of King's generation, defended the speech rights of the KKK. "One thing we must understand," he said, "a right is not a right in America until it is extended to every American. And even though they beat and brutalized us in seeking that right, if they take the Ku Klux Klan off [the air] today, they'll take the NAACP off tomorrow. . . . The problem with the Black struggle in America has been Black leaders like King didn't have the ability to communicate with the masses. Once they had that ability to communicate with the masses, things changed."[36]

Cancel campaigns may be legal under the U.S. Constitution, but they violate the Constitution of Knowledge. That they occur in the name of protecting vulnerable minorities is an especially ironic twist. Social justice activists who support censorship and social coercion invariably imagine themselves doing the censoring and coercing. Usually, that is a wishful assumption. Given everything the past couple of millennia have taught about the abuses committed by well-intentioned speech police, social-justice activists' confidence that they can be trusted to decide what others can say and hear is a sad display of ignorance and hubris.

Even more heartbreaking is that so many activists, in responding to what they claim is oppressive or unsafe expression, deploy exactly the same socially coercive tactics which were used so devastatingly against homosexuals and other minorities. We gay people are very, very well acquainted with canceling. Coercive conformity was weaponized, deployed, and perfected against us. We were denounced for our nonconformism, which was "unsafe" for the country and children and ourselves. We were shamed, and made ashamed, for who we loved and what we thought. We were made unemployable and socially untouchable. We were browbeaten to keep silent and stay in the closet. Anyone who stood up for us was also ostracized. ("Are you a faggot, too?") Oh, yes, we know something about canceling. We did not spend the last half century and more fighting against it so that we could turn the tables and make pariahs of others.

The society we fought for is a place of toleration and diversity, a place where *all* people, not just homosexuals, can express their truest selves and live openly as their conscience dictates, consistent with the rights which every person shares and under laws which treat all equally. As Martin Luther King Jr. said, civil rights are a single garment, and you cannot coherently defend your own without also defending those of your opponents. Coerced conformity has no place in a movement for liberty and equality. My activist friends should be fighting *for* the speech rights of those who maintain that homosexuality is wrong, that marriage is between a man and a woman, that gender is irrevocable from birth. They should be defending intellectual diversity even (actually, especially) when it offends them.

"So," I tell Theaetetus, "do not be deterred by claims that using your voice or defending others' voices oppresses minorities or entrenches inequality or 'enacts violence.' *You* are the advocate for the marginalized. *You* are making the world safer for minorities and less hospitable to violence. *You* are the friend of diversity. Minorities are always better off in a culture which protects dissent than in a culture which protects us from dissent."

The Burden Is Also a Privilege

Theaetetus still hesitates. Is it fair, he wonders, to ask minorities and the marginalized to bear the burden of encountering bigotry? Should Black people have to put up with white supremacism? Jews with Holocaust denial? Gay people with claims that they can be cured? Aren't those debates settled and far past the point where airing them does any good? Doesn't continuing them only force minorities to relive pain and suffer indignity?

In 2017 the manifesto by Middlebury's students made this point forcefully. Their deplatforming of a controversial speaker was "meant to challenge a college practice and policy which puts [an] undue burden on specific groups of students, asking them to continually

defend their right to exist in an academic community for the supposed intellectual enrichment of that same community. This practice
is wrong, one-sided, and must end." The manifesto added: "Supporting this event did not acknowledge the non-academic consequences
of the 'civil debate' in question, one that is exhausting, upsetting, and
deeply stressful for many in our community."

I understand where the Middlebury students were coming from.
Any American homosexual can attest that falsehoods and bigotry
can cause suffering and self-hate, and that batting them down again
and again can be "exhausting, upsetting, and deeply stressful"—
although normally it is more like a tax we pay on everyday social
transactions, a modest but persistent surcharge of explanation and
self-justification. And no, that is not fair.

But we can also attest that confronting and refuting bad ideas can
be invigorating, empowering, and deeply rewarding. There are benefits, not just costs, to being social educators. Minorities are always on
the front lines of moral progress. From our standpoint on the edges
of society, we have a clearer view of injustices and we feel their sting
more; seeing and confronting and rectifying them is a privilege as
well as a burden. I would not wish on anyone the war I waged against
myself as a closeted youth, yet I am grateful for the opportunities I
have had to spare others the same torments. Yes, having to beg for
the marriage rights which straights took for granted (and routinely
neglected and abused) was demeaning and tiring, but it was also the
most rewarding work I have ever done. It made society stronger, it
made marriage stronger, it made gay people stronger, it made me
stronger. If you offered me the chance to relive my life without the
fear and self-hatred of my first twenty-five years, on the condition
that I would be part of a complacent majority which took its place in
the world for granted, I would reject that deal.[37]

In his contribution to *I'm from Driftwood*, an online LGBT story
archive, my friend Nephi Niven recounts coming out at his university
and encountering a psychologist who prescribed conversion therapy.

> I told him that there was nothing wrong with gay people and they
> weren't sick, and they weren't gay because they came out of abusive
> families or situations, and they weren't abusers. . . . I think having

had that experience of standing up for myself and saying aloud the words that there's nothing wrong with gay people and there's nothing sick about them helped me realize that that was true for myself. And having stood up to someone who was capable of saying such mean and hurtful and hateful things, when you put yourself in a vulnerable position, proved to me that I had the strength to do that. . . . When confronted with any situation like that, standing up for yourself will give you strength moving forward.[38]

Yes, every time someone told me I could never marry because gay people are promiscuous or our unions are sterile or God disapproves, it stung; but every foolish or bigoted claim was an opportunity to make my case and shine by comparison. Every demonstration of hatred or ignorance was a chance to show love and speak truth. Every encounter, every explanation, moved the social needle a little bit toward justice.

Every time I hear a minority-rights advocate say that she should not have to debate haters who question her very right to exist, I say: on the contrary, that is exactly who you need to debate. The hearts, minds, and votes we need to win are those of people who do not already agree with us—a point which might seem obvious but is surprisingly easy to overlook. Recent research supports what activists like me learned firsthand in the gay-marriage struggle: deploring and denouncing people rarely changed their minds, but respectfully listening and talking to them often did. "If you want to change someone's mind," wrote Brian Resnick in *Vox*, summarizing recent research on how to reduce prejudice, "you need to have patience with them, ask them to reflect on their life, and listen. It's not about calling people out or labeling them fill-in-the-blank-phobic."[39] And, by the way, you will usually find that the "hater" is not hateful at all, though she may be incorrect or misinformed. If you give her a chance and approach her with a dose of humility, you might even learn something from her.

Maybe the most memorable moment in my almost two decades of advocacy for same-sex marriage happened in 2004. It was a year of setbacks, when anti-marriage ballot initiatives swept states across the country. I was arguing my case in a radio interview when a caller phoned in to tell the host, "I think your guest today is the most dangerous man in America." And why would that be? "Because he makes it sound so damn *reasonable!*" At that moment, I knew we would win, and I saw that my own oppression had given me gifts I would never trade away: a voice, a mission, and a chance to make a difference.

The Power of Not Protesting

Still, the emotional toll of confronting ignorance and animus can be high. Frank Kameny never backed away from an argument, but I often do, and so do a lot of other people who just want to get on with their lives and not be hassled.

"And then," asks Theaetetus, "don't the haters win?"

No, not necessarily. "Here's something you won't often hear on campus," I tell him. "If you elevate every offense and escalate every microaggression, you abandon the most underrated weapon in the information-warfare arsenal. Instead of protesting and punishing provocateurs, shrug and walk away."

Marginalizing bad ideas and foolish talk is the reality-based community's secret weapon. The history of science is littered with ideas which no one bothered to pursue, or which were examined and then dropped—and that was that. The reality-based community defends its boundaries mostly by deciding which propositions *not* to examine. Under the fallibilist and empirical rules, attention must be earned, with argument and evidence and a respectable track record. Without the oxygen of attention, bad ideas suffocate—not always, but much more often than not. Trolls and propagandists understand as much, which is why they take such extreme measures to outrage our sensibilities and defame our identities. By exploiting the urge to defend our commitments, they usurp attention which they could never earn on the merits. You need not be a professional propagandist to see that protesting or deplatforming someone is like putting up a neon sign attracting attention to her. After all, if an idea is dangerous, then it must be important; if a speaker is worth deplatforming, then she must have something interesting to say.

Competitive condemnation is a game we can choose not to play.

Next time you feel the urge to protest some piece of nonsense, to rebut it (and thus repeat it), to deplatform it, or to organize outrage against it, consider going out for a pizza instead. Don't feed the trolls. That provocateur who comes to campus to own the libtards? She is playing you. Stay home. An empty auditorium will slash her speaking fees. Most of the time, the best answer to a Holocaust denier is the chirping of crickets.

If you must respond, try dialing your reaction down to annoyance rather than up to outrage. Although it is true that both words and physical violence can be hurtful, the hurt is of very different types. If someone hits me with a club, I do not have a lot of choice about whether to receive a skull fracture, but if someone says something obnoxious, I can choose how to frame and interpret what I heard. The old saying I learned as a child, "Sticks and stones may break my bones, but names will never hurt me," is not literally true, as even a child knows; what it teaches is that we have agency in reacting to words. When someone says I am sick or sinful or shameful, I can steer myself toward feeling tedium rather than trauma. I can make a point of reacting with my liberal brain instead of my lizard brain. By doing so, I empower myself and disempower a provocateur or ignoramus. Whereas escalating every obnoxious encounter makes the information environment a playground for trolls. An easily offended society is a happy hunting ground for someone who takes delight in offending.

Or try humor, another underrated troll-killer. Any drag queen worth her salt can attest to the power of satire. "Counterintuitive though it may seem, ridicule and mockery have long been an effective way to disarm protesters who espouse bigotry and racial supremacy," reported the *New York Times* in 2017. "In Knoxville, Tennessee, residents countered a white supremacist march with a hastily assembled group calling itself the Coup Clutz Clowns. The clowns pretended not to understand the shouts of 'White power!' 'White flour?' the clowns cried, throwing some in the air. 'White flower? Tight shower? Wife power!' For wife power, some of them put on wedding dresses."[40]

Provocateurs would not be provocative if ignoring them were easy; they are expert at exploiting humans' wired-in compulsion to defend our tribes and our honor. Resisting outrage requires self-discipline and a thick skin. It requires us to remember that the Constitution of Knowledge imposes a double-edged civic obligation: try not to give offense, and try even harder not to take offense. It asks us to shrug and stay cool when every impulse urges us to shout and get hot. Ignoring or mocking trolls is difficult, but centuries of science, and decades of drag shows, prove that it works.

Never Truthiness, Always Truth

"One other thing you can do, while you are not shutting up," I say to Theaetetus. "Maintain your integrity by sticking to the truth.

"By 'truth' I don't mean truthiness. I don't mean what you wish were true, or what is metaphorically or narratively true, or what supports social justice or some other worthy cause, or what is true in your lived experience, or what seems authentic. I mean: to the best of your ability, stick to what the reality-based community has found to be factually accurate. Never cede that ground."

According to Merriam-Webster, the word "truthiness" was once a rare synonym for "truthfulness." In 2005, debuting *The Colbert Report* on Comedy Central, the comedian Stephen Colbert seized upon "truthiness" and repurposed it. "We're not talking about truth," he later explained. "We're talking about something that seems like truth—the truth we want to exist."[41] The word caught on, and for good reason; truthiness was spreading like wildfire in politics. Former House speaker Newt Gingrich provided a memorable example in 2016 when a CNN news anchor confronted him over his bogus claim that crime was on the rise.

> *Interviewer:* "Violent crime across the country is down."
> *Gingrich:* "No, that's your view."
> *Interviewer:* "This is the FBI statistics. They're not a liberal organization."
> *Gingrich:* "No, but what I said is equally true. People feel it."
> *Interviewer:* "They feel it, yes, but the facts don't support it."
> *Gingrich:* "As a political candidate, I'll go with how people feel and I'll let you go with the theoreticians."[42]

Truthiness was the stock-in-trade of Trumpiness. After Trump retweeted a falsely labeled and incendiary anti-Muslim video, the White House spokeswoman said, "Whether it's a real video, the threat is real." Trump himself continued maintaining that he won the 2016 popular vote "in a true sense."[43] In 2020 his intuition told him he won the popular vote in a landslide, so that was what he told the country. Trump's radical subjectivism—his claim that reality aligned with his feelings and intuitions—was nothing new for him; in 2007, asked in a legal deposition about his wealth, he had dodged by saying his net worth fluctuated "with the markets and with attitudes and with feelings, even my own feelings."[44] Explaining his 2016 victory, two of his senior campaign aides boasted that authenticity had trumped accuracy (pun unintended): "It didn't matter to the people who listened to Trump whether the boss had gotten the details correct. His words captured the way they felt. His was a language the left couldn't and wouldn't ever understand."[45]

Actually, the left understood his language perfectly well, having done much to invent it. For decades, a gaggle of influential academic doctrines—subjectivism, postmodernism, perspectivism, intersectionality, and more—had denigrated the idea of objective accuracy and the privileging of factuality. At Middlebury, the student manifesto asserted, "We contend that experiences and emotions are valid ways to see the world, and that the hegemony of rational thought-based perspective[s] found in a university setting limit[s] our collective creativity, health, and potential."[46] Another college told its students, "The most important indication of bias is your own feelings."[47] The idea that authenticity trumps accuracy suited unscrupulous conservatives just fine. Caught using a fake Lincoln quotation at the 2020 Republican convention, a Republican politician refused to back down, saying the quotation was authentic because "the sentiment rang true" and the politician "feels [it] deeply."[48] A prominent House Republican who circulated a deceptively edited video did not apologize when caught, instead saying that the video's underlying point was correct.[49]

Of course, relying on subjective feelings cannot root out biases; it only entrenches them. Subjectivism is the opposite of liberal science, whose entire purpose is to transcend "your own feelings" by outsourcing reality to interchangeable strangers. But because humans are wired to be subjective, biased, self-certain, self-interested, and social, the temptation to slide from truthfulness to truthiness is strong, especially when our friends are doing the same.

"Resist," I advise Theaetetus. "There may be political reasons to claim that transgender women of color initiated the 1969 Stonewall riot, or that American colonists declared their independence in order to protect the institution of slavery, or that a Black man invented the light bulb, or any number of other factually challenged propositions. Fight the temptation. George Orwell (a socialist) understood that subordinating truth to politics is a game which tyrants and bullies always win. In the reality-based community, accuracy is the only game in town. It is our common denominator and the taproot of our integrity."

The young Lincoln held that reverence for the law is the true north of America's constitutional culture. Reverence for facts is the true north of the reality-based community. Sometimes we get facts wrong. Of course. But we do not cheat. We do not cut corners. We hold ourselves accountable—to others, to our community—for rejecting convenient fictions and half-truths. Because factuality anchors our integrity and defines our community, we renounce propaganda and truthiness even if we are the only person in the vicinity who is doing so. And just by doing that, we make a difference. As the great Soviet writer and dissident Aleksandr Solzhenitsyn wrote in his masterpiece, *The Gulag Archipelago*, "You can resolve to live your life with integrity. Let your credo be this: Let the lie come into the world, let it even triumph. But not through me. The simple step of a courageous individual is not to take part in the lie. One word of truth outweighs the world."

"And so," I say to my friend Theaetetus, who wonders how to respond when others shush or disqualify him, "stand your ground, but also stand corrected. Check your facts, not your privilege. Stay civil and speak up. You will be surprised by your power."

A Fighting Faith

As I wrote in chapter 1, the Constitution of Knowledge is the most successful social design in human history, but also the most counterintuitive. In exchange for knowledge, freedom, and peace, it asks us to mistrust our senses and our tribes, question our sacred beliefs, and relinquish the comforts of certitude. It insists that we embrace our fallibility, subject ourselves to criticism, tolerate the reprehensible, and outsource reality to a global network of strangers. Defending it every day, forever, against adversaries who shape-shift but never retreat, can be, as the Middlebury students said in a different context, exhausting, upsetting, and deeply stressful. But we cannot afford to be snowflakes. Epistemic liberalism, like political liberalism, is a fighting faith.

My biggest worry is Lincoln's biggest worry: "If destruction be our lot, we must ourselves be its author and finisher." By themselves, the forces of chaos and coercion lack the strength to unseat the Constitution of Knowledge, and if they did unseat it, they would have nothing to replace it with except a Hobbesian war of each of millions of personal and tribal realities against all the others. What propagandists and social-media bullies and emotional safetyists and subjectivists and all the rest might succeed in doing, however, is to demoralize and confuse and intimidate, so that the reality-based community will lose heart and give ground. Mocked by trolls and mobbed by cancelers, denounced from the left for racism and colonialism and from the right as a deep-state conspiracy, the reality-based community feels besieged and looks fragile. Too many of its members may come to believe that disinformation is invincible, that objectivity is indefensible, that viewpoint diversity harms minorities, that words are violence, that canceling is merely criticism. When trolls and conspiracists and bots and U.S. presidents spew misinformation; when social media make shaming and shunning a fun desktop hobby; when supercomputers monetize our outrage and algorithms manipulate our attention; when more than half of university students and the general public are reluctant to express their real opinions for fear of losing their reputations or livelihoods—at such a moment, the enemies of intellectual pluralism and free inquiry seem to be ten feet tall. Which is just how they want to seem.

Yet the reality-based community has withstood much worse. It beat back the inquisitors who imprisoned Galileo, the dictators whose gulags spanned continents, and the racists and homophobes who sought to silence voices of freedom. "Tomorrow morning," said Socrates, "let us meet here again." The conversation he and his young protégé began 2,500 years ago continues, now spanning the world instead of just Athens, despite countless efforts to squelch it.

"Just a reminder, Theaetetus," I tell my student friend. "When we support the Constitution of Knowledge with our heads and our hearts—with reverence and reason, as Lincoln prescribed—and when others do the same, its enemies are not ten feet tall. We are."

Acknowledgments

The ideas in this book reflect research and conversations across the Brookings Governance Studies program. I am grateful to the Charles Koch Foundation for its financial support for this book project. The William and Flora Hewlett Foundation, Phil Harvey, and the Governance Studies Council have all provided valuable financial support for my larger research agenda and for the work of the Governance Studies team more broadly. I am grateful to Darrell West and all of my Brookings Institution colleagues, who make Brookings as close to the Platonic idea of a think tank as will ever be seen on this earth.

The list of people who contributed ideas, inspiration, and constructive criticism is long. It includes all of the people whose writings and interviews I have quoted and cited. Special thanks are due to the many people who generously made time to read and comment on drafts, including Bill Adair, David Barker, Peter Berkowitz, Carl Bogus, John Corvino, David Dalton, Mark Fabian, Bill Galston, Larry Haas, Jonathan Haidt, Adrian Hernandez, Eric Kaufmann, Aaron Kindsvatter, Kate Klonick, Brink Lindsey, Greg Lukianoff, Morgan Marietta, Jacob Mchangama, Ken McIntyre, Manu Meel, Richard Reeves, Dan Rothschild, Steve Schultz, Stuart Taylor, Mike Tolhurst, Rebecca Tuvel, Stacy Ulbig, Pete Wehner, Adam White, and Ben Wittes.

I was fortunate that Yuval Levin, of the American Enterprise Institute, allowed me to test-drive my ideas in an article in *National Affairs* magazine ("The Constitution of Knowledge," Fall 2018). I did foundational work on the book during residencies at the University of Nevada at Las Vegas and the University of Denver's Institute for Public Policy Studies, where Richard Caldwell has been a faithful friend. The American Enterprise Institute provided the valuable opportunity to workshop chapters with distinguished scholars, and the Institute for Humane Studies honored me with the support of its distinguished fellowship. Nick Mortensen provided valuable research assistance.

This book could not have been written without the insights, suggestions, encouragement, and constructive criticism of more people than can I list, or perhaps even count. Some, such as the philosopher and sociologist of science David Hull, are no longer with us. Others, such as Donald Downs, have been at my side since I was a young writer struggling to get *Kindly Inquisitors* into print. All tolerated my trespasses upon on their expertise and donated their knowledge and wisdom with a generosity I did not earn, and all have my abiding gratitude.

Notes

Chapter 1

1. Quotations are from the translation by Francis Macdonald Cornford, reprinted in *The Collected Dialogues of Plato*, Edith Hamilton and Huntington Cairns, eds. (Princeton University Press, 1961).

2. *Publick Occurrences Both Forreign and Domestick*, Boston, September 25, 1690. Text and reproduction can be found at the National Humanities Center website.

3. The titles I named are by Cailin O'Connor and James Owen Weatherall, Jennifer Kavanagh and Michael D. Rich, Lee McIntyre, and Michiko Kakutani, respectively.

4. Jeffrey Goldberg, "Why Obama Fears for Our Democracy," *The Atlantic*, November 16, 2020.

5. Kat Rosenfield, "The Toxic Drama on YA Twitter," Vulture.com, August 2017.

6. Jesse Singal, "How a Twitter Mob Derailed an Immigrant Female Author's Budding Career," *Tablet*, January 31, 2019.

7. College Pulse, "Free Expression on College Campuses" (Knight Foundation, May 2019).

8. Bill Schneider, *Standoff: How America Became Ungovernable* (Simon & Schuster, 2018), p. 261.

9. Lucian Gideon Conway, Meredith A. Repke, and Shannon C. Houck, "Donald Trump as a Cultural Revolt against Perceived Communication Re-

267

striction: Priming Political Correctness Norms Causes More Trump Support," *Journal of Social and Political Psychology* 5, No. 1 (2017).

Chapter 2

1. Ben Bradlee Jr., *The Forgotten: How the People of One Pennsylvania County Elected Donald Trump and Changed America* (Little, Brown, 2018), p. 247.

2. Jonathan Haidt, *The Righteous Mind: Why Good People Are Divided by Politics and Religion* (Pantheon, 2012), pp. 89, 91, 74, 76.

3. D. J. Flynn, Brendan Nyhan, and Jason Reifler, "The Nature and Origins of Misperceptions: Understanding False and Unsupported Beliefs about Politics," *Advances in Political Psychology* 38, suppl. 1 (2017).

4. Joseph L. Árvai, "Do People Vote with Their Hearts or Their Minds?" *Policy Options*, November 2, 2016. Also see Robyn S. Wilson and Joseph L. Árvai, "When Less Is More: How Affect Influences Preferences When Comparing Low and High-Risk Options," *Journal of Risk Research* 9, no. 2 (March 2006).

5. Ben Yagoda, "The Cognitive Biases Tricking Your Brain," *The Atlantic*, September 2018.

6. See, for example, Michael A. Cohen and Micah Zenko, *Clear and Present Safety: The World Has Never Been Better and Why That Matters to Americans* (Yale, 2019), and John Mueller, *Overblown: How Politicians and the Terrorism Industry Inflate National Security Threats, and Why We Believe Them* (Free Press, 2006).

7. Transcript of bin Laden's videotaped speech, *Al Jazeera*, November 1, 2004.

8. Good brief treatments can be found in, for example, Jason Altmire, *Dead Center: How Political Polarization Divided America and What We Can Do about It* (Sunbury Press, 2017); and Jennifer Kavanagh and Michael D. Rich, *Truth Decay: An Initial Exploration of the Diminishing Role of Facts and Analysis in American Public Life* (RAND, 2018).

9. The psychologist Gary Klein has argued that the term *fixation*—an overly stubborn attachment to our beliefs—is a more accurate term than *confirmation bias*. Gary Klein, "The Curious Case of Confirmation Bias," *Psychology Today*, May 5, 2019, and "Escaping from Fixation," *Psychology Today*, June 11, 2019.

10. Haidt, *The Righteous Mind*, p. 88.

11. Jeremy A. Frimer, Linda J. Skitka, and Matt Motyl, "Liberals and Conservatives Are Similarly Motivated to Avoid Exposure to One Another's Opinions," *Journal of Experimental Social Psychology* 72 (2017).

12. *The Economist*, "What Psychology Experiments Tell You About Why People Deny Facts," December 8, 2018.

13. Brendan Nyhan, "Fake News and Bots May Be Worrisome, but

Their Political Power Is Overblown," *New York Times*, February 13, 2018.

14. Dan M. Kahan, "Misconceptions, Misinformation, and the Logic of Identity-Protective Cognition," Cultural Cognition Project Working Paper 164 (Yale Law School, 2017), pp. 6–7.

15. Jay J. Van Bavel and Andrea Pereira, "The Partisan Brain: An Identity-Based Model of Political Belief," *Trends in Cognitive Sciences* 22, no. 3 (March 2018), p. 218.

16. Brian Resnick, "How Politics Breaks Our Brains, and How We Can Put Them Back Together," *National Journal*, September 19, 2014.

17. Dan M. Kahan, Ellen Peters, Erica Dawson, and Paul Slovic, "Motivated Numeracy and Enlightened Self-Government," *Behavioural Public Policy* 1 (September 3, 2013), pp. 54–86; Yale Law School, Public Law Working Paper No. 307, https://ssrn.com/abstract=2319992.

18. Monmouth University, "Impeachment Support Up Slightly but Trump Job Rating Steady," October 1, 2019, www.monmouth.edu/polling-insti tute/reports/monmouthpoll_us_100119/.

19. Lilliana Mason, "Ideologues without Issues: The Polarizing Consequences of Ideological Identities," *Public Opinion Quarterly* 82 (special issue, 2018).

20. Jonathan Haidt, "The Moral Roots of Liberals and Conservatives," TED talk (2008), www.ted.com/talks/jonathan_haidt_on_the_moral_mind/ transcript. Haidt speaks of *moral* beliefs and statements, as opposed to *identity-defining* ones; I take the concepts to be similar.

21. See Dominic Abrams and John Levine, "The Formation of Social Norms: Revisiting Sherif's Autokinetic Illusion Study," in J. R. Smith and S. A. Haslam, eds., *Psychology: Revisiting the Classic Studies* (Sage Publications, 2012).

22. Saul McLeod, "Solomon Asch—Conformity Experiment," *Simply Psychology*, December 28, 2018.

23. Interviewed by Sam Harris, *Making Sense*, podcast, October 8, 2019, 48:00.

24. Paul Starobin, *Madness Rules the Hour: Charleston, 1860 and the Mania for War* (PublicAffairs, 2017).

25. Van Bavel and Pereira, "The Partisan Brain," p. 215.

26. Josh Clinton and Carrie Roush, "Poll: Persistent Partisan Divide over 'Birther' Question Factuality," NBCNews.com, August 10, 2016.

27. Hugo Mercier, *Not Born Yesterday: The Science of Who We Trust and What We Believe* (Princeton University Press, 2020).

Chapter 3

1. Thomas Hobbes, *Leviathan* (1651/1668), Noel Malcolm, ed. (Oxford University Press, 2012), vol. III, p. 1202. Quoted in Teresa M. Bejan, *Mere Civility: Disagreement and the Limits of Toleration* (Harvard University

Press, 2017), p. 110. Hat tip to Jacob Mchangama, whose podcast history of free speech ("Clear and Present Danger") is invaluable.

2. I exaggerate, but not all that much. See, for example, Steven Pinker, *Enlightenment Now: The Case for Reason, Science, Humanism, and Progress* (Viking, 2018).

3. See Samuel Fleischacker, *Being Me Being You: Adam Smith and Empathy* (University of Chicago Press, 2019). Fleischacker argues that Smith's notion of empathy is distinctive in having a cognitive as well as emotional component: we can "enter in imagination into the circumstances of others . . . thereby gain[ing] insight into what it is like to occupy their perspective."

4. Brad S. Gregory, *Rebel in the Ranks: Martin Luther, the Reformation, and the Conflicts That Continue to Shape Our World* (HarperCollins, 2017), p. 10.

5. *The Complete Essays of Montaigne*, translated by Donald M. Frame (Stanford University Press, 1958).

6. Joseph Ben-David, *The Scientist's Role in Society: A Comparative Study* (Prentice-Hall, 1971), p. 73.

7. Charles S. Peirce, "The Scientific Attitude and Fallibilism," in Justus Buchler, ed., *Philosophical Writings of Peirce*, pp. 58 and 46–47. I used the Dover reprint of an edition published by Routledge and Kegan Paul in 1940.

8. Philip P. Wiener, ed., *Charles S. Peirce: Selected Writings* (Dover, 1966; reprint of 1958 Doubleday edition), p. xx.

9. Ibid., p. 398.

10. Peirce, "The Scientific Attitude and Fallibilism," p. 247.

11. James Hutton, *Theory of the Earth* (1785).

12. John Kidd, A *Geological Essay on the Imperfect Evidence in Support of a Theory of the Earth* (1815). Anonymous review in *British Critic*, September 1823.

13. Bianca Bosker, "What Really Killed the Dinosaurs?" *The Atlantic*, September 2018.

14. Noretta Koertge, "Belief Buddies versus Critical Communities: The Social Organization of Pseudoscience," in Massimo Pigliucci and Maarten Boudry, eds., *Philosophy of Pseudoscience: Reconsidering the Demarcation Problem* (University of Chicago Press, 2013).

15. Lee McIntyre, *The Scientific Attitude: Defending Science from Denial, Fraud, and Pseudoscience* (MIT Press, 2019); see various pages in chapter 6. McIntyre draws on histories of medicine by W. F. Bynum and Roy Porter.

16. See Barbara J. Shapiro, *A Culture of Fact: England, 1550–1702* (Cornell University Press, 2000).

17. Frederick Rudolph, *The American College and University: A History* (University of Georgia Press, 1962, 1990), p. 415.

18. Peder Olesen Larsen and Markus von Ins, "The Rate of Growth in

Scientific Publication and the Decline in Coverage Provided by Science Citation Index," *Scientometrics* 84 (2010), p. 594.

19. National Science Board, *Science and Engineering Indicators 2018*, chap. 5.

20. Caroline S. Wagner, Travis A. Whetsell, and Loet Leydesdorff, "Growth of International Collaboration in Science: Revisiting Six Specialties," *Scientometrics* 110 (2017), p. 1643.

21. Carolyn Y. Johnson, "Scientists Are Unraveling the Chinese Coronavirus with Unprecedented Speed and Openness," *Washington Post*, January 24, 2020.

22. COVID-19 Primer, https://covid19primer.com/dashboard.

23. Michael Polanyi, "The Republic of Science: Its Political and Economic Theory," *Minerva* 1, no. 1 (September 1962).

24. Helen E. Longino, *Science as Social Knowledge: Values and Objectivity in Scientific Inquiry* (Princeton University Press, 1990), pp. 73–74; I provided the italics. The previous Longino quotation is from p. 74.

25. McIntyre, *The Scientific Attitude*, pp. 92, 113, 148, and 91, respectively. For the anecdote, McIntyre cites Michael D. Lemonick, "When Scientists Screw Up," *Science*, October 15, 2002.

26. Jean Decety, Jason M. Cowell, Kang Lee, Randa Mahasneh, Susan Malcolm-Smith, Bilge Selcuk, and Xinyue Zhou, "RETRACTED: The Negative Association between Religiousness and Children's Altruism across the World," *Current Biology* 29, no. 15 (August 2019).

27. "Slow. But Sure," *The Economist*, November 2, 2019.

28. Jonathan Haidt, *The Righteous Mind: Why Good People Are Divided by Politics and Religion* (Pantheon, 2012), p. 90.

29. Larsen and von Ins, "The Rate of Growth in Scientific Publication," pp. 576 and 600.

Chapter 4

1. Thanks to Emily Chamlee-Wright for the concept of contestability.

2. Michael Hayden, "The End of Intelligence," *New York Times*, April 28, 2018.

3. Nada Bakos, quoted in Jefferson Morley, "What Happens When the Intelligence Community Decides That Trump Is Too Dangerous to Be President?," Salon.com, November 16, 2018.

4. Seth Borenstein, "NOAA Assailed for Defending Trump's Hurricane Dorian Claim," Associated Press, September 8, 2019.

5. Yasmeen Abutaleb, "Trump's 'Conscience Rule' for Health Providers Blocked by Federal Judge," *Washington Post*, November 6, 2019.

6. Supreme Court of California, *In re Stephen Randall Glass on Admission*, January 27, 2014.

7. Barbara J. Shapiro, *A Culture of Fact: England, 1550–1702* (Cornell University Press, 2000).

8. Glenn Kessler, Salvador Rizzo, and Meg Kelly, "President Trump Has Made 9,014 False or Misleading Claims over 773 Days," *Washington Post*, March 4, 2019.

9. Susan Haack, "Preposterism and Its Consequences," in *Manifesto of a Passionate Moderate: Unfashionable Essays* (University of Chicago Press, 1998).

10. "The Scientific Attitude and Fallibilism," in Justus Buchler, ed., *Philosophical Writings of Peirce*, p. 54. For emphasis, Peirce sets off and centers his dictum, as shown here.

11. See Jonathan Rauch, *Government's End: Why Washington Stopped Working* (PublicAffairs, 1999).

12. Hat tip to Susan Haack for the crossword puzzle analogy.

13. Francis S. Collins, *The Language of God: A Scientist Presents Evidence for Belief* (Free Press, 2006).

14. Suzanne Raga, "Eight of the Weirdest Gallup Polls," MentalFloss.com, November 18, 2017.

Chapter 5

1. Edoardo Tortarolo, *The Invention of Free Press: Writers and Censorship in Eighteenth Century Europe* (Springer, 2016), Kindle location 3419. Hat tip: Jacob Mchangama.

2. Barbara J. Shapiro, *A Culture of Fact: England, 1550–1720* (Cornell University Press, 2000), p. 89.

3. Not that the Founders were above exploiting fake news. The Boston Tea Party was instigated partly thanks to the Boston *Evening Post*'s reports that British tea contained a "slow poison" that caused "spasms."

4. Randall S. Sumpter, *Before Journalism Schools: How Gilded Age Reporters Learned the Rules* (University of Missouri Press, 2018), p. 94.

5. Ibid., p. 31.

6. Rick Sobey, "Harvard Student Government Sides with Anti-ICE Protesters against Newspaper," *Boston Herald*, November 11, 2019.

7. Jon Ronson, "How One Stupid Tweet Blew Up Justine Sacco's Life," *New York Times*, February 12, 2015.

8. Ali Vingiano, "This Is How a Woman's Offensive Tweet Became the World's Top Story," *Buzzfeed News*, December 21, 2013.

9. Jeffrey M. Berry and Sarah Sobieraj, *The Outrage Industry: Political Opinion Media and the New Incivility* (Oxford, 2014), p. 5.

10. Alex Kantrowitz, "The Man Who Built the Retweet: 'We Handed a Loaded Weapon to Four-Year-Olds,'" *Buzzfeed News*, July 23, 2019.

11. M. J. Crockett, "Moral Outrage in the Digital Age," *Nature Human Behaviour*, September 18, 2017, p. 2.

12. Marie Le Conte, "The Eye of the Storm," *The Critic*, July–August 2020.

13. Joshua B. Grubbs, Brandon Warmke, Justin Tosi, A. Shanti James,

and W. Keith Campbell, "Moral Grandstanding in Public Discourse: Status-Seeking Motives as a Potential Explanatory Mechanism in Predicting Conflict," *PLoS ONE* 14, no.10 (October 16, 2019). See also Justin Tosi and Brandon Warmke, *Grandstanding: The Use and Abuse of Moral Talk* (Oxford University Press, 2020).

14. Berry and Sobieraj, *The Outrage Industry*, p. 127.

15. "Dire Straights," *The Economist*, September 7, 2019, p. 28.

16. Berry and Sobieraj, *The Outrage Industry*, pp. 6, 13, and 127.

17. Soroush Vosoughi, Deb Roy, and Sinan Aral, "The Spread of True and False News Online," *Science*, March 9, 2018.

18. William J. Brady, Julian A. Wills, John T. Jost, Joshua A. Tucker, and Jay J. Van Bavel, "Emotion Shapes the Diffusion of Moralized Content in Social Networks," *PNAS* (Proceedings of the National Academy of Sciences), June 26, 2017.

19. Christopher Bouzy, "Is There a Targeted Troll Campaign against Lisa Page? A Bot Sentinel Investigation," *Lawfare*, January 22, 2020.

20. Nick Corasaniti, "How a Misleading Biden Video Spread," *New York Times*, January 7, 2020.

21. Lachlan Markay and Dean Sterling Jones, "Inside the Online Campaign to Whitewash the History of Donald Trump's Russian Business Associates," *Daily Beast*, July 5, 2018.

22. Elizabeth Grieco, "Fast Facts about the Newspaper Industry's Financial Struggles as McClatchy Files for Bankruptcy," Pew Research Center, February 14, 2020.

23. PEN America, *Losing the News: The Decimation of Local Journalism and the Search for Solutions*, November 20, 2019.

24. Richard Cooke, "Wikipedia Is the Last Best Place on the Internet," *Wired*, February 17, 2020.

25. Lee McIntyre, *Respecting Truth: Willful Ignorance in the Internet Age* (Routledge, 2015), p. 126.

26. Jimmy Wales, foreword to Andrew Lih, *The Wikipedia Revolution: How a Bunch of Nobodies Created the World's Greatest Encyclopedia* (Hyperion, 2009), p. xvii.

27. Lih, *The Wikipedia Revolution*, p. 111.

28. Alex Pasternack, "Twitter Wants Your Help Fighting Falsehoods. It's Risky, but It Just Might Work," *Fast Company*, January 28, 2021.

29. Regina Rini, "How to Fix Fake News," *New York Times*, October 15, 2018.

30. Pinterest news release, "Bringing Authoritative Vaccine Results to Pinterest Search," August 28, 2019.

31. Ben Collins, "Twitter Is Testing New Ways to Fight Misinformation—Including a Community-Based Points System," NBCNews.com, February 20, 2020.

32. I describe Duke's real-time fact-checking initiative in "Fact Checking the President in Real Time," *The Atlantic*, June 2019.

33. Anne Quito, "Jack Dorsey Admits Twitter's 'Like' Button Should Never Have Existed," *Quartz*, April 16, 2019.

34. Jonathan Rauch, "Twitter Needs a Pause Button," *The Atlantic*, August 2019.

35. Hat tip to Regina Rini, cited above, for this idea. In 2018 it was reported that Facebook was already rating trustworthiness, but only behind the scenes. Elizabeth Dwoskin, "Facebook Is Rating the Trustworthiness of Its Users on a Scale from Zero to 1," *Washington Post*, August 21, 2018.

36. Twitter.com, November 23, 2020, https://twitter.com/TwitterSupport/status/1331018136712261632/photo/2.

37. Sam Harris, Making Sense Podcast, January 16, 2019.

38. "Preparing the Way Forward for Facebook's Oversight Board," Facebook press release, January 28, 2020.

39. Per Baybars Örsek, the director of the International Fact-Checking Network, podcast interview by Jen Patja Howell for *Lawfare*, March 26, 2020.

40. For a roundup of steps taken by social media companies against misinformation during the pandemic, see Evelyn Douek, "COVID-19 and Social Media Content Moderation," *Lawfare*, March 25, 2020.

Chapter 6

1. Adrian Chen, "The Agency," *New York Times Magazine*, June 2, 2015.

2. Andy Szal, "Report: Russian 'Internet Trolls' behind Louisiana Chemical Explosion Hoax," Manufacturing.net, June 3, 2015.

3. Translated by Paul Shorey, in *The Collected Dialogues of Plato*, Edith Hamilton and Huntington Cairns, eds. (Princeton, 1961).

4. Joel Stein, "Milo Yiannopoulos Is the Pretty, Monstrous Face of the Alt-Right," *Bloomberg*, September 15, 2016.

5. Ashley Feinberg, "This Is the Daily Stormer's Playbook," *Huffington Post*, December 13, 2017.

6. See Erin Gallagher, "Advanced Meme Warfare—July 6, 2016," Medium.com, August 1, 2018, and related posts.

7. Ben Collins and Joseph Cox, "Jenna Abrams, Russia's Clown Troll Princess, Duped the Mainstream Media and the World," *Daily Beast*, November 3, 2017.

8. Michael Bang Petersen, Mathias Osmundsen, and Kevin Arceneaux, "The 'Need for Chaos' and Motivations to Share Hostile Political Rumors," preprint, May 2020, https://psyarxiv.com/6m4ts/.

9. Dudley Clendinen, "Conservative Paper Stirs Dartmouth," *New York Times*, October 13, 1981.

10. Dinesh D'Souza, *Letters to a Young Conservative* (Basic Books, 2002), p. 135.

11. "Belleville Woman Helped Cook Up Pizzagate," Toronto *Star*, December 7, 2016.

12. Abby Ohlheiser, "This Is How Facebook's Fake-News Writers Make Money," *Washington Post*, November 18, 2016.

13. This and succeeding quotations are from Renée DiResta, "Of Virality and Viruses: The Anti-Vaccine Movement and Social Media," Nautilus Institute for Security and Sustainability, November 8, 2018.

14. James Barragán, "Russians Spread Misinformation on Jade Helm Military Exercise in Texas, Former CIA Director Says," *Dallas Morning News*, May 3, 2018.

15. See Carly Nyst and Nick Monaco, "State-Sponsored Trolling: How Governments Are Deploying Disinformation as Part of Broader Digital Harassment Campaigns," Institute for the Future, 2018.

16. Dipayan Ghosh and Ben Scott, "#DigitalDeceit: The Technologies Behind Precision Propaganda on the Internet," New America Foundation, January 2018.

17. Thomas Rid, *Active Measures: The Secret History of Disinformation and Political Warfare* (Farrar, Straus and Giroux, 2020).

18. Claire Allbright, "A Russian Facebook Page Organized a Protest in Texas. A Different Russian Page Launched the Counterprotest," *Texas Tribune*, November 1, 2017.

19. Michael Lewis, "Has Anyone Seen the President?," *Bloomberg Opinion*, February 9, 2018.

20. Susan Haack, "Preposterism and Its Consequences," in *Manifesto of a Passionate Moderate: Unfashionable Essays* (University of Chicago Press, 1998), p. 191.

21. But there were incursions. Profiteers learned to create realistic-looking fake academic journals with pretend peer review, for example, and state-sponsored trolls showed interest in fake-science activity. See Alex Hern and Pamela Duncan, "Predatory Publishers: The Journals that Churn Out Fake Science," *The Guardian*, August 10, 2018; Alden Fletcher, "Is the Threat of 'Fake Science' Real?," *Lawfare*, August 5, 2019.

22. Yochai Benkler, Robert Faris, and Hal Roberts, *Network Propaganda: Manipulation, Disinformation, and Radicalization in American Politics* (Oxford University Press, 2018), p. 24.

23. Hannah Arendt, "Truth and Politics," *Between Past and Future: Eight Exercises in Political Thought* (Penguin, 1954), p. 239.

24. Sophia A. Rosenfeld, *Democracy and Truth: A Short History* (University of Pennsylvania Press, 2019), pp. 130–31.

25. Christopher Paul and Miriam Matthews, *The Russian "Firehose of Falsehood" Propaganda Model: Why It Might Work and Options to Counter It* (RAND, 2018).

26. "Kremlin-Backed Fake News Targets Britain," *The Economist*, April 19, 2018.

27. Joby Warrick and Anton Troianovski, "Agents of Doubt: How a Powerful Russian Propaganda Machine Chips Away at Western Notions of Truth," *Washington Post*, December 10, 2018.

28. Hunt Allcott and Matthew Gentzkow, online appendix to "Social Media and Fake News in the 2016 Election," *Journal of Economic Perspectives* 31, no. 2 (Spring 2017), fig. 1. For example, around 10 percent who saw a fabricated story that the Clinton Foundation had purchased $137 million in illegal arms believed the story, but an additional 40 percent or so were unsure.

29. Sabrina Tavernise, "These Americans Are Done with Politics," *New York Times*, November 17, 2018.

30. Trip Gabriel, "Trump's Fights Are Their Fights. They Have His Back Unapologetically," *New York Times*, August 25, 2020.

31. "KGB Defector Yuri Bezmenov's Warning to America," February 1, 2013, https://youtu.be/bX3EZCVj2XA.

32. Tim Wu, "Is the First Amendment Obsolete?," Knight First Amendment Institute, September 1, 2017.

33. DiResta, "Of Virality and Viruses."

34. See Lena H. Sun, "Trump Energizes the Anti-Vaccine Movement in Texas," *Washington Post*, February 20, 2017.

35. Isaac Stanley-Becker and Tony Romm, "Pro-Gun Activists Using Facebook Groups to Push Anti-Quarantine Protests," *Washington Post*, April 19, 2020.

36. Shelby Grossman, Khadija H., and Renée DiResta, "Coordinated Behavior across 18 Pro-Saif Gaddafi Facebook Pages," Stanford Internet Observatory, April 27, 2020.

37. David Leonhardt, Ian Prasad Philbrick, and Stuart A. Thomson, "Trump's Lies vs. Obama's," *New York Times*, December 14, 2017.

38. Glenn Kessler, Salvador Rizzo, and Meg Kelly, "President Trump Has Made 9,014 False or Misleading Claims over 773 Days," *Washington Post*, March 4, 2019.

39. Salvador Rizzo, "Anatomy of a Trump Rally: 67 Percent of Claims Are False or Lacking Evidence," *Washington Post*, January 7, 2020.

40. Christina Wilkie, "Hours after Trump Calls US Justice System 'a Laughingstock,' White House Denies He Ever Did," CNBC.com, November 1, 2017.

41. Dana Milbank, "Trump Concocted a Story about a Border Agent's Death. The Truth Won't Catch Up," *Washington Post*, February 9, 2018.

42. See Jill Colvin, "Trump Lashes Out as Scientists Whose Findings Contradict Him," Associated Press, May 22, 2020.

43. Anne Gearan, "On Weekend Dedicated to War Dead, Trump Tweets Insults, Promotes Baseless Claims and Plays Golf," *Washington Post*, May 24, 2020.

44. Lisa Rein and Tom Hamburger, "As Trump Removes Federal Watch-

dogs, Some Loyalists Replacing Them Have 'Preposterous' Conflicts," *Washington Post*, May 24, 2020.

45. Libby Cathey, "Beyond the Bombshells: Five Other Memorable Take-aways from Bolton's Book," ABCNews.com, June 18, 2020.

46. Pew Research Center, "Biden Begins Presidency with Positive Ratings; Trump Departs with Lowest-Ever Job Mark," January 15, 2021.

47. Glenn Kessler and Scott Clement, "Trump Routinely Says Things That Aren't True. Few Americans Believe Him," *Washington Post*, December 14, 2018.

48. Rush Limbaugh, "The Four Corners of Deceit: Prominent Liberal Social Psychologist Made It All Up," transcript of syndicated radio broadcast of April 29, 2013. Accessed via RushLimbaugh.com.

49. Rush Limbaugh, "ClimateGate Hoax: The Universe of Lies Versus the Universe of Reality," transcript of syndicated radio broadcast of November 24, 2009. Accessed via RushLimbaugh.com.

50. Quoted in "Hacks at Work," *The Economist*, February 23, 2008.

51. Alex Clark, "Breitbart's Boyle: 'Our Goal Is the "Elimination of the Entire Mainstream Media,'" *Breitbart News*, July 19, 2017.

52. Marisa Guthrie, "Fox News' Sean Hannity Declares 'Journalism in America Is Dead,'" *Hollywood Reporter*, January 26, 2017.

53. Amy Mitchell, Jeffrey Gottfried, Jocelyn Kiley, and Katerina Eva Matsa, "Political Polarization and Media Habits," Pew Research Center, October 21, 2014.

54. Mark Jurkowitz and Amy Mitchell, "About One-Fifth of Democrats and Republicans Get Political News in a Kind of Media Bubble," Pew Research Center, March 4, 2020.

55. Robert M. Faris, Hal Roberts, Bruce Etling, Nikki Bourassa, Ethan Zuckerman, and Yochai Benkler, *Partisanship, Propaganda, and Disinformation: Online Media and the 2016 U.S. Presidential Election* (Berkman Klein Center for Internet & Society Research at Harvard University, 2017).

56. Andrew M. Guess, Brendan Nyhan, and Jason Reifler, "Exposure to Untrustworthy Websites in the 2016 U.S. Election," *Nature Human Behavior* 4, no. 5 (March 2, 2020).

57. Andrew Romano, "New Yahoo News/YouGov Poll Shows Coronavirus Conspiracy Theories Spreading on the Right May Hamper Vaccine Efforts," Yahoo News, May 22, 2020.

58. Amy Mitchell and J. Baxter Oliphant, "Americans Immersed in COVID-19 News; Most Think Media Are Doing Fairly Well Covering It," Pew Research Center, March 18, 2020.

59. Marc Hetherington and Jonathan Weiler, *Prius or Pickup? How the Answers to Four Simple Questions Explain America's Great Divide* (Houghton Mifflin Harcourt, 2018), p. 150.

60. The quotations following are from pp. 356, 74, and 220 of Benkler, Faris, and Roberts, *Network Propaganda*.

61. Cato Institute and YouGov poll, published October 31, 2017. See Emily Ekins, "63 Percent of Republicans Say Journalists Are an 'Enemy of the American People,'" Cato Institute, November 1, 2017.

62. Dana Milbank, "The Latest Trump Defense: If It Swims and Quacks Like a Duck, It's a Piano," *Washington Post*, December 9, 2019.

63. Ryan Broderick, "Republicans' Conspiracy Theory–Ridden Counter-programming to Impeachment Is Working," *BuzzFeed News*, November 20, 2019. See also Quinta Jurecic and Jacob Schulz, "How the Schiff Report Deals with Disinformation," *Lawfare*, December 8, 2019.

64. David Weigel, "House Science Committee Chairman: Americans Should Get News from Trump, Not Media," *Washington Post*, January 25, 2017.

65. Jeremy W. Peters, "'Everything You're Seeing Is Deception': How Right-Wing Media Talks about Impeachment," *New York Times*, September 26, 2019.

66. Dana Milbank, "My Total Lack of Evidence Proves My Case!," *Washington Post*, December 11, 2019.

67. Claire Galofaro and Juliet Linderman, "One County, Worlds Apart: Bridging the Political Divide," Associated Press, January 25, 2021.

68. Dan M. Kahan, "Misconceptions, Misinformation, and the Logic of Identity-Protective Cognition," Cultural Cognition Project Working Paper 164 (Yale Law School, 2017).

69. Kate Starbird, "Information Disorder during and after the Trump Presidency," *Lawfare* podcast interview, January 21, 2021.

70. Andrew Guess, Jonathan Nagler, and Joshua Tucker, "Less than You Think: Prevalence and Predictors of Fake News Dissemination on Facebook," *Science Advances*, January 9, 2019.

71. Brendan Nyhan, "Why Fears of Fake News Are Overhyped," *Medium*, February 4, 2019; Andrew Guess, Benjamin Lyons, Jacob M. Montgomery, Brendan Nyhan, and Jason Reifler, "Fake News, Facebook Ads, and Misperceptions: Assessing Information Quality in the 2018 U.S. Midterm Election Campaign," a 2019 working paper for Democracy Fund.

72. Tommy Christopher, "New Poll: Republicans Trust Trump for Medical Information More than the Centers for Disease Control," *Mediaite*, April 10, 2020

73. Gary Marcus and Annie Duke, "The Problem with Believing What We're Told," *Wall Street Journal*, August 31, 2019.

74. Leticia Bode and Emily Vraga, "Americans Are Fighting Coronavirus Misinformation on Social Media," *Washington Post*, May 7, 2020.

75. Thomas Kent, "Activists against Digital Lies," *The American Interest*, June 2, 2020.

76. "Ben Nimmo on the Return of the Internet Research Agency," *Lawfare* podcast interview, September 10, 2020.

77. *The State of the First Amendment*, 2017 and 2019 editions, Newseum Institute.

78. John Koblin, "The Evening News Is Back," *New York Times*, March 24, 2020.

79. Cary Funk, "Key Findings about Americans' Confidence in Science and Their Views on Scientists' Role in Society," Pew Research Center, February 12, 2020.

80. Glenn Kessler, Salvador Rizzo, and Meg Kelly, "The Central Feature of Trump's Presidency: False Claims and Disinformation," *Washington Post*, June 2, 2020.

Chapter 7

1. Daniel Pipes, *The Rushdie Affair: The Novel, the Ayatollah, and the West* (Birch Lane, 1990), p. 249

2. Naomi Oreskes, *Why Trust Science?* (Princeton University Press, 2019), pp. 136–37.

3. Helen E. Longino, *Science as Social Knowledge: Values and Objectivity in Scientific Inquiry* (Princeton University Press, 1990).

4. Elisabeth Noelle-Neumann, "The Spiral of Silence: A Theory of Public Opinion," *Journal of Communication* 24, no. 2 (Spring 1974). Recent empirical research supporting the "spiral of silence" hypothesis, and finding that it applies to social media, is in Jörg Matthes, Johannes Knoll, and Christian von Sikorski, "The 'Spiral of Silence' Revisited: A Meta-Analysis on the Relationship between Perceptions of Opinion Support and Political Opinion Expression," *Communication Research* 45, no. 1 (2018).

5. Cailin O'Connor and James Owen Weatherall, *The Misinformation Age: How False Beliefs Spread* (Yale University Press, 2019), pp. 73, 74, 82, 83, 85, 86.

6. Alexis de Tocqueville, *Democracy in America*, vol. 2, James T. Schleifer, trans. (Liberty Fund, 2012), chap. 7.

7. Jonathan Rauch, "In Defense of Prejudice: Why Incendiary Speech Must Be Protected," *Harper's*, May 1995.

8. Ben Smith, "Inside the Revolts Erupting in America's Big Newsrooms," *New York Times*, June 7, 2020.

9. Alexander Aleinikoff, quoted in Dinesh D'Souza, *Illiberal Education: The Politics of Race and Sex on Campus* (Free Press, 1991), p. 152.

10. Conor Friedersdorf, "Suspensions for College Students Who Thwarted Free Speech," *The Atlantic*, July 19, 2017.

11. Jonathan Rauch, "Offices and Gentlemen," *New Republic*, June 23, 1997.

12. See, for example, Erwin Chemerinsky and Howard Gillman, *Free Speech on Campus* (Yale University Press, 2017).

13. Greg Lukianoff and Jonathan Haidt, in their 2018 book, *The Coddling of the American Mind: How Good Intentions and Bad Ideas Are Setting Up a Generation for Failure* (Penguin), use this more nuanced definition (p. 30): " 'Safetyism' refers to a culture or belief system in which safety has become a sacred value, which means that people become unwilling to make trade-offs demanded by other practical and moral concerns. 'Safety' trumps everything else, no matter how unlikely or trivial the potential danger."

14. Mattie Kahn, "An Activist at Yale on What It's Like to Be #Blackon-Campus," *Elle*, November 12, 2015.

15. Katie Herzog interview with anonymous interviewee, " 'What a Stupid F*cking Way to Have a Really Important Conversation': Reflections on a Yearlong White Fragility Training," June 22, 2020, in *Blocked & Reported* podcast, from minute 31.

16. Lukianoff and Haidt, *The Coddling of the American Mind*, pp. 7 and 9.

17. Robby Soave, "A Harvard Law Professor Is Representing Harvey Weinstein. Students Say This Makes Them Unsafe, Demand His Resignation," *Reason*, February 26, 2019.

18. Lukianoff and Haidt, *The Coddling of the American Mind*, p. 46.

19. Jeremy Bauer-Wolf, "Free Speech 'Meltdown,' " *Inside Higher Ed*, April 23, 2019. The Chicago principles express the university's "fundamental commitment . . . to the principle that debate or deliberation may not be suppressed because the ideas put forth are thought by some or even by most members of the University community to be offensive, unwise, immoral, or wrong-headed."

20. Darel E. Paul, "Listening at the Great Awokening," *Areo*, April 17, 2019.

21. Seung Min Kim, "Sen. Cotton Rallies Conservatives and Raises National Profile as Op-Ed on Military Intervention Causes Uproar," *Washington Post*, June 8, 2020.

22. Jacob Mchangama, "The Totalitarian Temptation Part II: The Untergang," *FreeSpeechHistory* podcast, episode 39, January 27, 2020. I am grateful to Mchangama for allowing me to consult his forthcoming book on the history of free speech.

23. Robby Soave, *Panic Attack: Young Radicals in the Age of Trump* (All Points, 2019), p. 94.

24. Rick Sobey, "Harvard Student Government Sides with Anti-ICE Protesters against Newspaper," *Boston Herald*, November 11, 2019.

25. Foundation for Individual Rights in Education, "Whale Done: Animal Rights Club Approved by Public University after FIRE's First Amendment Uproar," February 10, 2020.

26. Gretchen Rachel Hammond, "More than 1,500 at Dyke March in

Little Village, Jewish Pride Flags Banned," *Windy City Times*, June 24, 2017.

27. Brown Immigrant Rights Coalition, "Silencing and 'Free' Speech," *Bluestockings Magazine*, February 13, 2018.

28. Shera S. Avi-Yonah and Jamie D. Halper, "Students Filed Title IX Complaints against Kavanaugh to Prevent Him from Teaching at Harvard Law," *Harvard Crimson*, October 2, 2018.

29. Sam Budnyk, "Emory Students Express Discontent with Administrative Response to Trump Chalkings," *Emory Wheel*, March 22, 2016.

30. Neal Broverman, "NYC LGBTQ Center Cancels Event Hosted by Right-Wing Queer Group," *Advocate*, March 22, 2019.

31. Catherine Rampell, "Political Correctness Devours Yet Another College, Fighting over Mini-Sombreros," *Washington Post*, March 3, 2016.

32. Those phrases are among many identified as racial microaggressions in the pioneering article on the subject by Derald Wing Sue, Christina M. Capodilupo, Gina C. Torino, Jennifer M. Bucceri, Aisha M. B. Holder, Kevin L. Nadal, and Marta Esquilin, "Racial Microaggressions in Everyday Life: Implications for Clinical Practice," *American Psychologist* 62, no. 4 (May–June 2007).

33. See Julio Rosas at https://twitter.com/Julio_Rosas11/status/118249 3159449907200?s=20.

34. See Smith, "Inside the Revolts Erupting in America's Big Newsrooms."

35. Bari Weiss, "Jonathan Haidt on the Cultural Roots of Campus Rage," *Wall Street Journal*, April 14, 2017.

36. Juan Prieto, "Violence Helped Ensure Safety of Students," *Daily Californian*, February 7, 2017.

37. Olga R. Rodriguez, "Four Injured in Campus Riot over Milo Yiannopoulos Speech Sue Berkeley, UC Berkeley," *NBC Bay Area*, January 16, 2018.

38. Mari J. Matsuda, Charles R. Lawrence III, Richard Delgado, and Kimberlé Williams Crenshaw, *Words That Wound: Critical Race Theory, Assaultive Speech, and the First Amendment* (Westview, 1993).

39. For a full treatment of the fallacy that suppressing so-called hate speech reduces hatred, see Nadine Strossen's excellent *Hate: Why We Should Resist It with Free Speech, Not Censorship* (Oxford University Press, 2018).

40. Jon Ronson, "How One Stupid Tweet Blew Up Justine Sacco's Life," *New York Times Magazine*, February 12, 2015.

41. Jonathan Chait, "The Still-Vital Case for Liberalism in a Radical Age," *New York*, June 11, 2020.

42. Nancy Rommelmann, A Guide to Surviving Your Fifteen Minutes of Hate, *Reason*, February 19, 2019; Lizzy Acker, "#MeNeither YouTube Videos Create Backlash for Portland Coffee Company," OregonLive.com, January 11, 2019.

43. Julia Halperin, "Gary Garrels, the San Francisco Museum of Modern

Art's Longtime Chief Curator, Resigns amid Staff Uproar," *Artnet News*, July 11, 2020.

44. Sean Collins, "The Lessons of the Rebecca Tuvel Witch Hunt," *Sp!ked*, May 11, 2017.

45. Jesse Singal, "This Is What a Modern-Day Witch Hunt Looks Like," *New York*, May 2, 2017.

46. Justin Weinberg, "Philosopher's Article on Transracialism Sparks Controversy (Updated with Response from Author)," *Daily Nous*, May 1, 2017.

47. Nathan Cofnas, "Academics Are Trying to Get My Paper Retracted—and Some of Them Haven't Even Read It," *The Spectator*, January 31, 2020. The professor also tweeted, "You're about to learn why people generally avoid fucking with me."

48. Laura Gianino, "A Touchy Topic?," *New York Times*, July 30, 2017.

49. Pipes, *The Rushdie Affair*, p. 20.

50. Yarrow Eady, " 'Everything Is Problematic': My Journey into the Center of a Dark Political World, and How I Escaped," *McGill Daily*, November 24, 2014.

51. Conor Friedersdorf, "The Chilling Effect of an Attack on a Scholar," *The Atlantic*, July 20, 2020.

52. Shaun Cammack, "Steven Pinker Won't Be Cancelled—but You Could Be," *Sp!ked*, July 9, 2020.

53. See, for example, Richard Hanania, "Does Apologizing Work? An Empirical Test of the Conventional Wisdom," *Behavioural Public Policy*, October 23, 2019.

54. Rob Eshman, "The CEO of Holy Land Brands That I Know Doesn't Match the Social Media Monster," *Forward*, June 8, 2020.

55. Elizabeth Picciuto, "The Real Free Speech Violations," *ARC Digital*, July 8, 2020.

56. Hannah Giorgis, "A Deeply Provincial View of Free Speech," *The Atlantic*, July 13, 2020.

57. Pre-publication survey results were provided to the author by Aaron Kindsvatter.

58. Jeffrey M. Jones, "More U.S. College Students Say Campus Climate Deters Speech," Gallup.com, March 12, 2018.

59. Knight Foundation, *Free Expression on College Campuses*, May 2019

60. See, for example, Heterodox Academy, *Understanding the Campus Expression Climate*, Fall 2019; Foundation for Individual Rights in Education, *Student Attitudes Association Survey—Full Text*, January 2019.

61. Emily Ekins, "Poll: 62 Percent of Americans Say They Have Political Views They're Afraid to Share," Cato institute, July 22, 2020.

62. Jennifer Larson, Mark McNeilly, and Timothy J. Ryan, *Free Expression and Constructive Dialogue at the University of North Carolina at Chapel Hill*, March 2, 2020.

63. Heterodox Academy, *Understanding the Campus Expression Climate*.

64. José L. Duarte, Jarret T. Crawford, Charlotta Stern, Jonathan Haidt, Lee Jussim, and Philip E. Tetlock, "Political Diversity Will Improve Social Psychological Science," *Behavioral and Brain Sciences* 38 (2015).

65. Jonathan Haidt, "New Study Indicates Existence of Eight Conservative Social Psychologists," Heterodox Academy blog, January 7, 2016.

66. Mitchell Langbert, "Homogenous: The Political Affiliations of Elite Liberal Arts College Faculty," *Academic Questions*, Summer 2018.

67. Musa al-Gharbi, "Data on how Ideological (Under)Representation Compares to (Under)Representation Along the Lines of Race, Gender or Sexuality," Heterodox Academy blog, March 29, 2018.

68. Samuel J. Abrams, "Think Professors Are Liberal? Try School Administrators," *New York Times*, October 16, 2018.

69. Yoel Inbar and Joris Lammers, "Political Diversity in Social and Personality Psychology," *Perspectives on Psychological Science* 7, no. 5 (2012).

70. Uwe Peters, Nathan Honeycutt, Andreas De Block, and Lee Jussim, "Ideological Diversity, Hostility, and Discrimination in Philosophy," *Philosophical Psychology* 33, no. 4 (2020).

71. Nathan Honeycutt and Laura Freberg, "The Liberal and Conservative Experience across Academic Disciplines: An Extension of Inbar and Lammers," *Social Psychological and Personality Science* 8, no. 2 (2017).

72. Jon A. Shields and Joshua M. Dunn Sr., *Passing on the Right: Conservative Professors in the Progressive University* (Oxford University Press, 2016), p. 185.

73. Jon A. Shields, "The Disappearing Conservative Professor," *National Affairs*, Fall 2018.

74. Christopher Dummitt, "Confessions of a Social Constructionist," *Quillette*, September 17, 2019.

75. This and related ideologies have been called political correctness, wokeness, the successor ideology, critical race theory, and intersectionalism, among other terms. In general, the variants have in common a neo-Marxist structure in which the axes of oppression and revolution are translated from the realm of economic class to the realm of group identity, with persons of color playing the role of the proletariat, white cisgendered non-queer people playing the role of the bourgeoisie, and anti-racist and anticolonialist activists playing the role of the revolutionary vanguard.

76. Cory J. Clark and Bo M. Winegard, "Tribalism in War and Peace: The Nature and Evolution of Ideological Epistemology and Its Significance for Modern Social Science," *Psychological Inquiry* 31, no. 1 (March 2020).

77. Lee McIntyre, *Respecting Truth: Willful Ignorance in the Internet Age* (Routledge, 2015), p. 135.

78. Kenneth B. McIntyre and Stacy G. Ulbig, "The Diversity of 'Diversity': Support for Differing Conceptions of Diversity on the University

Campus," chapter forthcoming in Jack Simmons, ed., *The 21st Century and its Discontents: A Philosophical Analysis of Shifting Social Norms.* Manuscript provided in 2020 by the authors.

79. A 2017 survey by the Foundation for Individual Rights in Education found that only 1 percent of students said that they might use violence or disruptive actions to prevent an event from occurring, and only 2 percent said they might participate in drowning out a speaker. There may be a gap between students' abstract approval of disruptive or violent tactics and their personal willingness to use such tactics. FIRE, *Student Attitudes Free Speech Survey*, 2017.

80. Italics in the original (p. 46).

81. "Free Speech at American Universities Is Under Threat," *The Economist*, October 14, 2017.

82. According to the Environmental Working Group's online farm subsidy database, accessed July 13, 2020.

83. Mancur Olson's two seminal works are *The Logic of Collective Action: Public Goods and the Theory of Groups* (Harvard University Press, 1965) and *The Rise and Decline of Nations: Economic Growth, Stagflation, and Social Rigidities* (Yale University Press, 1982). I explore both books and their implications for government in my book *Government's End: Why Washington Stopped Working* (PublicAffairs, 1999).

84. Haidt, "New Study Indicates Existence of Eight Conservative Social Psychologists."

85. Stephen Hawkins, Daniel Yudkin, Miriam Juan-Torres, and Tim Dixon, *Hidden Tribes: A Study of America's Polarized Landscape* (More in Common, 2018).

Chapter 8

1. Yuval Levin, *A Time to Build: From Family and Community to Congress and the Campus, How Recommitting to Our Institutions Can Revive the American Dream* (Basic Books, 2020).

2. The story, retracted, alleged ties between a Russian investment fund and an associate of President Trump.

3. Kim Parker, "The Growing Partisan Divide in Views of Higher Education," Pew Research Center, August 19, 2019.

4. Morgan Marietta and David C. Barker, *One Nation, Two Realities: Dueling Facts in American Democracy* (Oxford, 2019), pp. 221 and 225. I have omitted the authors' italics.

5. Thomas Simpson and Eric Kaufmann, "Academic Freedom in the UK" (Policy Exchange, 2019). I added the italics.

6. For a summary of existing laws against political discrimination, see Susan Milligan, "How Should HR Handle Political Discussions at Work?," *HR Magazine*, Spring 2020.

7. Utah S.B. 296, section 10.

8. The Fairness for All Act was not acted upon in the 116th Congress.

9. Trader Joe's, "A Note about Our Product Naming," blog post, July 24, 2020.

10. The term "moral clarity" in this context was popularized by the journalist Wesley Lowery.

11. See, for example, Erik Wemple, "Dear Mainstream Media: Why So Liberal?" *Washington Post*, January 27, 2017. A survey of a national probability sample of U.S. journalists in 2013 found that "most journalists said that they consider themselves to be either 'leaning left' (38.8 percent) or 'middle of the road' (43.8 percent), and only 12.9 percent described them[selves] as 'leaning right.'" See David H. Weaver, Lars Willnat, and G. Cleveland Wilhoit, "The American Journalist in the Digital Age: Another Look at U.S. News People," *Journalism & Mass Communication Quarterly* 96, no. 1 (2019).

12. Jen Patja Howell, "Pete Strzok on 'Compromised,'" *Lawfare* podcast interview, September 11, 2020.

13. Zolan Kanno-Youngs and Nicholas Fandos, "D.H.S. Downplayed Threats from Russia and White Supremacists, Whistle-Blower Says," *New York Times*, September 9, 2020.

14. Valuable reform suggestions are in David Frum's 2020 book, *Trumpocalypse: Restoring American Democracy* (HarperCollins); Paul Rosenzweig and Vishnu Kannan, "Repairing the Rule of Law: An Agenda for Post-Trump Reform," *Lawfare*, September 7, 2020; and Bob Bauer and Jack Goldsmith, *After Trump: Reconstructing the Presidency* (Lawfare Institute, 2020).

15. Conor Friedersdorf, "The Princeton Faculty's Anti-Free-Speech Demands," *The Atlantic*, August 4, 2020.

16. Donald Alexander Downs, *Free Speech and Liberal Education* (Cato Institute, 2020), p. 145.

17. Cato Institute book forum, "Is Free Speech Still Alive on the American College Campus?," September 10, 2020, at minute 42.

18. As of 2020 the organization's website said, "According to those who choose to self-identify, 16 percent identify as conservative, 17 percent as progressive, 29 percent as centrist, and 26 percent as libertarian."

19. See Robert E. Litan, *Resolved: Debate Can Revolutionize Education and Help Save Our Democracy* (Brookings Institution Press, 2020).

20. "A Letter on Justice and Open Debate," *Harper's*, July 7, 2020. I was one of the signatories.

21. Middlebury College students, "Broken Inquiry on Campus: A Response by a Collection of Middlebury Students," March 12, 2017. Published by 150 Middlebury College students online at https://brokeninquiryblog.wordpress.com/.

22. Eric Cervini, *The Deviant's War: The Homosexual vs. the United States of America* (Farrar, Straus and Giroux, 2020).

23. In June 2009, the U.S. Office of Personnel Management—formerly known as the U.S. Civil Service Commission, the same agency which had fired and blacklisted Kameny (among many others)—presented Kameny with the department's most prestigious award, the Theodore Roosevelt Award, along with a letter which said, in part, "In what we know today was a shameful action, the United States Civil Service Commission in 1957 upheld your dismissal from your job solely on the basis of your sexual orientation. . . . Please accept our apology for the consequences of the previous policy of the United States government." The award was presented by the agency's director, who was openly gay. Kameny's response: "Apology accepted!"

24. Chris Bodenner, "The Surprising Revolt at the Most Liberal College in the Country," *The Atlantic*, November 2, 2017.

25. The exchange could be viewed on YouTube at https://youtu.be/Sgyb8dH5vFQ.

26. Matthew Reade, "Students Demand Administrators 'Take Action' against Conservative Journalists," *Claremont Independent*, April 17, 2017.

27. Louis Michael Seidman, "Can Free Speech Be Progressive?" *Columbia Law Review* 118 (2018), p. 2239.

28. Elizabeth Siyuan Lee, "Discord at Middlebury: Students on the Anti-Murray Protests," *New York Times*, March 7, 2017.

29. Ulrich Baer, "What 'Snowflakes' Get Right about Free Speech," *New York Times*, April 24, 2017.

30. Erwin Chemerinsky and Howard Gillman, *Free Speech on Campus* (Yale University Press, 2017), p. 27.

31. Nadine Strossen, *Hate: Why We Should Resist It with Free Speech, Not Censorship* (Oxford University Press, 2018), p. 81.

32. See Chemerinsky and Gillman, *Free Speech on Campus*, for these and other examples.

33. See Strossen, *Hate*, p. 89.

34. Ibid., p. 87.

35. Human Rights Watch, "A Ruling Inspired by U.S. Anti-Pornography Activists Is Used to Restrict Lesbian and Gay Publications in Canada," February 1, 1994.

36. The undated clip of Williams making those comments on the *Phil Donahue Show* appears in the documentary *Mighty Ira*, about the former American Civil Liberties Union executive, Ira Glasser, from minute 48.

37. See my memoir *Denial: My 25 Years without a Soul* (Acorn Abbey Press, 2019).

38. *I'm from Driftwood*, http://imfromdriftwood.com/nephi_niven/.

39. Brian Resnick, "How to Talk Someone out of Bigotry," *Vox*, January 29, 2020.

40. Tina Rosenberg, "Neo-Nazis in Your Streets? Send in the (Coup Clutz) Clowns," *New York Times*, September 6, 2017.

41. Adam Sternbergh, "Stephen Colbert Has America by the Ballots," *New York*, October 6, 2006.

42. Interviewed by CNN's Alisyn Camerota, July 22, 2016.

43. Josh Feldman, "Trump Continues Pushing Claim He Won Popular Vote in 2016 'In a True Sense,'" *Mediaite*, September 1, 2020.

44. Kiran Khalid, "Trump: 'I'm Worth Whatever I Feel,'" CNN.com, April 21, 2011.

45. Corey Lewandowski and David Bossie, *Let Trump Be Trump: The Inside Story of His Rise to the Presidency* (Center Street, 2017), p. 86.

46. Middlebury students, "Broken Inquiry."

47. Christian Schneider, "A Year of Discontent on Campus," *The Dispatch*, February 6, 2020.

48. James Hohmann, "The Daily 202: Republican Convention Offers Apocryphal Quotes amid Revisionist History," *Washington Post*, August 27, 2020.

49. Quinta Jurecic and Jacob Schulz, "Thirty-Six Hours of Cheapfakes," *Lawfare*, September 3, 2020.

Index

Abrams, Stacey, 171
Abrams v. *United States* (1919), 92
academics and academia: cancel culture and, 11–14, 211–12, 215, 220–27, 247–48; Chicago principles in, 235; conservative media on, 175; integrity of, 18; mobilizing against conformity in, 19, 236–38, 242–45, 250–51; political discrimination in, 223–27; positive epistemic valence of, 121, 134; reality-based communities and, 100–102; viewpoint diversity in, 220–27, 236–38
accountability, 6; anonymity vs., 128, 129; digital media and, 134, 140–43, 150; in liberal science, 15; in reality-based communities, 104–05, 234; Trump and, 171
Adair, Bill, 152
Adams, John, 48, 82–83

ad hominem attacks, 127, 134, 212, 219
Administrative Procedure Act (1946), 102
AdSense, 146
advertisers and advertising: bias exploited in, 28; digital shift of, 137–38, 149; disinformation campaigns and, 161–62; internet and, 125; Twitter and, 149; Wikipedia and, 139
algorithmic media filters, 124–26, 132–33, 145, 148, 152–53, 263
Alien and Sedition Acts (1798), 253
alt-right, 159
ambition and political power, 81–85
American Academy of Arts and Sciences, 69
American Association for the Advancement of Science, 69